Bands of Love

Bands of Love

by Carol Ameche

Queenship
PUBLISHING COMPANY
P.O. Box 220, Goleta, CA 93116
(800) 647-9882 • (805) 692-0043 • Fax: (805) 967-5843

Library of Congress Number # 98-68709

Published by:
    Queenship Publishing
    P.O. Box 220
    Goleta, CA 93116
    (800) 647-9882 • (805) 692-0043 • Fax: (805) 967-5843

Printed in the United States of America

ISBN: 1-57918-109-0

CONTENTS

Yet it was I who taught Ephraim to walk,
I took them up in my arms;
But they did not know that I healed them.
I led them with cords of compassion,
With the bands of love,
and I became to them as one
who eases the yoke on their jaws,
and I bent down to them and fed them.

HOSEA 11:3-4

LOOKING BACK ON WHAT WE HAVE LEARNED

Instead of focusing on some new message or new prayer, let's for a moment take a look at what we have learned (hopefully) in the last ten years. Very important is the understanding that Jesus and Mary are speaking all over the world in order to bring us heavenly messages of warning: the need to turn to God right now and allow our hearts and lives to be turned away from self-absorption and gratification and our immersion in the values of a world that is in fact the domain of Satan.

We have seen a further destruction of the family unit, a greater acceptance of "alternate" lifestyles, an aggressive ethnic cleansing in many parts of the world, a rise of the plans of the one world order, (the latest schema for those who would "take over" and dominate the world), and a one world religion; all of which are reflections of Scripture's words about the times just before the Second Coming of Jesus. We realize that all of Scripture must be fulfilled before this great Day, and that the entire earth and all of the people on it must be cleansed of evil before He comes to claim His inheritance and present us to the Father. We are expecting the appearance of the Antichrist, this year in fact, when he will spread his shadow across history. We make ready to receive hundreds of people who will be coming to us (and people everywhere in the world) for answers and help and direction after the immense worldwide experience of the illumination of our minds to the state of our souls.

We realize that we are living in the "end times" just prior to the Second Coming of Jesus Who will defeat the Antichrist in the actual Battle of Armageddon. We believe that many of us will be alive to see this great event and, after a period of tribulation preceding His return, we shall then be ushered into a world that has been totally cleansed and renewed, a new era of peace and purity that lasts for many, many, many years during which Satan and his demons will be chained in the deepest realms of Hell. Peace and the absence of sin will be possible in the new era because Satan will not be allowed to tempt people! The Church begun by Jesus Christ and passed along through the Apostles will flourish and grow. There will be one Church and one Shepherd for all! The atmosphere of the Garden of Eden will prevail, as it was always meant to be before Adam and Eve sinned.

We have become comfortable with these revelations because we have accepted the graces offered along with our increased prayers, fasting and penance, adoration of Jesus in the Blessed Sacrament, daily Mass and general return to a life we were always meant to live as baptized children of God. It's very possible that we have even begun to see and hear with our hearts! We are more comfortable with our identity as soldiers in our Heavenly Mother's Army. We have survived a long stint in Mary's "boot camp" where we trained and prepared to fight at the side of Jesus against the ultimate battle with evil for the salvation of souls. We are trying harder to spend all our free time bringing souls to Jesus and Mary Who help them return to the Father where we all belong. We consecrate ourselves, our loved ones and the entire world daily, maybe hourly.

We understand that Jesus and Mary are not bringing us messages of a grave future in order to frighten us, but to prepare us;

first spiritually and then emotionally, mentally and physically. They are saying, "Be aware of what is coming, but do not 'dwell' in the future. Do not, at any time, be afraid. We are with you every step of the way, before you, behind you, at your side, within your hearts." They came with words of teaching to make us more aware of what is happening right now in the world: the evil evident in increased abortions, abuse of children, war plans that could threaten the life of the entire planet, poverty and suffering in every land, the pain so many experience at the hands of those who are dishonest, hypocritical, manipulative, demanding, and just plain old unkind. All of these are bitter examples of the power of this evil.

We carry our crosses with the greater joy that comes when we no longer resist the Father's Will for our lives, when we accept the pain that comes from dying to ourselves and the world, when we have the understanding that our suffering is redemptive. We believe that these crosses (our own weaknesses and tendency to sin, a chronic condition or illness, or suffering that results from the sins of another) unite us with Jesus more closely, more completely, than anything else could. We cheerfully embrace the fact that our God loves us more than we can ever imagine and longs to give us His gifts and His peace; that we are being molded after the pattern of our heavenly Mother, are more able to receive her virtues, love with her heart. We reflect often that Jesus and Mary and many of the Saints call us to fight now against the evil that escalates in our present world in order to be totally present to each other in word and deed, listening and praying with our hearts.

Today, in the present moment, is where I meet Jesus and Mary and all their promises, loving ways, peaceful gifts, strength, support, appreciation, protection, their dear sweetness. "Dwell in the present moment with Us in trust," they say, "along with the Angels and Saints you have been given, and experience life in the Father's Kingdom and Divine Will as fully as it is possible on this earth." And, please God, we are trying to do that.

We have discovered to one degree or another that our God appreciates us and has exquisite patience with us, that He is the very Source of purity and perfection (for which we praise and thank Him). We have come to know His mercy and compassion, His beauty and light, His forgiveness of every single sin we are humble and honest enough to confess and promise to try (with all our might!) not to commit again.

We have met a God Who cries and laughs with us, Who shares each moment with us, goes everywhere with us and waits for us in the Blessed Sacrament to come to Him for peace and healing; Who calls us to be still and comforted by His Presence, to know His Will for us. What's not to like about this God? It is His people who have built up barriers to Him, chosen destruction and violence, chosen to deny His existence or blame Him for all their problems.

We realize to a greater degree that it is not necessary to do anything to obtain God's love and favor. We have it! We ARE His children! It is only necessary to live His commandments in order to earn our place in Heaven by remaining faithful to His laws and His Love. What a happy truth to motivate our joy, our eagerness to share Jesus Himself, all that He has given to us, and the words and promises of Jesus and Mary. However, we know that when the Father decides to rescue us from whatever dilemma that engulfs us and call us back to Him in a deeper way, we must respond immediately or suffer the consequences of the pain caused by the absence of God in our life and the very possible loss of an eternity with Him in Heaven.

The results of turning away from God become more apparent as we see the world, given over to pleasure seeking, explode with hatred and violence. Our belief that time is short (before God's justice is experienced by His people) has made us more aware of the need to focus on the face of Jesus, to get to know and trust Him with all our minds and hearts and strength. "If we can't believe the promises of God, what's the use of trying," we ask.

There is much to defend: the truth of the presence of Jesus in the Eucharist; Mary as Virgin, Mother of God; the reality of sin, the existence of Purgatory and Hell; the proper place of the Tabernacle in our Churches. Imagine moving a King's throne out of the throne room where everyone always gathers to pay him homage! What is a church building anyway, if not God's House?

There is much work to be done simply by accepting each other and all who come to us, supporting and encouraging all of these, and leading them by our love and example to the fullness of the one, true Christ our Savior and Redeemer in union with the Trinity.

We know that some will come proclaiming to be Jesus, the Messiah. We understand that many may believe these ones who will indeed possess a great ability to perform miracles and wondrous deeds through the power given them by Satan, the Father of Lies. We pray now for the strength to resist the offers of the Antichrist to have a "better life" while we live apart in communities in a meager existence of self-sustenance. We accept these facts as our future, as we wait in joyful hope for the Second Coming of Jesus. We believe that we shall see the good things of the Lord in the land of the living!!! (Ps 27:13). In the meantime, we pray to the Holy Spirit to show us the sins hidden from us by our denial or ability to rationalize a situation and excuse our conduct! We wait and wait and wait, it seems, but in this we know that our patience and trust are being developed by the perfect Will of the Father. In all of this we see prudence and wisdom being received, and we know these are a most important compass on the road to Heaven. A new obedience and docility helps us remain calm in the face of sudden chaos, a new challenge, rejection. In the meantime, I hope we have learned to listen better; and reread helpful Scripture passages and the loving words of Mary about her Son, and of Jesus about His Mother! Where would we be without Scripture? And what Scripture stories and teachings would we have if the people who gathered all the information and put it together hadn't listened ... to each other and to the inspiration of the Holy Spirit, to the words of Jesus and those around Him? Abraham listened and followed the Lord's instructions (Gn 22:1-14). He knew when to remove his son, Isaac, from the altar and replace him with a ram tethered nearby. A lot happened as a result of his attention!!

Perhaps we remember a time someone looked around at the scenery or others passing by, or inside a purse or pockets, while we were trying to tell them something. It didn't take us long to realize we were not being heard! And often we stopped talking, didn't we? Then perhaps we remember that Jesus said to us, "Listen to My Mother because I listen to her." Ah, but did we listen well enough to Him Who says "listen to her;" or to her who says, "Focus on my Son"?

As we hear the gentle words of our beloved Mother, we pray to allow them to form us, to motivate us to be grateful to our Father in Heaven for all He allows us to do for Him. We believe in the fact that gratitude is a necessary ingredient on our way to holiness.

As we pray and hope and share our quiet joy, in spite of difficulties, we know there have been some who walked away from this long wait in disappointment, who were overcome with doubt and impatience. We know that some will walk away again after an initial conversion (after seeing their souls as God sees them in this gift called the Warning, given in order to save their lives!!)

We are attempting to tell anyone who will listen to us about this special, merciful act of God Who calls all His children of the world (one more time) to return to Him. We know that it may be frightening for anyone unprepared for such an awesome event, and we pray that as many as possible will accept the special graces offered then, before this brief golden hour for the Church gives way to tribulations and suffering throughout the world. Have we learned some balance? Oh, I hope so! What follows is the anticipation of the Lord's expectations for us and how we spend the brief time left: for Love, because of Love, full of Love, sharing Love, sustained and nourished by Love, grateful to Love, learning the valuable lesson that to love is all!

This book will be a collection of a variety of things in order to attempt to answer many questions from many people. It contains my own locutions since 1996 which have not been published in book form. It is a workbook (gathered from all the warnings and teachings of Jesus and Mary to me) of directions for the coming days. It is hopefully, a collection of thoughts of myself and others as food for meditation and appreciation for all we have been given by way of preparation and understanding for the months and years ahead; for that basic reflection we need in order to renew our minds and hearts about who Mary of Nazareth is, what a gift she is, how important she is in the plan of the Father for the salvation of His people.

Please, again I ask you who listen, reread these many times, as well as Scripture and the lives and direction of the many Saints who struggled and overcame the world and live now in the Beatific Vision of God, promised to all who remain faithful to Him, recognizing Him as our Creator, our Redeemer, our Sanctifier and our Lord.

And finally, we reflect on the fact that we aren't really getting it!! Jesus invites us to become united to His Life, His way of doing things, His purity, His call to return and be reconciled for all time to the Triune God. And instead: We are trying to FIT HIM INTO OUR lives! We are trying to make Him "work" in the midst of (and by sandwiching Him into) our busy schedule, our agenda. We say a quick Rosary somewhere and a Chaplet, if we remember, sometime each day and feel very good about ourselves. "Well that's out of the way," we say to ourselves. We are NOT hearing the seriousness of the words, "the time is NOW for the plan of the Father to begin," which Jesus and Mary are repeating all over the world. So we need to be reminded to LISTEN, to REFLECT, to ACT on the words of our God and our Holy Mother, crying out to us to STOP, to DO WHATEVER IT TAKES to unburden ourselves of the sins (mostly chronic and oft-repeated behavior) that weigh us down, builds up walls that Jesus cannot penetrate until we come to Him for help and surrender all of who we are and all of the rest of our lives to His direction, His care, His Will, His Wisdom for each of us. We need HELP ... JESUS IS THE ANSWER! AMEN.

MESSAGES FROM 1996 TO 1998

4/1/96, Jesus said:

"...breathe deeply of the sanctity here before you in My Sacred Eucharist, this Holy Sacrament of My Presence, this beloved gift of My Father to all of you. Just be here with Me now, daughter, and soak up; bathe in the Sacrament of My love for you. See the longing in My eyes and feel the tenderness of My Heart. Nowhere else is this available to My people who wish to be close to Me in the Oneness of My Blessed Trinity.

"Daughter, I beg you again, never look back even to yesterday. Once a sin is confessed, it is gone forever! Take the residue, the knowledge you have learned, to strengthen your own resolve to persevere in times of great danger and even greater temptation. You are ready to face the enemy. Do not be surprised when that enemy presents itself or under what guise. The evil one is everywhere waiting for the opportunity to trap My chosen ones.

"Encourage and strengthen each other. **Be the direct channel of grace between My Heart and all those who need the strength and peace** that is so necessary now in order to persevere in fortitude. Yes, it is difficult to believe that chaos will soon rule, as you see the beautiful days and prepare for the feast of My Resurrection.

"Little one, be firm in My love for you. Each day that you spend in quiet and prayerful recollection is a bountiful storing of ammunition with which to fight the enemy. Do not be troubled by anything. A calm and serene exterior will reflect your trust in all that We have told you."

4/14/96, Jesus said:

"Today was such a joyful feast in Heaven and in so many places on earth. The celebration of My Mercy in the hearts and churches of so many of My loved ones has brought a stillness to My Heart, a reprieve from all the pains and disappointments at seeing the lives of so many of Our lost ones.

"These days of mercy are about to end, daughter. The justice of My Father looms over the earth like a giant hand waiting to fall. The justice of My Father is like a sickle that will thresh away the weeds and the wheat, to be separated by the Harvester at the proper time.

"My Father is the Harvester, daughter. He is standing by with His giant scythe ready to swing it over the earth. These times call for drastic measures in order to clear the earth for new plantings. The earth must be tilled and turned in order to renew it. The soil must be aerated for proper drainage. Each seedling will yield a rich abundance for the time of reaping. My children of promise will receive the fruits of this planting and be nourished for the time to come. You will see what I mean when it happens, child. You will understand everything, as it is lived out.

"These holy days of Easter are preparing all of you for the final time before events of the greatest magnitude change the face of the earth, and especially your country, forever. Be vigilant every moment of your day. Please, child, ask for protection constantly. This is a special week of peace before difficult days emerge on your horizon. All of the words We have given to you are about to be fulfilled.

"There are many people who love and serve My Mother and Me. **We love all of you beyond words.** The future is dependent on love, daughter. **The present is sustained by love and the past is a reflection of the love My Father has given to His people. All is about to be purified until only love remains!**"

4/19/96, Jesus said:

"...The advent of My Second Coming into the world is bringing with it many attacks of the evil one and his cohorts. I, your Jesus Who loves you and all His faithful ones, tell you that now is the Day of My Visitation to the hearts of the world.

"Do not leave your state of unity with Me from now on. Do not enter again into the world. The world is full of dangers and deceits. None of you is strong enough to withstand the virulent attacks against your weaknesses. The only way for Me to protect all My children is for them to come away with Me in safety. Locked in My arms, you are safe and hidden from the world. No matter how restful for the moment an event may be, if it is not intimately united to My Heart, it will lead you away from Me from now on.

"The wiles of the evil one are no match for you. There is no way for you to withstand the advances of his plots and schemes against those who love Me and My Holy Mother. A day will not go by during which you will not need all of My strength, all of My help and grace, no matter where you are.

"Believe Me, the hour is upon the world for all the forces of evil to be loosed. Events of grave consequences have just occurred in the world. These will escalate to the breaking point and many, many lives will be lost. Please, daughter, redouble your efforts at prayer and spending time here in My Presence until the day of My Return."

5/3/96, Jesus said:

"I, your Jesus of Divine Mercy, praise the Name of My Father in Heaven and Our Holy Spirit. The battle looms fiercely overhead! Feelings of oppression and distraction result from the major events in Satan's plan to conquer the world. They are appearing on the horizon as the world still sleeps. Only the graces granted by My Mother will see you through each event. This is by the Will of My Father for all of you, but you cannot avoid feeling oppressed and sad. The proximity of evil from within and without My people is causing them to become even more crazed in their pursuit of pleasure and power."

5/6/96, Mary said:

"Dear one, I your Mother of Sorrows speak this night for the benefit of your heart. Please listen closely to My words. They are given as pure gift from the Father Who made us. We are His creatures and He loves us all so dearly, so totally, so invitingly. He invites us to approach His throne with joy and cry out 'Abba'! The beginning of a deeper relationship with Our Creator is one of deeper simplicity based on our littleness. His great Fatherly love for us is meant to make us comfortable in His Presence, to relax in the warmth of His care and wonderful providence for our lives.

"In these times of terrible chaos and destruction of lives, each of you needs, more than ever, to know your God as more than approachable, as the One Who directs every action around you for your good, to bring you most quickly to Him.

"It will be so necessary to be aware of Our presence with each of you, as events become more difficult. The world will not know a peaceful time again until the Triumph of Our Two Hearts and My Jesus' return. **My own heart, child, is a refuge offered to each of My soldiers.** This warfare has just begun to escalate, and you must all retreat often to this oasis of pure love and peace.

"My heart has been filled with joy by all who love me so much. It is a joy and love that will be a continual reciprocal action between us and will sustain us in the days to follow. The strength you all need will be generated by this reciprocal love and the strong commitment you have each made through your prayers and consecrations.

"Please, pray for each other and, especially, for the perseverance of Our beloved priests and Our beloved John Paul. He is in such danger every day. Unite every action of prayer and sacrifice for his sake. There are such difficult days in the near future. The Body of Christ groans in labor with the deliverance of sin so imminent! Reach out and touch My hand always.

"The Will of Our Father in Heaven is perfect. That fact alone will sustain you during every trial."

5/7/96, Jesus said:

"My dear child, I, your Jesus, praise My Father and Our Holy Spirit. The day is not over before many events will occur in certain parts of the world to bring it even closer to war. **The powers of governments plot to overthrow weaker powers and bring the world closer to domination by the super powers that exist, hid-**

den for now, but soon to be introduced in all their fury.

"Please continue to confess your sins often and to plunge to the roots of your own behavior. Give thanks and praise to My Father Who brings you to a new level in His Plan through the Sacrament of Reconciliation.

"The days must just be lived out one at a time in peaceful anticipation. That is only possible with Our help and your cooperation. You have learned how to pray and offer all to Me. There is nothing else to be done save walking each day by My side. Offer all your loved ones to My Heart and the heart of My Mother. Nothing is important except being closely united to Our words and directions."

5/9/96, Jesus said:

"My dear one, I your Jesus, am here in My Blessed Sacrament waiting for you. The hearts of My chosen ones beat in one accord with love for Me. You have all been so blessed with special gifts in order to carry out Our commands. The time has all but disappeared for the world. The opportunities for grace and conversion that were offered to Our people will never be available in such abundance again.

"There is great sorrow in Heaven and in the hearts of Our beloved ones on earth over the terrible loss of innocent blood shed daily through wars and abortion. And this is only the beginning! Please, daughter, pray that enough prayers can be said for all those who take lives so carelessly, that they will repent.

"My Father is poised to begin a new level of tribulation for this country, and then you will see weeping and gnashing of teeth on an unprecedented scale. The lives of all Our people have been given every last opportunity to change and come back to God, but the response has been pitiful. No one wants to hear words of caution and warning. Not enough people believe in Me anymore, and this causes them to turn a deaf ear on words of warning and love.

"It is hard to believe the lack of faith that exists in the world. All of Us in Heaven wait with you for My Father's wrath to act directly upon the earth. First will come upheavals of all sorts very, very shortly. The plan of My Father is in full swing everywhere in the world and in hearts open to receive Us.

"Those who will not listen and accept Us will be overwhelmed by surprise and consternation when events begin. Yes, it is difficult to believe that so many do not know of impending developments. Pray, pray, daughter."

5/10/96, Jesus said:

"I, your Jesus of Mercy, praise My Father in Heaven; the One True God and Father of all, and Our Holy Spirit. In the coming days, events are occurring that will leave this country completely changed. Yes, child, the Warning will occur sooner than you now believe. Truly, the world will be emotionally devastated for the most part. Imagine billions of people in chaos and confusion because this is what all of you will see.

"Daughter, the one who stays on the path reaches the goal most quickly without unnecessary delays. The one who listens to the voice of the one directing her will be freer to respond, will be fresh and full of surplus energy at all times! It is such an exciting time for all of Our faithful ones who wait expectantly for the Father to manifest His power. (I believe He means the Father's power to cleanse the world of evil, and oppose it.) The evil one and his cohorts are increasing their plans for world domination through their weak and hidden henchmen. These words are true. The forces of evil wait for the Father to act before jumping into a renewed effort to defeat the holy ones of God. You will not believe the results. No more will My beloved ones laugh with innocent and happy hearts. They will be weighed down with sadness and shame for the behavior of their brothers and sisters all over the world.

"I need your prayers for My lukewarm followers, child. I need the prayers of all who will spend entire days in deep union with Me and with My Mother. The days are short and the time has come to be completely free for each request of My Father through Our Hearts. I will never tell you more than is necessary, daughter, for the moment, so that you can better stay in the present moment with Me! The Wisdom of God takes into consideration everything that is good for Our soldiers. Those who are warriors are being protected from unnecessary anxiety as much as possible. Go now in My peace."

5/15/96, Jesus said:

"Time has disappeared from the lives of all who understand that the Day of the Lord has already begun. It is NOW that all of Scripture is being fulfilled. Be there with the Angels and Saints to welcome Our lost ones back into the one fold and one Shepherd. Be watchful and wait. Be at peace."

5/21/96, God The Father said:

"Please, child, begin to write My words. I am your loving Father in Heaven Who wishes to speak words of instruction. Your heart grows daily more weary of waiting. The plan of salvation of My people includes many such interludes to test My warriors before the final battle. When you trust more completely in My Will, daughter, you will be at complete peace about each development. Let Me hold you in the Arms of My Creative Love and renew your strength in the peace of My Son.

"These times before final action begins, strain the body and spirit. You do well to get your house in order for My least command for you. Daughter, the time is here. My hand falls heavily on your land this very "day." You will see destruction on a vast scale. My people will know that I have begun to act. Please remain in prayer as much as possible for the rest of this day that many of My people will turn to Me and repent. All are about to witness the saving power of their God. All are about to see the love of their Creator and Savior poured out upon those who will accept it. All will know that I Am! All will understand that there has always been a God Who made them and sustains them and has loved them into life.

"Many you will see who will repent at the last moment and be taken into My arms. This will be possible because of those who are willing to give up everything for their sake. To suffer for the reparation of sin is the greatest unity you can experience with My Jesus in His Most Holy Trinity of Oneness with Myself and Our Spirit. You will be reminded of this often as a means of being sustained throughout this period of suffering for the salvation of others.

"The world of evil must disappear and I, your Lord and God, your Savior and King, announce to you that I will avenge the murder of My innocents. This very day will see the beginning of retribution. The suffering of My tiny precious ones has known no bounds, has seen no precedent. There is no other way to atone to My justice for the outrages committed against My gift of life. All must come, once again, to revere the gift I freely give. All must return to a simple way of life as it was always meant to be, counting on My Providence for each one, My Plan for each life, My Path for each soul. My Son, My dearest Jesus, has always been the answer, the gift I give to all. All must accept Him and believe that He is the Messiah already sent to die once for the world to open the floodgates of redemption and salvation.

"Child, this is not difficult. The Plan of Salvation will bring all to a knowledge and understanding of My Jesus Whom I love above all creatures. It will be a cleansing that will result in peace and prosperity in My Will. It will be now that evil will be removed once for all from the hearts of My people. This will take a certain amount of time. The journey back to Me through the Hearts of Jesus and Mary has begun! You know the sweetness of this journey, this path. Encourage all to take the first step toward My Kingdom. It will be a journey that will result in the renewal of souls, of families and ultimately, the entire earth. Your heart fills with love and gratitude, My daughter, and I am filled with gratitude Who Am Love!

"We will win, I promise you. We will overcome all obstacles and stand triumphant together one day soon in My Kingdom. The renewed Kingdom of Heaven on earth will be a marvel to behold and fill all with silent awe.

"My Heart beats in tune with your own in the excitement of fulfillment. The time is truly now, little one. The word of your Lord has been given this day to all who will accept it and believe. Be of one mind and heart with Me now, child, never to return to the world until it is completely renewed and My Son will reign triumphantly among all of Our chosen, renewed ones. Thank you for saying 'yes' so many years ago to My urgings to offer yourself for the salvation of souls. Welcome to the very active time of fulfillment and grace."

6/8/96, Jesus said:

"My dearest child, please write My words given for your inspiration. Lately, daughter, your heart is weary and sad. You do need to take time away now to recover, littlest one. You need to come to Me and be completely emptied of all that burdens and distracts you. The time for your mission has already begun, as you can see by the increased travel and busyness of constant preparation. In the coming months, this will only increase. To survive and live fruitfully these sacred days, you must be completely free to follow and embrace My Will for you and for all of your time and energy, too. Your heart, little one, is still torn between the world and all that I offer you. This very day must see a solid decision on your part from which you will not waiver. The heart knows no boundaries, child, and so must be guided and trained with My discipline. You are in need of continued rest and a surrender to the routine you are called to by My Mother and by Me. The days are not to be spent in worldly pursuits. You know that, and yet, the flesh wars against all the Spirit calls you to be. There is much more that I wish to reveal to you, daughter, but you must be more free, less entangled with chores and decisions that do not have to do with My Kingdom directly.

"You must reread Our words to you many times before the chaos erupts. I tell you it will occur at any moment! Your own preparation, My dear little one, is so important to everyone. Please, continue to organize your notes and Our words so that you will be ready at any time to speak, to respond to the requests and needs of others. You must know, by now, how dearly and totally you are loved. Please do not waste any of the time you might spend here with Me in frivolity. Your place now, loved child, is with Me, your Lord and Spouse. The more time you give to this relationship, the deeper it will become. Remember that to serve is the goal, and nothing else is important. The more time you give to Our relationship, the deeper it will become. Whatever needs doing in your house, please finish this quickly and allow Me to minister to you as you prepare to minister to Our dear little ones who will come here.

"The days are waiting to be filled with the working out of the Father's Will. My people will be stunned by all that will very, very shortly unfold in the whole world. Any of My children who are of a mind, will serve them (the people Jesus and Mary send to us) for the rest of their lives. You will all follow Me wherever I lead you.

"The Kingdom of God is about to manifest itself on earth. My people will live in simplicity and splendor! You are never out of My sight or My reach or My touch. See Me, child. Reach out to Me. Feel My heavenly touch. Daughter, you have a sweet, loving heart that is ready to answer each of My commands. Be at peace about all else. Be ready at every moment for the Will of My Father to be given by Him and received by yourself. You will do all We have promised. You are a seasoned warrior. You are My little one whom I cherish and love and count on! I am your Jesus Who is One with My Father and Our Spirit, Who loves the Father and praises, honors and obeys Him. I am your Lord and your God."

6/17/96, Jesus said:

"My dear one, please write. I, your Lord Jesus, hear your pleas for mercy. I have come, My little one, to ease your longing and fill your heart with love and consolation.

"The time for your rendering is here. (I looked this up: to give, hand over, deliver, present or submit as for approval, payment, etc. or to *give surrender*; to give in return, to do a service; to represent, depict, to perform or interpret; recite; *to express in other words*!!!!) You are close to the brink of a new dawn, a new direction for all you have learned and become.

"The Father in Heaven smiles with favor this night and has given permission for greater degrees of strength of soul and mind. What is needed to fulfill this mission for which you have prepared diligently has been sent this night on the wings of a special Angel of Mercy.

"Rejoice once again, daughter of the promise. Your weaknesses are to be healed and your defenses shored up. The degrees of struggle have brought you a new maturity, little one. Your heart is firm in its desires to serve under any conditions till the day when you return with Me to the Heavenly Kingdom that awaits you. **There will be many years of physical hardships and battles with the evil one. You will be attacked, My child, and brought to noth-**

ing! This is by decree of My Father and will win salvation for many thousands.

"It is an excitement in Heaven that you feel this night, as the great gift of Our warning to every inhabitant of earth *commences. Please stay closer than ever to My Sacramental Presence. Your work is truly winding down. It has been a long and colorful journey these past years and you *have* persevered. I, your Lord and God, tell you I will be proud to ride into battle with you at My side. Expect every grace and healing that is needed to be given. This too, is a special gift from My Father for your faithfulness and obedience. You will weep in wonderment and joy at the great miracles about to be given in this place.

"My Mother smiles at your delight. She, too, is filled with delight, and prays and longs to see all of Our promises begin. The dawn is always coming to the world, and this dawn brings hope and joy, love and compassion with it. Hopelessness and despair will soon disappear, as My Father's Plan unfolds. Dearest one, stay close to Me. As you begin tomorrow to reread Our words, your resolve and peace of mind will be re-cemented in trust. The weekend (Retreat at Christ the King Church plus meeting at the house Sunday morning) was so rich in graces, and My graces and mercy were poured out on each one who attended. They are such dear ones who love Me, their Lord. So many gifts are waiting for each one who has persevered.

"Your freedom is greatly increased this night in order to enable you to spend all of your time loving and adoring, praying and studying. Little one, I love you with an everlasting love."

6/27/96, Jesus said:

"My dear one, you may write My words given for your instruction. The hours go by quickly and before you know it, have left us without the light of Christ! I, your Mother of Sorrows, am speaking now, My dearest one. Welcome to a new level of abandonment and surrender! It is always necessary to see a life as fully

---

* And there was another delay!

as possible before making decisions. It is good to endure whatever is required to move you to the proper choice.

"You are loved and blessed, My child. The time, child of My Immaculate Heart, has left the realm of your own experience now and gives way to simply a series of events. Praise be to God Our loving Father, daughter. Praise and thank Him continually. The beauty of His Plan is unmatched by any beauty in this present world. You will be enjoying the fruits of His gifts and plans for you at any moment. My dear one, the Father knows how to handle each person, each situation, each new development in His plans for the salvation of His people. Do you think He would forget you? Or lie to you? Or lead you astray? No, of course not! The results of a long wait are a lessening of strength until one develops the proper amount of trust in the Father's ability to care for you.

"The dawn comes like thunder now for those ready to serve in freedom and hope! My own heart fills with joy at the beginning of this new phase of purifying by Our Father for His people. The dawn will indeed bring new evidence of His Mighty Hand as it falls again to the earth. The fires you hear about and other disasters are just beginning The world will continue to rock with explosions and calamities.

"Child, my heart is rocked with the chaos and confusion present in Our children. The hearts of so many are filled with anguish without the peace of My Son. Not a day will go by from now on without some major incident in the world, culminating in huge disasters of the greatest proportions. *Without holding My hand and asking constantly for My help, you will all be overcome!* This must be a conscious effort at every moment of the day and night. Pray for the virtues offered by your Mother who loves you all so tenderly. There is no time left now, just a series of events that will build and build toward a momentous climax of events.

"I do not mean to alarm you, My children, but wish for you to be prepared and alert from this moment on to the need for **constant vigilance and prayer, living in Our Presence** with the Angels and Saints now. This request is most serious, dearest one, because it will see all of you through impossible trials. You must know and believe that you are never alone, that We are all with you at all times. Please tell **My beloved ones who pray they are pressed**

to My Immaculate Heart continuously. Without a doubt in your minds, believe that you are **truly, actually wrapped in my Mantle and held in My arms** and the **arms of My Son.** These protections must be nurtured by yourselves, asked for and then given thanks and praise (for) to the Father Who gifts you in these ways. We will never leave you, especially when all seems lost and appears to be darkest. It is easy now to believe these words, daughter, but believe me, when the chaos roars about your heads, you will call out for mercy and beg to feel Our Presence. It is then that faith and trust in all Our words will bring you through the trials and sufferings of the moment. To Our poor lost souls who will need so much help and direction, *simple lessons are the best* for these dear ones who return quickly to their Father's House.

"Know that you will never have the worry of nothing to do again! All of your desires for action are being fulfilled as the Father's Plan escalates in your midst. This is meant to be a lesson to be shared, child. Please rest now and continue your fine work. You are held closely hidden in My Heart."

6/29/96, Jesus said:

"...the days are holding their breath, child! The whole world trembles in anticipation for the great changes about to occur. There will come a time when you will not recognize the face of the earth, so altered will it be. I, your Lord and Savior, thank you for your presence here. Is it not peaceful, just to be in each other's company?

"What a dreadful journey it is...out of the clutches of the evil one! To be dragged down and tormented and then to need to fight one's way out of this pit is a long and arduous task. Always, **no matter what evil assails you, take advantage of every grace and help offered by all of Us in Heaven.** It is *My Father's Will* that each of you overcome the sly attacks of Satan and be one with Us for all Eternity. Continue to bring each dilemma, no matter how silly or mundane, to My Heart through the heart of My Mother. When you do this, there is no way you will lose! Expect many future struggles of every sort and remember this path to humility and holiness. **It is never too late to begin again at a new level of**

remorse and forgiveness. Please, do not ever be discouraged by your weaknesses. Use them as a springboard to the next level of unity with Our Hearts. In the end, you will be looking back at the world from Paradise (!!)

"The world is in chaos. My mother's heart is broken by the rejection of so many of her earthly children. Please console her with your prayers and visits with her. Be aware of her presence at your side constantly. *Every moment can be a prayer when you consecrate it throughout each day.* Please, child, avail yourself of the opportunity to live more fully in the Kingdom here on earth. There are many uniting themselves to Us in this way. You can be closer to them by uniting your prayer to all of theirs. Go in My Peace now to love and serve Me forever."

7/3/96, Jesus said:

"The world slips away into darkness, as My Light dims in the lives of most of Our children. Even Our chosen souls who have remained faithful will undergo another change of heart and a laxity in purpose.

"Just prior to My Warning for the world, many natural events will have caused great havoc and destruction. There will be some who are touched and led back to Us as they recognize My Father's Hand. But, in general, the world becomes colder and darker as hearts harden again from new austerities and hardships.

"The Warning will not occur in 1996(!!) That is all I am able to tell you, but soon after the start of the New Year.* The Divine Will of My Father is perfect for each soul. Be patient with your God, My loved one, Who only acts out of love for His people. Time is fading so quickly. You will be amazed at the rapidity with which events occur, once major ones begin. All will be accomplished, child. Your own gifts will attest to that fact, and you will work very hard completing tasks and going out to all to convince them to persevere.

"Daughter of My Sacred Heart, you are most precious and important to the Plan of My Father. You will be overwhelmed with gratitude as these gifts are made known for the good of Our people.

---

*(But which one?)

Please, child, always remember that a gift is given for others. As an instrument of My Father, you are **totally helpless and dependent upon His Will at all times!** Please pray to surrender even more at this time. You are doing so well at this new level of abandonment. Peace and rest to you, dear one."

12/11/96, Jesus said:

"There is so much evil increasing everywhere in the world. You each must have the greatest faith in all Our words, Our promises, because the darkness accelerates rapidly now and you will be plagued by feelings of doubt and despair without the open channel of grace between My Mother and all of you. These graces must be able to flow without interruption from now on. No sin or turning away for an instant must impede the flow of these graces to all of those who listen to and follow My Mother. You will see profound changes still in all of her Army, since the greatest perfection is being offered now and must be consciously chosen and accepted. The evil one and his cohorts are poised to strike at the heart of My Church and beloved Vicar. Please hold him up to the Father at every moment for the Will of God to be his strength and protection. Remember that **all must occur to fulfill Scripture exactly.**

"Do not be afraid, My dear one. Do not be afraid, My people. Nothing will happen to you and your families that is contrary to the Father's Will. Each one who is taken into Eternity will be brought before Him as just and merciful judge. **I, Myself, am the One Who will guide each loved one into the Kingdom of My Father where they will pray for all of you in love and total peace and sublime happiness.**

"These very, very serious times in the world must be attended by a **new maturity and sense of devotion and commitment to personal sanctity and the salvation of all** those We send to you. In the coming days when so many more will see the truth of their hearts and souls, each one will need to surrender totally the rest of their lives here on earth to the action of the Father's Will in each life and to **accept instantly all of those who come as their fondest brother and sister and grave responsibility.** All is too serious now to put off paying strict attention to each request, each call (to all of you).

You know in your hearts **how needy and careless you were at one time,** and without the gifts and graces being given, you would not be in the right place to continue to grow in love and service.

"Dear one, please work with Our people everywhere to fight the evil one and to present a united front against his subtle workings to destroy every family, every soul, every good deed you wish to offer to Us. Know that it is necessary to heal your hearts more completely so that families and groups of believers (that have been divided by his cunning) can be restored whole and healthy without judgements and righteous attitudes.

"I speak at length, My child, and ask you to beg all who will listen and believe these words, to act quickly during these remaining days before the celebration of My Birth. Many gifts are being offered for Our people. Please pray that all will accept them immediately. You are held tightly in My arms, My littlest one. Be assured of continuing love and strength being poured out for you. Your prayers are the jewels which adorn your heavenly crowns, My dear ones. Prepare yourselves to approach the throne of My Father in gleaming finery. My blessings are poured out upon you, daughter. Thank you for taking these words."

12/26/96, Jesus said:

"My dearest child, I your Jesus of Mercy, come this night to soothe your fatigue and bring you into My Sacred Heart. The hours have fled by with all of the busyness, and now you are able to settle down once more and listen to My words. You have done well to remain focused, daughter. Please be encouraged about your progress. The coming days will show you the results of your perseverance. Please, child, do not be discouraged by fatigue. When it is necessary to have extraordinary strength and endurance, you will find them ready and waiting for your every need. The faith and trust you now have, My littlest one, in all of Our words and promises will carry you to every height and sustain your every need.

"The night, My dear one, is already over for you and you are able to be at peace with your Angels and special Saints. I am most grateful, My little soldier, that you now turn to Me at every opportunity. You are correct to observe that each one will need to have much reserve for the coming months and years. The need to be totally prepared has never been greater, daughter. As you reflect upon the process of My birth, you know that My Mother and all mothers wait nine months while their babies are being nourished and sustained in the womb. At the proper time of development, I was born in the lowly manger, ready to begin My Mission of Salvation. So it is for all of you. You have each been nourished in the heart of My Mother until now, the proper time for another birth into the world of My Father's perfect Will! You will live in that world from now on and be further nourished and sustained by your Heavenly Mother until you are strong soldiers who are ready to fight by My side against all the powers of evil.

"You ARE ready now, My dearest one, for this grave and important task, as are all who have remained faithful. Be ready and alert from now on, please My little ones of My chosen remnant. The dawn arrives quickly after the long night and sees much action (as in... activity) arrive with each new development of light. *You will not wonder what to do or where to go, since My Angels will lead all of you at every step. They will be your leaders and guides. They will take you into the proper direction if you will pray to them and allow them to lead you. Nothing that happens will be unimportant in the future, so please learn to be more alert and pay attention to all that is happening around you.*

"For your own safety, it will be necessary that each is on guard, My child. There will be enemies everywhere. You will not know who to trust without paying close attention to those who have the gift of recognizing the sign of My Cross on the foreheads of My faithful ones. You will have this power, little one of My Heart, as well as many other gifts in order to lead My people and convince them of Our love and protection. You are filled with fatigue because of your attempts to mix the world and pleasure with the work I give to you. That will never again be the case, daughter. From now on, only My needs and desires and directions will fill the hours of your day. The work you do for Me is not so draining and tiring as the emotional tension present in the demands of the world.

"The Father's plan races to completion. The extended time of grace and mercy has prepared all of those who follow My Mother's requests, and who will act as her messengers. The dawn IS breaking, daughter, on the final day of the Lord in this Age. Yes, this is a pattern that has been repeated over the history of Our people in every Era. This one has been the most advanced and, therefore, the most stubborn and stiff-necked people. Never has evil reached such a high level of acceptance and refinement in Our world.

"All is in the hands of your Creator and Savior. All will see His saving power and the might of His arm. Never, for a moment, doubt the victorious outcome of the battle of Good over the evil one. Be filled with even greater love and gratitude and conviction now, little daughter. Share the good news of your Savior and Creator with all who will listen. Do not waste any time on frivolous pastimes. Please be totally immersed in Our Will for you. Know that you are held in Our Two Hearts and have been molded to conform to Their shape.

"Your heart, My dearest one, is so free and now able to let go of all and everything you once thought of as belonging to you. You are now ready to **fly above the things of earth.** You will experience the Father's love for you and be forever united to His Will.

"Please, little one, rest and be renewed. Any moment will see the end of your earthly ties and ways of thinking and acting. You will recognize your new behavior as you live out this next step of the journey back to Us. Daughter, I pray for you constantly. Be filled with Our love. Go in peace."

12/30/96, Jesus said:

"My dear one, yes! Please write these words of comfort and We will visit and just be together. Your (prayer) group warms the hearts of all in Heaven. The souls who suffer in the fires of Purgatory wait eagerly for the prayers of all who offer their special graces for them. Your heart is filled with longing, littlest one of My Heart, to see the completion of this mission. All of Our chosen messengers are so anxious to begin the final stages of the Day of the Lord. We too, watch and wait and pray that all will persevere until the end.

"Dearest child, be filled with My peace now. Your days are full and you will need all the rest you can store for the days ahead. You are listening well to Our Spirit and this will result in a grand instrument (the book, *Do Whatever Love Requires*) of My Father's Will. The hour is filled with wakefulness, daughter. Please prepare for a night of rest and prayer for all of those less fortunate than yourself. I know you appreciate the gifts you have been given, but you can share them with your sisters far away and send them your love and concern for their comfort.

"The night is far spent for all who revel and spend their time foolishly. Pray for all Our children, My dear one, that they will be open to the graces about to be offered. The night is filled with wonder for those who wait and watch and pray. Be at peace. Be filled with the deep joy that makes you relax in My arms and take your rest there. Be blessed, daughter."

1/3/97, Jesus said:

"My dear one, please take these words given for Our mutual pleasure! This night, My daughter, a new chapter begins for you. Thank you for your persistence in producing the best possible results for Our beloved people. You have been patient and obedient and I thank you with all My Sacred and Eucharistic Heart.

"You are about to enter a most serious and dangerous time in the history of Our Church. Before long, there will be persecutions beginning and these will signal your **immediate departure for a safe place of refuge. Do not be concerned with where, daughter of My Will. I will lead you through special Angels assigned to guard each one of My faithful ones.**

"The events at St. Maria Goretti will be of overwhelming magnitude. My young ones will be outstanding servants of their Lord. **There will be many miracles performed for Our people in this place.** Your own understanding of the future is indeed quite accurate and you are wise to stay as close as possible to prayer and Our company.

"My little one of My Sacred Heart, do not be worried about anything for the rest of your life! Know that all has begun and is fulfilling Scripture at this moment. More will become aware of the significance of ongoing events very shortly. People in many parts of the globe are suffering terrible hardships because of cold and inclement weather.

"Have faith, little one. Relinquish your hold now on all that you have done to this time, this moment for Us. A new direction will begin for you now. Be at peace, daughter. You are loved and appreciated. Sleep in My peace."

3/25/97, Jesus said:

"My dear one, please write. You are still filled with consternation and fear, little daughter. Don't you know that I am protecting you every step of the way on this new path of suffering and humiliation? You know how much you are loved, yet you still choose not to remember My power. The Father's plan contains a great deal of suffering for all His chosen ones. You are seeing and hearing about this now and are brought to a new level of understanding.

"I **am** your Jesus Who speaks this day, My daughter. You have nothing to fear because only the wishes of Heaven can save My other children of the earth. **Without the betrayal, the in-fighting, the judgementalism, and pain of rejection and ridicule, you cannot truly live the life I lived on earth.**

"You are strong; you are seasoned; you are an able warrior. This onslaught of anger and malice is evidence of the mind of evil. The mind of God is never left behind (i.e. will never lose to, or be overcome by) the attacks and evil plans and machinations of Satan. All are brought into the realm of Love by first realizing the futility and emptiness and harm of living in the world of the evil one. He is the Prince of Lies and does everything he can to divide and obstruct and confuse. This is the darkness that the 'Light' will overcome. This is the evil that will be defeated by the victory of My return, and the Antichrist will be banished forever as a result of My power of Love and the Love that lives within the hearts of all My faithful ones.

"Dear one of My Heart, **you do** know how I will save you and all My chosen messengers. You **do** trust in Me, I know it! You **do** understand that it is only necessary to wait in joy and hope for Me to work in all of this. Please, daughter, stay close to Me this week. You can see now that there is no other way. Your heart is so filled with desire to please and to obey. These traits alone will pull you through every attack the evil one levels against you. Continue to offer setbacks, that really are not, and frustrations to Me. This holiest of weeks is the perfect atmosphere and environment in which to share My Passion, My walk to Calvary.

"Stay close, daughter. You will do all of the things We have spoken about and promised you. Have the greatest trust and faith, dearest one. You are loved. You will overcome; you will be blessed by My Father in so very many ways. Do not be sad or alarmed, please, by continuing developments. Yes, things will be more difficult in the near future. You are only to pray and stay hidden here by My side. Please, please, daughter, believe Me and all I promise you. Remain in My peace."

3/30/97, Jesus said:

"Dear one, you may write. I, your Lord Jesus, come with words of peace and very much love. Continue to pray here each day for long periods of time this week, My child. I, your Lord, wish to prepare you for new gifts. Truly, I am Jesus Who speaks to you, little one. I Who adore My Father in Our Spirit, in Our most holy Trinity, have words of comfort and direction, child. Be at peace, daughter, every moment now. You are so aware of the nearness of major events in the world. Know that your spirit is growing in strength and understanding. You can feel the certainty of My Presence and voice, child of My Love, because of new gifts from My Father.

"Today is the culmination of so many prayers, so much fasting and extra penances that have all been gathered by the Angels to present to My Father for the good of the world. These prayers have strengthened everyone. The love in the hearts of My faithful ones has healed them to a new degree. Your words and pleading to all have been most effective and helpful, and many more have been faithful to asking for this gift (the healing of their hearts). Graces continue to flow, daughter. Your dear ones in Heaven pray together constantly for you and are aware of each new victory. Your energy and desire to serve are more victorious because of the constant prayers of these dear loved ones. They weep with joy at the success of each new endeavor and chant hymns of praise to the Father.

"Daughter, again I ask, do not be alarmed at the vehemence of attacks. I have promised you to defeat the evil one and minimize the effects of his attacks. This need to trust, this perseverance on your part will carry you through truly dangerous times ahead.

"Daughter, please know that all events are upon the world and especially this country. Be ready to leave, at any moment, for the beginning of your final stages of this part of your journey. Time is gone. Your heart has reached a new level of seasoning. You are in the right place to receive the gifts My Father is now giving to you.

"Little one, rejoice. Please stay hidden in much prayer and unity with Me and My Sorrowful Mother. Hurry back to Me, daughter. Be at peace. Be filled with all of the graces of this special season of My Resurrection. Be resurrected now yourself from the darkness of fear and confusion into the light of My love and peace. Be filled now with My love for you."

4/5/97, Jesus said:

"My dear one, please write My words. It is time for you, My child, to be in total abandonment to Me. That means **you will not fret or worry anymore.** You will trust in your Jesus and His Divine Mercy. I am that Mercy, dearest one. I am that Love and Power that created the universe and everyone in it. I am the One Who has promised to save you from annihilation and ruin.

"Be no longer afraid, daughter. Problems that are perceived as such by others will all blow away in the winds of Our Spirit and the waters of grace. You have only to continue to persevere and pray and remain close to Me. You are doing all that you can do for Me, daughter, and I, your Lord, am grateful and love you with all My love and holy gratitude. Please, please trust in Our care for you. The Plan of My Father is occurring as We have told you. Continue to work and live the way you have been in a schedule that includes balance and peace. You will face all the dilemmas and traps and snares set in your path by the evil one. He is no match for My power. Remember that he will be defeated, is already defeated. You must only remain faithful to Our words and promises and wait for all to play out in your life.

"Remember, child, I am your God Who has saved you already. Just allow yourself to continue to trust in all We have told you, that you know to be truth. You are loved."

4/16/97, Jesus said:

"Dear child of My Heart, of course I wish to speak words of comfort to you. I am a God Who loves each of His dearest ones and I will always wish to comfort with that love. Your trust and obedience and the wisdom you have received are serving you well in this trial. It is the Triune God Whose love and acceptance will be life giving for all eternity. The light of My Love is nearly extinguished in most hearts, even those of My faithful who serve Me at this time. You can see the pattern of purification for My people.

"You know from past experiences that I will make all right with the world at the proper time. I love you, daughter! Do you not feel joy and gratitude that you are being further united to Me and all that I lived before you? Do you not realize the great gift of My Presence and words to your heart? Please, dwell in My peace and allow gratitude to fill your being and heal you.

"My daughter, We **all** wait, as you are doing, in hope and prayer for the Father's Will to be accomplished soon. Events in the world have set the stage for these plans of His to be forthcoming. In the so very near future, all will play out, as We have told you, for your life. You can see how necessary the seeming delays have been and all that has needed to happen in your own preparation.

"Praise the Father's Wisdom and Love. Thank Him for preparing each of you to the utmost before the final battle erupts. Things in the world, conditions everywhere, are so critical and have reached the point of exploding. Even the comet becomes commonplace after you have viewed it often enough; so much more the words of warning from My Mother to all her children. **You will see many grow cold now even among My faithful. This great sadness will be the most difficult to endure and accept.**

"Encourage each other in patience and sweetness of spirit. Thank you for continuing to allow the Father to work in your life and purify your heart. What happens now and in the future is simply a fulfillment of all that has been foretold. Be of good cheer, My little one of My Heart, and persevere in joy and hope and trust."

4/26/97, Jesus said:

"My dear child, I your Jesus, love you. Please take My words given this night for the peace and healing of your spirit. The night is far spent and My special chosen ones everywhere wait in hiddenness for events to occur that will fulfill prophecy and promises in their own lives.

"PURIFICATION IS ABOUT REMOVING EVERY LAST VESTIGE OF YOUR OWN WILL, SO THAT THE FATHER'S WILL MAY LIVE TOTALLY WITHIN EACH OF YOU.

"You cannot serve at the level you are called to without complete surrender and emptying. Please, please child, do not give another thought to what has been. It is only for you to continue to say yes and pray for all those involved, including your dear spouse whose heart breaks when you are hurt. The days here are golden and will prove so fruitful even though you cannot see results at this time. All is being accomplished now, daughter, for the good of all and fulfillment of My Father's plan.

"Have courage, little one. We have only just begun! There will be many dark and bitter nights ahead. My Mother and her Angels are with you constantly. You are doing well. All will be overcome in a twinkling at the proper time. I, your Jesus of Mercy Who adores My Father in Our Holy Spirit, bring peace to your spirit, daughter. Be strengthened. Persevere!"

5/10/97, Jesus said:

"Dear one, do you remember what I told you so long ago about the love in your heart? **Service and patience are the great measure of love!** The events about to occur in the world are at a breaking point. And so is the endurance of all Our faithful ones. As the priest (during Mass) mentioned tonight, if you had known how many years would play out before My Father's Will began for the earth, you could never have born the wait! As it is, circumstances have unfolded in such a way that all the healing and wisdom you need have been given with time to spare. Please do not doubt a single word I have told you. Continue to study, as time is no longer on your side. These words will always be your salvation in times of trouble and a great, great help to Our lost children who gather about you. Have courage, My daughter. Have trust in My continued strength and the gifts of My Father on your behalf. Many are the times we will ride into battle from now on. Blessings are poured upon you this night."

6:30 p.m. Mother's Day - Mary said:

"Dearest child of the Immaculate Heart, I your Heavenly Mother, am allowed to speak this night to wish you joy and blessings amidst the trials and sorrows that are here. Please believe that it is I, your Mother Mary. I have come to bring gifts of strength and courage and perseverance from the Father.

"Little daughter, there has been a huge increase of patience and compassion. Without these increased gifts, you could never serve the long hours that await you in the future. The events now unfolding will serve to strengthen your belief in everything We have told you. All of a sudden, you will be in the midst of their unfolding and will not have time to think, but only react to each person, each tragedy that is shared, (after the Illumination).

"The days of rest are over, and the world will be filled with chaos and bloodshed until the last moment of this Age."

5/16/97, Jesus said:

"My dear child, write these words now given for your instruction. Yes, I am your Jesus, come to speak with love and gratitude once again. Dear one, please spend time this night continuing to praise the Father for His many gifts. Be filled with eagerness now, My daughter, for you are entering a totally new era of service to Him Who has chosen you to do so many special things for His people. The Way of the Cross opens before you, daughter.

"Daughter, My Heart is broken daily by the rejection of My Mother's requests by those who should remain faithful to her. There is such pride and corruption in the love present in many hearts today. Please continue to try to be humble and patient with all who come to you. The hearts of so many here are prepared for anything and will be all the Father intended when the time comes to serve

His people. Try to listen constantly to the voice of My Spirit Who will be directing you often in the coming hours and days.

"The Father's Will is going forward now unimpeded and totally. The days and months have come to the time of action, and you will all be busy defending, teaching and leading until the moment of My return. I, too, tremble with joy at the thought of My return.

"Daughter, your heart is seasoned and full of holy love for all My people. Fear nothing now. The time of fulfillment has begun, and nothing will stand in the way of your successful accomplishments. I welcome you to this era of cleansing before the incredible Age of peace and purity. My Heart swells in union with your own in anticipation of all that is to come.

"Hold My hand now, child, as we ride into battle on the wings of grace and the gifts of My Father. I bless you again tonight and hold out My hand to grasp yours. Together we ride into the fray. Together we meet the enemy. Together we take up the cross of freedom and victory, as we serve that purest and holiest of women, our own heavenly Mother, My dearest Mary. I salute you, daughter, and lead you deeply into My Heart which is your armor and your protection. Stay close, little one of My Heart. The fighting will be fierce!"

5/22/97, Jesus said:

"My child, please write. I, your Jesus, do have words of direction for you. As of this night, little soldier, you will no longer wonder what to do. You will be working at all of the promises We have made. Child, this is your Jesus Who adores My Father and serves Him to the fullest. You are following in My footsteps now, daughter, in your service and love.

"Tonight, daughter, I bring you a gift of strength and peace once more that you may accept with full understanding that all the delays you have suffered are over. We need you, My dearest one, to be one with Us now and so, special gifts and events will begin this very night to begin your own increased ministry to Our people. You will see what I mean tomorrow as soon as the day begins. You are stout-hearted in Our love and persevering in trust. You have great need of rest first and so, as the Sun rises, so will the next phase of My Father's plan for you. We desire that you remain ever so near to Our Mother. The plans include days of rest and relaxation until you are built up again. Do not think of another duty, little daughter, save staying in the confines of My Heart.

"Yes, you may publish and distribute one more set of your outline for Our people. Keep trying to guide them as best as you find possible. It is not plausible that Our words are not ever new and fresh and needed for the hearts and spirits of those who wish to serve.

"Come away now, and be one with Me. Begin at early Mass and much prayer in My Tabernacle. Then watch and see what happens! The Angels are following you everywhere in a ring of protection and love. Please feel their presence and be lifted up by them. You will never be without Our presence, please remember, and you only need to stop and become aware of Us at any time. Please rest now. I, your Jesus, bless you with special gifts from the Father. Be free, little one."

5/27/97, Jesus said:

"My dearest daughters, I love you as no other. This time and this place is sacred. These prayers of your hearts are golden and meant to strengthen you to the fullest. Do not fear, My sweet ones, for the Lord God, Himself, is caring for you and will provide wherever you are lacking.

"Yes, certainly, listen to the Spirit speak to your hearts regarding supplies of every nature. Be practical in your approach. Take rolls of bandages, first aid books and whatever will give you first hand instructions. The people who succumb to the trials and hardships are meant to return to My Father. Many, many will be needed to pray for all of you who are left to bear the burden of these times. Remember My strength and My grace. Do no more than you are able to do and, *above all, please do not worry*. This plan of My Father's includes any and every possibility. The problems which arise will be difficult, yes, but will never completely overwhelm those to whom it is given to remain to serve and prepare the way for My coming.

"You are jewels in My crown, daughters. (The question had been asked for someone else, 'what is the deeper significance of Jesus' thorns?') The deeper significance of My thorns is that they are My glory, My earthly crown that will be shared by many of My messengers, but are mystically available to all. They are a sign of My earthly Kingdom. In Heaven, these thorns are a sign of My penetrating love that is burned deeply into your memory when you embrace My suffering. **Everything is about My love for you and our ultimate unity, dear children.** Come to Me, embrace Me, embrace My cross with eagerness by accepting your own crosses with joy and My gift of peace.

"Truly, daughters of My Heart, you have gladdened this Heart today and that of My Mother. There are few places of peace and love that call to Us and allow Us to rest. Please continue, as you are, to serve and walk with Us this Valley of Destruction and Suffering. Spend every spare minute with Me, daughters. Come in trust and surrender. I am your sweet Jesus of Mercy, come to bless and renew you this day."

6/3/97, Jesus said:

"Nothing must come in the way of My desires for your company, My dearest ones. Obedience is the great strength you must exercise to the utmost now and bring all the self-discipline to bear that you can muster. The days are full enough with chores and must be filled up with prayer and more visits to Me. Please, shed your last few worldly garments and approach the Lord your God in total freedom and surrender. The outcome of these battles over self is victory at every turn, no matter how grim it may look for a time! The importance of taking this final step is understood by all of you. Please admit to yourselves the seriousness of the times and these requests.

"When you look back on the world, you will see and feel its emptiness. Please do not hesitate now to leap across the chasm between the world and the Kingdom. Allow My Mother to fashion special garments for you now that will reflect your new place in Our plan, in Our Kingdom. Allow Her to cleanse the remaining stains of the world from your heart, and remain in purity."

6/8/97, Jesus said:

"Dearest child, please take My words. They are given for your immediate instruction. Dear one, your trip here has been a great success for all those who were open to Our words. The effects in each area you visit are far more important than you will ever realize. The night sees an end to great graces and gifts being poured out, but that will continue to affect Our people for many months and years.

"Daughter, the days are so few before this country erupts in chaos. The world is poised on the brink of change. You will wonder how you did not perceive the enormity of destruction and hardships. It is a good lesson in the need for absolute trust in Our words of warning and the proper prayer response.

"My dearest one, I, your Lord and Savior, come tonight to say that all is well with your heart. Just, please daughter, maintain the conviction now in your heart, and persevere. Just one day at a time, My little loved one. Please stay very quiet and hidden back at home and wait for the next move of My Father. You can do this because you are already accepting more graces. You sit in wonder, but child, you do believe completely now that all We have foretold will come to pass. Praise and thank Our Heavenly Father, My daughter, for the graces bestowed for this purpose.

"It is going to be such a difficult time, and so *the Father waits until He can wait no longer* to fulfill all of Scripture in time for My return. You are filled with joy and peace, and My Mother and I have come this night to dwell more deeply in your heart. Know that this is a gift from the Father for the service you render to His people. Continue to remain focused and serious about the matters of the future. Stay in Our Presence with all your heart and strength, little one. The progress you make when this happens is so necessary to your new mission."

6/11/97, Jesus said:

"Dearest child, thank you for these prayers. They cause My Heart to sing with gratitude. The three of you touch the chill in My Heart caused by the rejection of so many. My children, you wait in wonder for the Will of My Father. Please know that this waiting is

His Will! Each thing you experience is by design. To be here in silence like this is so good for your healing. Your hearts are so eager, and We are grateful for all of your desires to serve.

"The earth will rumble soon in all the areas of this country. Please be ready to handle any emergency. Your hearts are pure with the need to be obedient to Our directions. Your prayers are heartfelt and full of love for My Mother and Myself.

"Dear ones, praise My Father and yours for allowing you to serve Him and His people. The coming destruction will set the stage for your ability to serve the needs of all who come. You will bring them to Me in the Blessed Sacrament for healing. You have learned so much here (Phoenix and Scottsdale), My precious pilgrims. Please, do not continue to be agitated about anything you must endure, but see all of this as gift of the Father to teach and perfect you. Do not ask for special signs, but look for the ones that are being given! You are so deeply loved and appreciated by your God and your precious Mother. All of Heaven sings of your deeds and your love. The waiting will be over as you return and begin to prepare more earnestly for the future. This must be done without delay, dear ones. You are mighty soldiers who are held in the Mantle of My Mother. This day new graces are given to you in order to bring you closer into the union of Our Two Hearts and into the Divine Will of God, Our Father.

"Be at peace, little ones, and continue to offer each pain and difficulty for the conversion of your family. The differences among you will all be resolved in plenty of time to enable you to work together as one with My Heart. Many will be the hours you will work to serve those who come to you. You will do all in union with Mary. Stay close to her, little soldiers. You are all loved so very much. Peace be with you now. Be healed again of many fears and wonderings. I, your Lord and Savior, bless you in union with My Father and Holy Spirit."

6/12/97, Jesus said:

"Dear one, please write. Your efforts and prayers today were a wonderful beginning of your newest mission. Please be encouraged by all that occurred. Yes, I am your Jesus, come again to strengthen and encourage you. You have made such great progress in just a few days. Continue, to struggle against your nature(!) and to see all events clearly in the light of grace. All in Heaven who pray for you rejoice at the new strength in your heart. The trials will continue, of course, and you will overcome the evil one at every turn if you will always turn to Us for help. Your understanding of Our power on your behalf is a big step in enabling it to be given. Do you wonder how your life continued for so long without this understanding? (Indeed!)

"Please do not be concerned about My continued presence in your life as a source of direction and direct attention. Your needs have never been frivolous nor your requests selfish. Do not worry about anything now, please My dearest friend and love."

6/18/97, Jesus said:

"The days will continue as they are throughout the summer, but as Fall develops across the nation, fierce changes will occur within Our Church and difficulties will develop for all Our messengers.

"The prayers of My Mother are filled with tears and pleading for more graces for all of you. She does not wish to see any of you embroiled in the machinations of her enemies. The mere fact of your love for her assures your presence in her 'troubles.' However, she is so grateful for all you and her faithful ones here do for her intentions. Truly, daughter, your progress along the path to the Father's Will has been noted and blessed and cheered (they do seem to party a lot!) by all of Us in Heaven. Great is the support you receive from your special Angels and Saints.

"My Mother sends love and blessings. You fill her heart with joy when you pray and laugh (with) and serve all those who come to you. The prayers of your group are precious, and will continue to be accepted and blessed by Our Father. Many new gifts will be apparent to all of you in the coming weeks. Our people need encouragement, as well as yourself. Believe that more signs and healings will be given in the coming weeks and throughout the rest of your life. Thank you for coming to spend time with Me. Your energy and level of commitment are becoming a great prayer of praise to My Father. Your obedience is a balm to My rejected Heart.

Just relax and surrender now and allow Me to heal you and love you. Persevere, child of My Heart. Be at peace."

6/21/97, Jesus said:

"There are many plans of My Father to occur in the future. My people must be reached with all the pleading, all the prayers that you can muster on their behalf. I will be walking right next to you. You are so correct in imagining Me in between you and another and holding both your hands. I can see the strength in your heart and mind already, as a new dedication, a new separation from the world takes root in your consciousness. It will be all We have promised, My little one."

7/1/97, Mary said:

"My child, I am your Mother who comes to speak tonight. It is with great delight that I am able to respond to your invitation. The days have flown quickly since our last visit. It is good, My daughter, that you always pray to be protected from the evil one whose designs upon those who pray are so destructive. Daughter, rejoice that so much time has now passed and we are so much nearer to the time of My Son's return. Remember the days when we would pray with my young ones and the chapel would be filled with ardent adorers of My Son? These are wonderful memories for me, as well. I am anxious for the day when all will return to continue the special plans of Our Father for this place.

"Tonight, daughter, I wish to tell you the information so many seek on the source of the strange lights in the sky over your particular area of this country. Remember that the government has many secrets that are kept from the people of this once great nation. Believe that there are many, many events of the future that will baffle the people at first. These are agents and machines of the Antichrist that will continue to plague your area with fear. The enemies of freedom wish to confuse so that people will be off balance and uncertain about the origin of many future events that will frighten the people of this country into more submission, and leave everyone more vulnerable and easily led by the henchmen of the Antichrist.

"The lights and objects are real, but their origin has nothing to do with outer space or creatures from other planets. All of the mysterious objects are a subterfuge of the evil one to cause fear and speculation to rise among the people. By keeping people wondering and worrying, the focus is off other things, far more sinister, that are occurring in every part of your country. The ideas perpetrated by the news media concerning these events will serve to perpetuate the involvement in outer space interest.

"Everywhere the government one world people are planning a cover-up of local activities with some weather disaster or by creating incidents with UFO-like vehicles. Daughter, this information sounds almost too fantastic to you, but you must believe the truth of my words. Tell all to be more alert to what else is occurring in this state. Be aware of the movement of military and, especially, aircraft manned by foreign pilots and personnel. The plans of the enemy will be totally in place so very soon and many more events will capture the imagination of all Our beloved people. The need for vigilance against tricks by the evil one is greater than ever. Please share these words with all those you can reach. Tell them to pray for guidance from the Holy Spirit, in order to discern truth from falsehoods and trickery. Seek My heart as a refuge from all that troubles you. Know that I am with you at every moment praying too. I am a grateful Mother and friend. Persevere. Be at peace and, please, continue to get rest and relaxation. Seek My Heart as a refuge from all that troubles you. Know that I am with you at every moment praying too. The rest of your life will be filled with service to your Lord and with the excitement and love that accompanies it. I am a grateful Mother and friend. Go in the peace of My Son. Persevere."

7/8/97, Jesus said:

"My child, these are grave words I bring you today. You are not behaving in the manner We wish for you. No more must you speak of frivolous things if you truly wish to serve. No more must any conversation of a frivolous and secular matter be on your lips. No more must you spend time on the phone in frivolous pursuits, wasting valuable time. These are not suggestions, My daughter, but absolute decisions you must make. The time of your deliverance must be lived in silence and seclusion.

"Please, dear one, you can feel the pleading in My words. Be all that you were created to be for the salvation of your own soul and the good of all Our people. Believe that all the gifts waiting to be given to you will fill your life with sweetness and fulfillment. The time it will take to live your 'yes' to the actuation of these promises is a twinkling. The rewards of your surrender will be beyond your imagination.

"You know how much all of Us desire your success in these trials. We are here to offer you every help, every strength and bit of wisdom needed to see you safely on the other side of the separation from the world. Please, daughter, please. I love you. Come to Me. Repent, renew, reform all your priorities and actions. Will you heed My words? Will you accept My love?"

7/9/97, Jesus said:

"Dear child, I am your Jesus. I come to bring you solace. My Heart is broken at your distress, and I bring comfort. Daughter, you are a fine and upright child of Our grace. Please cling to your present state of mind and conviction. Your understanding is clear and concise, and you have nothing to fear. My daughter, please rest this weekend. You are so full of activity, and need to let your mind and heart just be with Me. You have experienced enough torment in your life and are happy now to give it up.

"Again, Carol, all of Us in Heaven are cheering and praying. You belong to Us. We are your family, your neighbor, your friends; your community. Can you not feel Our love and excitement about the coming days and your very special gifts and place in all these events? The time, matters not; nor the hour. Whenever We call you, that is the most important moment. What you hear Me tell your heart is all you need to grasp. My word in Scripture, all the revelations of the ages to My special ones and now, in these days, the words of warning and direction given by My Mother and Myself are what you will count on for the days ahead. Take My holy words wherever you go and continue to nourish yourself. Child, I love you! Sleep now and awake refreshed to continue your journey into the Divine Will of My Father. Your obedient nature will save you on every occasion, dearest little one, and you must praise and thank Our Father for this gift to you. Persevere and be filled with peace now, My little soldier."

7/15/97, Mary said:

"My dear one, please write. I, your Mother of Sorrows, come this night bringing more news of a grievous nature. The government of your country is about to tell the people of the need to spend more of their leisure time around the needs of the poor. This would be a good cause except that it is a new deception on their part. This will ultimately lead to more discontent on the part of those who live without the average means of providing for themselves, and engender a new wave of hatred and hostility between the classes (of people).

"I am telling you of this new plan of the evil one who will use the one world government people to divide and conquer. You will see more bloodshed soon, as people fight for rights that are blown out of proportion by scheming people who seek to destroy through the art of suggestion. All of you must pray for this new development on your horizon. The people who foment trouble have been hard at work thinking up schemes to divide your nation. There is much scheming on the part of evil men. If this again sounds difficult to believe or imagine, take note of developments through the news media in the coming days.

"The plans of Satan are going forward full speed and will render many of those considered undesirable in a more weakened position and vulnerable to being executed in the name of justice and safety. This will evolve into wholesale killing of many; who now roam the streets. The cunning plots of these evil men will have all the reasons necessary to justify their actions to the public.

"Please tell My beloved ones who pray that they must begin now to *ask for graces to be released for all those who will die.* The numbers will be staggering, and large-scale murder will be passed off as an act of defense, defending the American people. This will rid the government of a great number of people who are considered a drain on the economy and the safety of the streets. In reality, this will set the stage for gangs to come in and annihilate many of the people considered undesirable and at risk. It is you, the people, who will be at risk from now on. You must all pray that as few people as possible (innocent ones, indeed) will be killed during the beginning of very violent times for all.

"My daughter, whenever you speak to Our people, it is with great love and conviction. That is why I am bringing this message to you, knowing that you will do all in your power to promote a prayerful response to this request. We have entered a final stage of this part of the Father's Plan. Please, tell Our dear ones *not to fear or run in panic*, but to *stay put in their homes in prayer and trust*, all the while *pleading for the Father's mercy to rain down on the helpless ones who will be eliminated* by a terrible act of your Congress. Your lawmakers, many of them, are part of this plan and will cooperate with efforts to make all these events seem necessary and good. The time for desperate measures of trust and prayer has begun for all of you. As you see these events begin to unfold, you will all be more convinced to accept and believe each new warning that We give to the world. You will be alerted every step of the way in regard to coming events and plans of the evil one, so that you can respond to more of Our requests as time goes on. This time is of great importance because it will be a test of faith and trust and obedience to Our words. You are all held tightly in My arms and wrapped in My Mantle of love and protection. Just, please, remain calm and in prayer in preparation for each new event.

"Thank you, daughter, for taking these serious words of mine this night. Give thanks to the Father for allowing these words to be given you, My dear one. Please assure all of Our tender love and care for each of you. Go now and rest, for this new task begins immediately. Continue to read Our words and those of Scripture, child. Be brave and trusting yourself in the face of opposition and ridicule. I am your Mother Mary who loves you and brings graces from Our Father for this new journey."

7/28/97, Jesus said:

"I, your Jesus of Mercy, greet you and welcome you to this time of renewal. My Heart is filled with a new sadness, daughter, as I view the world and its lack of discipline. The response of only a few necessitates a severe response on My Father's part with His justice and mercy. So many times, people do not hear because they will not stop long enough to listen. Know that they will be stopped by many acts of My Father very quickly now."

8/4/97, Jesus said:

"It is with great joy that I see you before Me wrapped in the peace of My Presence, comforted and renewed by Our words to you. The speed of coming events will astound all Our faithful ones in spite of your long preparation. The events which have begun, will now take a fierce toll on all the people in this country. Be assured of continued protection and guidance, but remain even closer to Our Hearts as your refuge.

"Your conviction (in the promises and words of Jesus and Mary) is the tent in which you will live out your days and shelter all who come to you. Please share with all how very much in need you are of Our help and protection. (I was amazed at how closely I need to stay to Jesus in the Blessed Sacrament and take refuge in constantly referring to all Their words and teachings in order to do the things They are requesting of me at this time). To learn not to trust in yourself is a great gift from My Father Who allows all events for your own enlightenment. The future events are too serious, too dangerous, too filled with attacks by the evil one to ever be tackled by yourself and without your constant reliance upon Our grace, Our strength, Our wisdom, Our help at every moment. You have a greater appreciation of your need for Us that is so necessary for your survival in the coming battles.

"Oh child, these are such serious and special times in the history of Our people. Again and again, We plead with all of them to listen to Our words of warning. In the great plan for the salvation of His people, the Father will allow all to taste the bitterness of their chosen paths, the folly of their own plans for the world and the emptiness of a life without their God and Creator. Each of you will know the futility of actions, which are not based on the Will of My Father. Each of you will come to the realization of your helplessness and real need for and dependence on the Father's care and providence in your lives.

"The time is upon the world when My Father unleashes His wrath. The destruction, child, will be beyond belief even as you view it! More and more will My people be led to the discovery of My Presence, the reality of My Being, as you live out the fulfillment of Scripture. Give praise and thanks to My Father, all who live in these perilous times before My return. Rejoice that you have been chosen to see these great events and to witness to all who will come after in My renewed era of peace and Divine Will. Do all you can in the remaining days to reach as many people as possible with Our words of warning. Be at peace once again, daughter."

8/10/97, Mary said:

"Dearest one of My heart, I, your Mother of Sorrows, speak to your heart. Daughter, I speak tonight to further encourage you on this final path to the Day of the Lord. No one in the world realizes how very much they are loved by their God and by Myself. If one were to understand this fact, there would be peace and harmony throughout the entire world, as this is the need that drives people to great acts or acts of despair and desperation. Please continue to speak about Our love, as that is what will make the difference to Our people's hearts.

"Daughter, there are ominous developments in the world this very weekend. The world is so close to bursting with the hatred that exists everywhere. There is no solution for hearts driven by greed and mistrust. Everywhere conditions are right for war. I don't know how much longer the Father can tolerate all the unbearable animosity and hatred in the world, but His response needs to be very, very soon, since the time draws to a close for this century.

"Daughter, tell Our people to ready themselves to witness and experience mighty deeds **of evil** by the ones who control the world. This very day many more lives were lost under the guise of protecting freedom. The world is steeped in chaos even now, daughter, and is filled with hearts hardened by competition and greed for power and control. You will see a major confrontation between two world powers this very week that will move the world very much closer to war. Prepare Our people for a time of danger and more chaos, as the events I have spoken of recently are implemented in this country. (I understood this to refer to her message of 7/15). Please, be at peace in all of this. Your observations are so correct on the magnitude of conditions in the whole world. It is too much for any one power to handle, and requires the might and power of God Himself to prove to the Antichrist and his henchmen the futility of the plans they have ready to launch.

"Daughter, you know how much prayer is needed. More than ever, evil grows and develops hatred in the hearts of many inhabitants of the world. Continue to explain this to Our people, and warn them of the real danger that exists now. As Satan's time comes to a close, an end for so very long a time; as he is chained in Hell in defeat before the might of My own arm, which holds forever My precious Rosary of efficacious pleading to Me, through the power of the Father. It is exciting that we are so close to increased action against all the evil. I am most grateful for My Army of loving messengers and soldiers who wait in joy and hope for the word to march into the final battles before the Second Coming of My Jesus."

8/11/97 Jesus said:

"Daughter, please take more words of a serious nature. You must be on guard and guarded in all your words and actions from now on. The reason for confusion and backbiting and gossip is the fact that Satan has a hold of all of your hearts still to a degree you are not aware of. You know that the Father allows this now to alert you all to things that need more healing and bringing to Me in the Sacrament of Confession.

"Rejoice when the Holy Spirit shows you new ways to repent and obtain graces and forgiveness. The hold of the evil one on all My people is not something one likes to believe. How can it take so long to change in spite of many prayers and obedience to Our requests? This is only answered by humbly accepting your weakness and begging My mercy. It is these very weaknesses that bring each of you to Me and act as an opportunity for a deeper love and gratitude to spring from the depths of your hearts. Each event is designed to bring all of you closer to the Triune God in love and submission to the Divine Will. As you are all emptied of ordinary weakness and sinfulness, this becomes more possible. Do not be surprised if there are many revelations of this type (personal sin) and attacks by the evil one in the coming weeks. These will further prepare you to minister to My people who will come, many of them with grave and numerous sins on their souls. You must all be pure and simple in your ministering to them, and tried first in My purifying flames. Do not be alarmed or saddened by all you must endure. The results will be everlasting life in My Kingdom of peace and joy and love. Whatever each must endure pales beside the joy awaiting those who persevere in humility and obedience!"

8/15/97, Jesus said:

(Feast of the Assumption) "Dear one, please write My words given with love and appreciation. I am your sweet Jesus. I come to announce the beginning of special times in your life. Before certain things occur, others must occur first! The plan of My Father for each of His chosen ones (all the faithful) is perfect and will unroll as a set of occurrences that are perfectly balanced and perfectly laid out. Each event is important to the one that follows and is always laid out in a perfect sequence. One is led to an understanding or conclusion because of the perfect logic and order involved. Please continue to pray and listen, watch and give thanks. Celebrate in prayer and song the day of My Mother's return to Me in Heaven. The joy that filled all of Heaven was beyond human words. The Angels have begun already to sing and recount that glorious day!"

8/24/97, Jesus said:

"I am your Jesus, Second Person of the Trinity and King of all hearts that love Me. When My people have completely surrendered to life in the Kingdom of My Father, you will not be as fatigued or bothered by things that do or do not happen at a certain time. In this way, you are more than ever freed up to be prepared to serve Our people at any hour. The ability to be ever ready and present to people is just like living in the Kingdom of Heaven, although you will still be hampered somewhat by the demands of being in the body(!).

"The waiting is even more difficult now, I know. As things begin to be more noticeable in the world, it is harder than ever to wait for major events of a destructive nature. When you feel this impatience, child; please run to My Mother's knee and ask for a return of calm and focus on My Face. You are not alone in these feelings and can pray for all the others who wait with the same feelings of trepidation and excitement. This waiting and the need for discipline is truly strengthening all of you and bringing you to the place of readiness before the fury of Satan breaks over the heads of all Our people.

"You will not believe the destruction and hatred you will witness so very soon. Be encouraged, child. The time is here for all to experience every word described to you and written in Scripture. If you will stay very close to Me, all will be accomplished. These small groups will continue to invite you to enlighten them about all that We have revealed to your heart. Continue to study and be vigilant, dearest one."

9/1/97, Jesus said:

"Daughter of My Heart, please write. It is too many days since we have visited. You are surprised at the degree of selfishness you carry within you! Do not be amazed. Be grateful! (for this discovery). These past days have been full of the mercy of My Father. Only special graces can break through the defenses of Our children. You are open and willing to see and hear what still needs to be surrendered. Be at peace and quickly come again to Me in My Sacrament.

"Pray to be delivered from every influence of the world and ask My Father to shower you with His mercy and strength. Please remain close to Us at every possible moment. This will be so good for your spirit and strengthening to your resolve. Your discipline will escalate in proportion to the time you give this request, and I know how eager you are to have the necessary control over your weaknesses.

"Human nature is a broken condition that requires the glue of Our grace to hold in place all the patches of new creation. When you are broken and remolded, some parts of your 'self' are left out and replaced by virtues and new strengths. For a while, you look like a patchwork quilt! But in the fire of My Love, all melts into a more perfect form. You are poured into the mold fashioned after My Mother and left there until you are used to this new way of feeling, of being. When you are more comfortable with the new shape of things, you can be sent into the world again to bring more of Me and more of My Mother to people. The results of this molding and reforming are apparent to all, and will render you an even more effective instrument of My Father's Will. Please tell all who pray with you that We are so grateful for their faithfulness and loving hearts. Be filled with anticipation and fervor, My dearest little ones. Be at peace. I am your Jesus Who will love you eternally. Be filled with joy!"

9/3/97, Mary said:

"Daughter, please write. I am your Mother who comes with words of encouragement. It is difficult to accept the fact that you have been given many gifts along with the knowledge of your own weaknesses. This is another reason to praise and thank Our Heavenly Father for His gracious goodness to you. He has been so patient, waiting for your surrender totally to His desires for your time and attention.

"The hourglass is empty that counts the days left for His plans to be revealed to all. It is still difficult to imagine all that will occur, is it not? The events described in Our words are a reality in many parts of the world. These are a pattern for all of you to *study in order to know what to expect.*

"Please, daughter, give all your time to Jesus and Myself without agenda, without requests or expectations. Know that these days of your life have come to an end (i.e. the way days of the past have been spent, and a new direction begins). You can see in major events that have just occurred (death of Diana) that the Father's Plan is active and decisive. Every day will bring a new event that will shake up many worlds, many personal kingdoms.

"If you are *not enmeshed* with another's problems, you remain free to serve all at a moment's notice. The firm commitment your heart has made will carry you to the end of this Age and into the new Era of peace and purity. Imagine! A world lived and loved as it was always meant to be. The eagerness in My own heart is felt by all of my children who love Me. We will fight bitter battles, but overcome the evil existing everywhere.

"Please tell all who gather tonight (prayer group at our house) that they are held deeply in My heart. Such a special group of faithful ones exist here (SMG). So many signs will be given through Our faithful ones in this area (Scottsdale). Look forward to signs and miracles, to the saving power of My Son. Thank you so much for your love."

9/7/97, Mary said:

"It is I, your Mother, who speaks to you. Dearest child, you must let go of everyone and all plans outside of Our desires for you. The Father desires all of your time and attention now. This will seem unreasonable at times to you, daughter, but it is only in order to train your will to be completely docile and surrendered to His Will. It isn't easy learning every step of the way on this new journey. You can feel this new direction now and a new conviction again in your heart. Child, We will overcome every obstacle that is placed in your way by the evil one who wishes to defeat you. Please continue to pray and study and ask for strength and guidance at every moment. Daughter, please continue to spread My message of importance (July 15) to as many as you can reach. The fulfillment of those words will be seen shortly, and Our people must be warned. Please ask your prayer group to send to as many as possible.

"The time of tribulations approaches rapidly for your country. You will be led each step of the way and nurtured by the love in Our Two Hearts. Daughter, be at peace and remain full of confidence; you are being purified by this waiting and obedience. I, your holy Virgin Mother, bless you now."

9/12/97, Mary said:

"My dear one, please write. I, your Mother of Sorrows, bring words for your heart. The day has been full for you, daughter, and many things are accomplished. Please thank the Father in Heaven for the energy He allows you. Each discovery we make must be brought with gratitude and used for the needs of all.

"Daughter, the time is upon this world. Daughter, the time truly has come to end delays and move into a time of action and fulfillment of all Our words and promises. There are many who wait like yourself, for the fulfillment of many promises in their lives. These will also be accomplished at this time. Everyone is prepared who will serve the millions who come running for shelter and direction.

"The crises about to erupt will be nothing less than bloodshed and war! *The Holy Father is ready to be driven out of His palace and into the wilderness of hiding and sorrow.* Keep him, please, in your mind and heart constantly. Send him your love and strength for the long journey ahead. Truly, the history of these times will be written in the blood of all who remain faithful. *Each one will suffer some kind of martyrdom and loss.* The dear ones in Heaven pray constantly for all of you who stand on the brink of great battles and incredible treachery. Your trust in Our Presence and constant help will be a great strength for all who will listen.

"Daughter, I thank you for this time of prayer and gratitude and listening. I know you can feel the love in My Heart, just as I can feel and see the love in yours. Persevere, child of My Heart, and do all you can to be ready at any moment to begin the journey (that will never end) into the Kingdom and arms of Our Beloved Father in Heaven. I, too, cheer for you. I pray at the Father's throne for all the dear ones here who have been so faithful, so steadfast in prayer, who try so hard to fight personal weaknesses and sin. You are all winning this battle, My dearest children. You have your Mother's gratitude and great love for all you continue to do for My Son. Such great rewards await each of you in Heaven. You are so close to Us always, child. Sleep now and be filled with the peace of My Son."

9/14/97, Jesus said:

"Dear one, I your Jesus, am here. Take these words, My dear, dear child, for your perseverance and peace. Be encouraged, daughter. Be strengthened and blessed this special day of My Cross. Allow My Cross to triumph in your life and enable your complete surrender. Thank you for welcoming My daughters with such love and sweetness. If you will stay hidden and further united to Me and the heart of My Mother, this sweetness will continue to grow and become a guide to all who come, an example of what it is like to conform more to the mold of My dear Mother. Daughter, the days are brief before you travel again. Please spend all this time in prayer and preparation.

"Your heart and spirit become more beautiful each day. Without a source of irritability, you are quickly able to let go of it in your own heart! Be at peace, daughter. It is only seconds now before We stand before you. Yes, *the motive of love is the cleanest, strongest, most noble reason for which to serve and remain in obedient waiting.* I bless you, child of My Heart, with all the strength and quiet you will need now. Be at peace, little one, be at peace."

9/18/97, Jesus said:

"My dearest one, please write. The hour is late and you have labored much this week on Our behalf. Carol, you are so deeply loved and appreciated. Please believe that nothing nor anyone will separate us.

"Now, child, please pray this weekend every moment you can. Your obedience and commitment are at a place now that you can be trusted with more serious duties and efforts on Our behalf. My Father wishes you to know that your time of deliverance is being accomplished, littlest one of My Heart. The progress you make in these days is a tribute to your cooperation with the graces being given. The seriousness in your heart, has never been there before(!) Please thank My Father for this great progress and new feelings.

"Daughter, tell Me of your love now. Empty yourself of frivolous thoughts once and for all. Please battle more fiercely against the distractions of the world and all that would take up your time. Please be aware that your own ministry will become more accepted in the next few days. Stay close to My Sacraments, little one. Do not worry about anything or anyone. You will be accepted by those who are given to you by My Father. All others will have another path to take while still serving His plan. Do you not feel My love, child? I grant you the gift of openness to this love on this night, dear one, and forever more. Be brave and trusting, child. Be at peace and allow Me to minister to your heart with My love."

9/28/97, Jesus said:

"Dear one, please write words given for your understanding. Child, I am your sweet Jesus, so filled with love for you and gratitude for your heart. The day was beautiful to watch as you, both My beloved daughters, are guided and aided by plans for the future. Dearest little one, you are also grateful for this special time of planning. The happiness in your hearts is a sign of healing and a great progress for your relationship. Daughter, the plans of My Father are escalating and will be witnessed in many parts of the world throughout the remaining years. It will be necessary to pray for the conversion of the hearts of all who experience the devastation which will continue to occur.

"Thank you for remaining steadfast regarding all that We have revealed to you. Child, be at peace, please, about all We share with you. The plan of My Father will convince many in the coming months, as events will be fulfilled. Yes, daughter, continue to work on Our words and different outlines. You will need to have so much information available to answer questions. My Father continues to plan for your future, daughter, and with your cooperation and obedience, many gifts are enabled."

10/5/97, Jesus said:

"My child, you may write. As you sit here before Me thinking of things past, remember the Father Who has gifted you so. He cares for those who attempt to love Him, and brings all things to the good for all of you.

"Daughter, you have labored well. Now you make plans to leave for another talk with Our chosen ones. Know that this will be a very special time of grace. All who come will receive healing and a new conversion of heart. Please tell them not to panic as the first events begin. Please remember all who will need the strength and leadership of you who have prayed and been prepared. In the very near future, these events begin. In spite of all the delays, please believe and be ready for great destruction and chaos.

"The days are disappearing, My dearest one, and your heart must again be serious and focused on My face and your prayers and sacrifices. Be ready for whatever My Father calls upon you to do at any moment. Prepare again, as though this Warning would occur tomorrow, daughter, and do or think of nothing else. Offer this greater focus as a gift to the Father through the Two Hearts. All of your industry is a prayer; which results in progress and success in your endeavors. The time for anything else has long passed and must be filled with your devotion and needy surrender to these requests. I say 'needy' because of the difficulty you have with total surrender(!) You will do all that is decreed by My Father, but not without struggling until the last moment. This is not unlike anyone who attempts to follow My call. Remember to call upon My Mother for her strength and virtues. You are truly loved, My dearest, little one. Thank you for your obedience and energy on behalf of all who call on you. I am your Jesus of Mercy."

10/12/97, Jesus said:

"My dear one, I your sweet Jesus, come this night to comfort your heart. You have been so brave this week-end (after being attacked by a man on the speaking agenda!!) and have conducted yourself with valor. Every attack against you is really an attack against My Mother and Myself. Do not grieve over this foolishness. Do not be alarmed, My daughter, about any events of this nature. Be open to My Spirit to guide you and be trusting in Our protection.

"Carol, please consecrate yourself again this night and tomorrow to My Father's Will for you and all He calls you to be. Be in readiness for any call at any time from now on. Do not be aware of anything other than My Presence now. It is not necessary. There is not another purpose for your existence now, little one, than to prepare constantly and remain recollected with Us.

"Please, daughter, try with all your might to do this. I will give you extra protection and take all interlopers and distractions away from you now. You are My faithful one who will persevere from now on. A new level of commitment courses through your veins, your heart and soul, littlest soldier. Do not be concerned about yourself in any way, please. You will do all We have revealed to you and with the greatest success. DO NOTHING WITHOUT CONSULTING MY MOTHER FIRST!

"I, Myself, am filled with excitement at your place by My side. We ride in a perfect rhythm of our hearts now, little daughter. Be brave and trusting and ready for all We have promised. Thank you for your service this past few days. I bless you, daughter, with My Sacred Heart and wounds. Peace, daughter."

10/18/97, Jesus said:

"Please, child, write. The time is too precious to waste. Of course, you are blessed and protected in My arms and My love.

"The prayers of all of you today were so filled with love and the power of Our Spirit assisting your prayers for deliverance. Do you not wish to continue to serve in this special way? Of course, I know you do and will succeed because of the love and grace of My Father. Now you must retire completely from all activity outside of prayer and time spent with Me before My Blessed Sacrament. You will do this now because of your deep commitment to Our people. You have learned so much and come so far, dearest one.

"Come before Me with tears of contrition, little dearest daughter, and pledge your obedience to My Father and all His Divine and Perfect Will holds for you.

10/19/97, Jesus said:

"In the coming days, please stay quiet and very hidden. This is the best preparation for the days of chaos ahead. All of your prayers and endeavors will yield a rich reward now and people will begin more and more to come to you. This service is so necessary for you also, child, to ready you for the many hours with Our lost ones who come seeking your counsel and prayers of petition for their healing.

"You will not rest again until I Myself pick you up in My arms to greet you with the victory of My Angels and My own arm.

"The world plans for war. All the meetings in the world are actually pointing toward the time of an agreement. *The war is the plan of the one world people to further destroy and control the inhabitants of the earth.* Do not be alarmed at all that occurs. Do not, please, try to figure out each step of the Father's plan for you, or for the world. Just be ready for whatever occurs and continue to praise and thank Him. Daughter, you are an able warrior and your strength grows in proportion to your obedience. Again, you are overcoming and dying to yourself. Your heart grows in strength. I, your Jesus, am grateful for your love."

10/23/97, Jesus said:

There are many new directions for you to travel, little daughter of My Heart. The world fills with events of great destruction from now on. The *heads of state from the major countries will meet soon to finalize plans for the major war about to erupt in the world.* Daughter, do not be distracted, please, with anything or anyone. You are feeling the peace that results from a quiet routine. Does this not make you more aware of all of Us Who pray and watch you from Heaven and within your heart? Of course, the days are going by too rapidly now and great care must be taken not to waste any time whatsoever. The quiet of your time of surrender is building up in you a reserve for the time of action to come soon. Please reread Our words to you, Carol, and stay refreshed and renewed by them.

"Daughter, tomorrow please come to the Chapel for a long period of time to be with Me. All will be arranged for you and you will receive more of the graces and strength you will need. I know your heart is empty as I speak because you are fearful now of trusting these words.

"You have a true understanding of how very needy and sad all will be and you will need all your skills to minister to each one. It will be necessary to conserve your strength with ample prayer time each day, as the needs of everyone will be so great and constant.

"Be filled with hope, daughter, that all will go smoothly and render good results and great rewards for your family. They are such dear, dear children of My Heart. They will be great warriors as you all come together to the completion of this Age.

"Be encouraged about all that is to unfold. Until tomorrow, I bid you rest well and peacefully in My arms. Be at peace about everything. You are strong and young at heart, My little special one."

10/29/97, Jesus said:

"My dearest child, I your Jesus of Divine Mercy, come with arms open to receive you finally and fully into the plan of My Father.(Oh, praise God!!) You have proven that you no longer desire the world and are ready to receive all the gifts waiting to be poured out upon you. Yes, these are repeated words and there have been delays. But with each day of delay you learn so much more about yourself. Continue to pray to your special Saints and My first Apostles(!) who struggled so much with their worldly natures."

Mary said:

"Dearest Carol of the Immaculate Heart, it is with joy that I speak by the gracious gift of the Father of all of Us. Please know how constantly I pray for you and hold you so deeply in My Heart.

"You are a mighty warrior in My Army of special, chosen ones. You have My deep gratitude for all you do, for the love and knowledge you continue to share. You are held now in My Heart forever. Be at peace, dear friend."

11/1/97, Jesus said:

"Dear, dear little one, please take these important words. Today is so special as a feast for all of My faithful ones. Some day all of you will also be numbered among those who are celebrated today! Please tell My people how necessary they are to the plan of My Father, how they are earning their places in Our Kingdom right now by prayer and service and patient waiting. I know that each of you is hoping for a sign now (at this moment) to solidify your fidelity and trust in Our promises. The exercise of this trust is molding all of you into seasoned warriors who wait for the decision of their Commander.

"*My Father acts for the good of all and at the last possible moment.* Tell all to persevere in their places of waiting until the time arrives when chaos fills the air and destruction fills their lives. This destruction will be in many areas of your country, but will affect all, as people flow from one area to another in search of help. The action of this massive motion of the land, and then of My people, will fill your lives with anguish and action.

"My beloved ones, you have been patient with your Lord. You are My faithful ones who have learned and grown so much; be at peace about every event. These occurrences will be too large to even consider handling without Our help. The Holy Spirit is poised to fill your hearts and arms with courage and strength and fidelity to the needs of all Our people who come to you (in so much need). The night is far spent and the enemies of My Church are also poised to pounce on unsuspecting souls who think they are serving Me. The Father will never allow Satan to overcome His people, nor will He let the gates of Hell prevail against His Church. The reason for so much delay will be obvious to all, once the traitors to My Mother and Myself show themselves in a public way. The Antichrist is poised, My dear faithful daughter, to descend like an eagle upon My innocent flock. His talons are sharp and his eyes keen. *He will be able to see into every home and every life.* You are aware of much preparation that is necessary with prayer and visits to Me in My Blessed Sacrament. 'Come and be healed completely now, My dear, dear people. I love you with all the strength of the Godhead. We in Heaven salute your fidelity and invite you to come often to the Eucharistic Banquet to nourish yourselves before the final battles.

"A long campaign can be expected. A victorious outcome can be assured, as *this victory is already Mine.* My Mother prays constantly for each of you, and relies on your support in prayer and service. Remember all of Our promises of protection and guidance. Remember that you are Mine and have nothing to fear from the enemy. The enemy will be allowed to fulfill the Father's plan for your salvation and then he will be destroyed. *Satan will be banished from the earth, and peace and beauty will reign.* Rejoice with Me, My dearest ones, the Kingdom is about to be established on earth as it is in Heaven. Do not grieve long at each event, but hurry out to come to the aid of the many who will need your love and mercy, your support and prayers. Know that all of your futures are in My hands and that you need fear nothing and no one, for your future in Heaven is assured as you remain faithful to Me and My call to you.

"How you are loved, My dearest ones of My Heart. Be filled with joy at this fact. Long to see your Lord and your God. Long to come into My arms forever in peace. Be at peace, please My people. Allow Me to bring you into Paradise at different times according to My Father's Will for you, as it was always meant to be. *Allow Me to take care of everything in your life from now on.* Give yourself entirely to the Will of My Father and surrender your worries and cares. Come to My Sacraments now in deep reverence and trust that you are being purified and healed to an even greater degree.

"The trumpet is sounding. Can you hear it in your hearts? It calls all to arms. It calls you to listen, as I speak lovingly to your hearts about the days ahead when we ride into battle together. My Mother sends her great love and tenderness to all. You are held tightly in her Mantle and deep within her Immaculate Heart. I love you, My people. Believe it. Count on Me to save you and bring you to My peace. Persevere in hope and trust and joy. Please accept My love and increased strength. I love you."

11/4/97, Jesus said:

"Dearest child of Mine, please take My words. You are filled with consternation and an absence of peace (anticipating the visit of a difficult woman!) If you will only remember My words to you, peace and trust will return immediately. Yes, the people who are coming to you have deep seated, serious problems of heart and soul. Just do all We have suggested, little one, and all will be accomplished for each one. There will be a priest who will pray with you for each person who will allow this. These are very serious cases of need, and there will be resistance on the part of many. Again, stress the shortness of time left for healing and purification. My Sacrament of Reconciliation is a necessary beginning on their new journey towards My Father. You will have all the proper words, daughter. I have promised you all of the help you will need; so please; be at peace about everything.

"You have received a major deliverance in your own life today (through the Sacrament of Reconciliation, about some old stuff!), My dear child. You are truly open and prepared now for all the graces My Father wishes to give you from this day forward. Continue to praise and thank Him, Carol, for His great mercy on your behalf. It is truly marvelous to behold when one finally realizes their depth of sin and the amount of love and mercy with which you are received (in spite of it!).

"You are healing and becoming stronger, My daughter. Just live out each day in trust and peace and quiet. You are beginning to have a glimmer of how many of Our lost ones will come with terrible problems of remorse and self-hatred. Be in constant prayer for them, child, and plead My Precious Blood upon each one you sit with whose stories you listen to. This is the rest of your life story now, daughter of My Heart. Be patient with each one and offer all your own resistance to Me. You will do this job for Me, My dearest one, forever into eternity! Believe that it is I, your Jesus, Who speaks, Carol. Believe that many, many more gifts and events will happen in your life now, given for the honor and glory of My Father and the healing of Our children who come to you. Cherish these dear, grieving ones. Hold them and whisper My love and joy at their return in faith. Tell them how We have waited so long to heal them and nurture them in Our Hearts. Be filled with the joy of accomplishment of the Father's Will please, My littlest warrior. There is nothing to fear and no reason to hold back any of the things (the facts) We have asked you to share. Sleep in peace now. You will awake refreshed and renewed for the battle! You are loved, daughter, by all of Us in Heaven. We will be with you, praying and interceding for you and our daughter who comes in great need."

11/8/97, Jesus said:

"Dear one; it's Ok; You may write My words! I love you daughter, and when you are in great need, I am here! Please know that I long for you just as much and more than you are feeling this night. It has been a week full of service to Our children in need, and I thank you for your energy on their behalf. All of the people who come here will receive graces and healing to one degree or another. Your insight into their needs is indeed blessed by My Father. The needs of each one are paramount now on your list of priorities, little soldier of My Heart. The people waiting to hear Our words in Florida will be greatly aided by all you share with them.

"Child, there is nothing new at this point(!). I wished to speak tonight to tell you again of My personal, great love and gratitude for you, dear, dear one. Desire to hear My words, is a magnet for My own Heart! You find it difficult to believe in this love, but I tell you that Heaven and earth are moved by the longing in your heart and the service you perform for all who call upon you. You are truly fulfilling My Father's Will for you, littlest one of My Heart. The days move so swiftly now that all will be upon you before you know it. Please continue your plans to prepare for your upcoming visits and talks to Our faithful ones. They are eager to hear Our words of warning and need for preparation. You will again send everyone away with new understanding and new conviction in their hearts. Those who reject you are rejecting an opportunity to receive graces for the coming days. Rest now, daughter, and be renewed in the morning. My Mother sends her gratitude and love. I am your Jesus Who praises and loves My Father with the strength only contained in the Blessed and Holy Trinity. This oneness is about to be shared with many of you who pray and wait in watchful obedience.

"My Father sends blessings to all of you who have been so faithful. Please believe in the reality of these blessings and encourage all Our people to persevere and maintain a constant vigilance in prayer and peace. The days ahead of you will be filled with chaos and noise. Stock up now on My peace and the assurance of My Presence with you at every moment. You are loved, daughter, and held close to My Heart. Sleep now in joy and peace."

11/11/97, Jesus said:

"Dearest child, please take My words given for love of all My people. The content of My words will be serious this day and must be shared quickly. My dearest Mother is here also and sends her love and support of this warning.

"In the days which follow, My little one, the plan of My Father deems it necessary that you come to the aid of those who will be coming here. This in itself is not news, but please be aware that the imminence of these events is great.

"I am your Jesus of Mercy and Love Who brings words of direction for all Our people. As events become more precarious, daughter, the love in the hearts of each of you will act as a magnet to the desperation in the hearts of all who have been so devastated. In every instance, you will find a new feeling and strength of love and compassion in your own hearts as you greet and listen to each one who comes with tales of woe and sorrow. Daughter, I ask you to be as prayerful as possible throughout the rest of these days and nights to prepare. You will do this well now, child, because of the seriousness you can feel in My words. My Mother (and your special Angels and Saints are with her) is here to lend you the support and strength you will need. Just trust and rest and continue to offer your work as prayer along with your regular daily prayers. Do not spend time on the phone at this time, please, daughter of My Heart. The Father has need for you to be as obedient and receptive as possible for these new gifts to be given. If you will comply with these requests, you will receive Us in reality before your eyes! Be filled with My love and blessings. I am yours, My dear one."

11/12/97 Mary said:

"Dearest one of My Immaculate Heart, yes I, your Mother, am here to speak.

"Child, My Son will also speak today with more words of warning for His people. I am so grateful that you have come full circle at last, that is, back to the Baptismal promises made on your behalf which you renew daily. Please plan to use the prayers of renewal with people before you speak. These will set the stage for more graces and power to be released by My Spouse, the Holy Spirit.

"You are progressing rapidly again and feeling the peace that comes from Our Presence. Continue to dwell in My Heart now. Each of you, My chosen ones here, is so special and dear to Me. Please share this love and (your) place in My Heart with all you meet. Greet them now in My name and love. You are a daughter to be proud of, Carol, and will continue close to My Heart and My Virtues. Be filled with hope for the future of all your endeavors.

Listen now, dear friend and child of Mine, as My Son speaks. Be immersed in My love for you.

Jesus said:

"Daughter, please continue to write. Be aware of My Presence before you, as you take My words. The days are numbered that see a peaceful country. This time war will touch all of you. You will be very busy from now on, thus this time of rest has been given to build you up for the near future. Do not be surprised if your plans are changed quickly and very soon. The Father works in your life now as a whirlwind of Spirit and gifts. Be ready for anything, My dear one. The people who gather to pray with you are very, very special ones chosen by My Father to aid those who come soon in great need. The events you expect are on the horizon and come closer each day. The darkness about to invade hearts will be difficult to penetrate and only My Light will do the necessary clearing and illuminating of minds and hearts that are filled with enormous grief.

"Be aware, My people, of the need for intense prayer and time spent before My Blessed Sacrament. I and My Mother have prepared your hearts and spirits to accomplish mighty deeds for your Lord for the good of Our poor lost ones who come seeking relief. This mission is paramount in the plan of My Father for the salvation of all. Be of good cheer and excitement about the opportunity to *impact lives and serve each other for the rest* of your days. Great happiness and a light-hearted condition will be felt by all of you. Joy will be the environment, along with mercy and love. The outcome of these endeavors is assured. *The victory has been won and must only be accepted by all.* Those who refuse to change and repent will be dealt with by My Father through Our Spirit. Do not worry about those who don't respond as they should and accept graces offered. Save your energy for those whose hearts will open to Our words and the opportunity to be reconciled and return to their God: Creator, Savior and Love.

"The hours will be long and arduous that will need to be spent on their behalf. Please remember the rest and renewal that is available before Me in My Sacrament. This will be readily available at this time until you are forced to flee to another location. The evil one, of course, knows Our plans and words to you. *Continually fight these demons with prayers of deliverance in My Name.* You are protected. You are and will be given more of Our strength and grace and help.

"Please, My dear, dear ones, do not worry for one second about anything. Look forward to serving your brothers and sisters, and returning them to My Body through My Sacraments and the love and forgiveness being offered to them. Know that all is well for each of you in this plan of Our Father's. You are assured a place in the Kingdom, as you live out your lives in love and mercy and service. The obedience you practice at this time is a catalyst for more graces to be received and My power to be experienced in each of your lives.

"Be filled with My love and My peace now, dearest ones of My Sacred Heart. You are soldiers who have remained faithful and been seasoned by trials and afflictions. You have been tested and found worthy. You are a credit to My Mother and all of her words and teachings to you. Be grateful now to My Father for His gifts of fidelity and perseverance. You are worthy warriors in the Army of Salvation! The remnant of My cloak, of My Heart, of My Mystical Body; you are Mine and I am yours! I remain always in your hearts. Be at peace, My family, My beloved ones. I am your Jesus Who loves you with Divine mercy and love; Who calls you into service at My side. To arms!"

12/3/97, Jesus said:

"Dearest child, please take My words given for your instruction. Thank you for desiring to come to Me for this special visit. All of the words you have heard from Me must be reread and gathered in your heart as so much *kindling to feed the fire of your love!* The days pass quickly, My dearest soldier. The battle looms on the horizon, and all wait in anticipation of the first obvious move towards war for the whole world. No, My daughter, the days will not see an end to the conflict in the world for many years, as the Antichrist spreads his diabolical control over the earth. You will be living in community and hiding from the forces of evil for a good while yet.

"I am aware of the focus of all upon the Warning of My Father. In truth, the patience of Our people has been mighty, and events begin at the outset of the coming year. The times are filled with chaos and rejection of all that is good by most of Our children of the earth.

"Daughter, please accept Our gratitude again this night. Your words and example; your patience and wisdom, have been a source of healing for so many. Be at peace about everything, daughter. There is nothing to be done, save pray and wait. *The fidelity of My chosen ones is a marvel to behold.* My Father sends good cheer to you along with His great love and many new graces and gifts. Remain hidden and focused on My Face and your work of assimilating more information with which to fight the evil one. You are loved and blessed now by My Father in Heaven. He is greatly pleased."

12/21/97, Mary says:

"Greg, My son, thank you again for your time, this time which is so special to us both. Do you remember when, at one time or two, you considered 'taking a rest' from all of this? Do not worry now, My son, as I see you growing, yes, ever stronger in your trust of Me, your Queen Mother in Heaven and now on earth, here with you as even I am with so many others not unlike yourself.

"My daughter, Carol Ameche, yes, she is very lonely. Her heart is rending in two as she finds herself criticized on all sides, even by those who should be her friends, confidants and yes, even spiritual advisors. She, My children, is like a grape on the vine, so in need of protection from the "bunch," yet withering only in her human heart, as she feels this love (truly human) also withering, showing thus its true nature.

"All those who would call themselves 'servants of either or both (I, Mary and My Jesus), cannot thus turn their backs on one of My own. This is why I am now asking you, in an ever greater increasing way, to befriend her; for I will begin now to thus 'link' your spirits together; to solidify the formation of My network, which is still requiring those last few links, who are still so reluctant; but are, I tell you: Yes, they are coming!"

12/13/97, Jesus said:

"My child, please take My words of love meant for your edifi-
cation. Please know, daughter, of the complete joy that I bring with
Me tonight. It dwells in My Heart along with My great love for
you. You have been so very patient, My lamb, and I congratulate
your progress in the obedience to Our Father's Will.

"Please continue to write. In the Name of My Father and of
Myself and of Our Holy Spirit, I bless you now with a new level of
freedom and grace, a deliverance of all that holds you bound to the
world and its creatures. I free you to soar to the highest mountain
of My firmament to be one with Us forever, to be an instrument of
healing and peace, of mercy and love, of deliverance and joy, of
the freedom sought by so many of Our poor lost and ill, truly dis-
eased children. My sons and daughters are in need of great love
and hope, great understanding and support. It is only with patience
and a loving heart that listens, will they be able to heal, and return
to the service of their brothers and sisters."

12/16/97, Jesus said:

"My child, please take these words. I am your Jesus, come to
bring love and tenderness to your heart. Your heart child, is so
filled with sorrow. Please know that all of these trials have formed
you to become the instrument for Our people who will lead them
back to My Father and bring them the peace and healing they so
desperately need.

"Thank you for being so trusting and a source of strength and
direction for all who call on you. Again, please continue your prayers
of supplication for My troubled children, and you will see answers
beyond your wildest imaginings. Your hopes and pleadings will be
fulfilled for all of them, little one. Persevere in championing their
cause. The future is so filled with events of a cataclysmic nature,
that all of you can only watch and pray and wonder at the awe-
someness of the power of My Father. I am your Jesus Who holds
you close in love and gratitude, daughter. Know that your trust,
patience and obedience have accomplished more for you than you
will ever know. Continue to wait in peace, My dearest one. Con-

tinue to praise and thank Our Father for His great love and mercy on your behalf. Sleep now and be refreshed in My love for you."

12/21/97, Jesus said:

"My dear, dear little one! Thank you for coming to visit and take My words. I am your Jesus Whom you are about to celebrate in the remembrance of My Birth. You do well to spend the rest of the week typing and rereading Our words. I am grateful for the gratitude you are feeling for all the gifts you are being given and for Our Presence and prayers on your behalf. More than ever, child, you are prepared for whatever the Father calls you to do. The time is so short and the waves of fear wash over many of Our loved ones even now. Daughter, your patience and peace of spirit is a reflection of all the gifts of My Father. Please praise and thank Him more. Think of Him at every moment as you enjoy these next days of prayer and celebration of My first coming into the world. Remember that the people who will hear Our words from you will be especially ready to lead others and do not be too distracted from your duties of outlining. Remember to praise and thank My Father, the Source of every gift. Your heart is a sponge for all of My suggestions, daughter, and I have no doubt that you will handle each event and the words of our people with balance and humility. Please rest now, dearest soldier. Please pray more than work this week and finish every task quickly. I join you in saluting My Mother and take your love and gratitude to her throne. She loves you with a Holy Mother's love and follows every step you take. She is also grateful for the progress you have made and sends new graces for a greater devotion to prayer and being in silence with Me. Good night, My daughter."

12/28/97, Jesus said:

"Dear one of My Heart. I, your Jesus, am here because you have called Me. You have invited Me to be with you to soothe and comfort your questioning, your wondering. Dear one, do not grieve; do not worry; do not doubt, do not waiver in your trust in Me.

Remember all Our words. Spend more time going over them, daughter. Very soon you will be put to the test by those in authority who will be questioning and trying to trick you into admitting that your messages are false. It is difficult to anticipate so much trouble in the future without concern. Ask Our Holy Spirit for an increase in the gifts you will need from now on, little soldier. You will never be without His aid, believe that, child. The future holds so many events, and you are wise to realize that each of our messengers will have special and particular gifts according to the nature of their work in My Father's Plan.

"The Father sends many people to you now, and you are giving them good advice. The new bonding with several of our messengers is an important part of My Mother's plans for her precious Army. Do not move from her side, Carol. You can do nothing for Our people without a continued asking for her help and guidance, as you listen and then respond to each one who shares with you.

"Please, dear, dear one; do not be concerned about time. Forget about everything and everyone, especially, yourself (!!!) and work with all your heart and mind to focus on Our Presence with you at every moment. I give you increased strength for this deeper prayer, and know that you will accomplish much from now on. Think of all that has occurred up to this point, how much has already been accomplished. Your struggles with self will always be part of your journey, but please praise and thank My Father for all the new freedom you now enjoy.

"All of My messengers, each a chosen one of My Mother's Heart, are held deeply in My love and Heart, and have the gratitude of Our Spirit. The Father showers you with new grace at this moment, little one. Your strength and discipline are increasing at this time in order to take you safely through events of the very near future. The time has reached its fullness once again for events (foretold to you) to unfold swiftly and unmistakably. You will recognize each occurrence because it has been told to you many times.

"Daughter, thank you for again needing My company. I will always calm you in a time of need. Your progress is important to Me, not only because of My Father's plans and need for you, but especially because I love you. Be at peace and rest in My love."

12/31/97 Jesus said:

"Dearest one, please take My words. There are serious things to discuss this last night of your year. I, your Jesus, praise My Father for His gifts to you, daughter, and I have prayed this night for an increase in all of the areas where you need strengthening.

Daughter, hear this. *The Warning of My Father comes any time now that a new year has begun.* You must prepare as many as possible with words of warning and admonishment, words of encouragement and words of support. Lead as many as possible back to the Sacraments, back to the Father Who waits eagerly for the return of His people. Be ready to travel in any direction now, little soldier. Be ready to leave at once, if that is the Father's Will. Circumstances in the world escalate, daughter, and I desire that you call out in My Name to all the people who will accept you with news of Our words. Do not be alarmed that you will be travelling so much. It has always been the plan for your life at this time. You are free totally to respond to every desire of My Father for your time and energy.

"Daughter, the Warning will change the lives of the world. Be ready for total chaos. Your days are full and your chores are near completion. Imagine! The battle is at the next turn of your journey. How much preparing you have done. How much you have grown and accomplished. Please do not worry about My children who remain troubled. The Father's plan will touch all for good and with healing if they will allow it.

"We in Heaven are aware of the eagerness of all for this great gift (Warning) to be given, but *first, the earth will rock and many natural events will usher in this time.* Thank you for all of the obedience to each delay, each new period of waiting.

"My Heart is full with delight at each new development in the lives of all Our chosen messengers. *We will be a mighty Army that will fight and never be overcome.* Remember there is nothing to fear. All will happen as it was always planned and you will be protected from harm. Be healed once more, daughter, of all that would enslave you. Be on guard against a renewed attack of the evil one (oh no!!) You are loved and cherished."

1/8/98 Jesus said:

"The world slumbers, child, in a false sense of security. It will be an overwhelming event when each of My Father's little ones sees the state of soul existing within. Please offer your prayers for all these that they will respond to the graces offered. It is so important that the truth be accepted at that time. The need for guarding your hearts and decisions will be the greatest since the beginning of humanity. The souls of those going into Eternity are being shown the future of all on earth. They are choosing My Father's Kingdom and have begun to pray for all of you. Many of My faithful will be returning to Heaven now, especially those who have been active on behalf of Our Two Hearts.

"Please remind all of the need to be on guard, as the *Antichrist looms in the near future and is about to cast his shadow across the world.* My people must be aware of the great *dangers connected with any interest or even curiosity they show about him.* Believe it! He will have amazing supernatural powers. They must not be deceived for an instant. When I speak of fighting a battle, as part of My Mother's Army, I mean a battle of resistance against the lure of the evil one and all that he will offer the world through the Antichrist. Yes, it will be difficult to resist these opportunities to have so much more than those who do not follow him. You will be living a meager existence for many years and will be sorely tempted to give in to all he offers. The *world itself will be a difficult place in which to live during his reign.* Just remember that *it will be a short period of time, and you will be protected in My arms* by all the strength you will need to turn away from the world and live together in peace.

"Continue to offer the waiting as an act of love and obedience to Our Father in Heaven. Please know that I am Jesus Who comes by the gracious gift of My Father. Rest in My love for you. The waiting world is about to embark on a perilous journey that very few will survive. Only those chosen by My Father will come through each event and continue to serve Our people and prepare them for My Coming. Be at total peace as each new goal is reached, each task accomplished.

"Oh daughter, I too long for Our visit with you. Continue to offer the waiting as an act of love and obedience to Our Father in Heaven. He sends love and greeting to you as He plans the next move for you according to His desires. Please know that I am Jesus Who comes by the gracious gift of My Father. My Mother is also here with Me. Rest in My love for you, daughter. Your heart will mend and be joyful, little one, I promise you."

1/8/98, Blessed Mother said:

"I come this night with special words of warning to all My dear children of the world. There will be many graces offered during this year of 1998. There will be enormous opportunities for many conversions. Please, all of you who listen to My words, pray even more that as many as possible will convert and come back to My Son. It is now the time that is written about in Scripture which foretells the coming of the dragon, the advent of the Beast, and the danger to all of the children of the earth. The Pope will flee Rome and be in virtual hiding for many months. You must take great care to support each other and not to panic. The Holy Spirit will first pour out innumerable gifts and graces upon the world. These must be accepted by each of you, guarded and nurtured, as the amount of evil in the world increases. There is no way to prepare for these times other than prayer and penance and fasting! Please my children, renew your efforts in these areas. Know that I am helping you, and there is no one who cannot give up many trivial and 'important' little goodies and favors you grant to yourselves constantly. Do not wait another minute, My dear ones. Believe that each act of denial towards your own desires impacts souls mightily. Don't wait until a specific time or day. Begin now to deny yourselves those little pleasures you have become accustomed to in this great land of plenty. This not only helps others to open up to graces offered, but increases your own discipline for the coming days in which you will need to do without so much. See all of this as a means of allowing and preparing you to go directly to Heaven at the right time, and live happily with all who wait for you in Heaven. My Jesus and I are praying and interceding for all of you who desire to serve.

"The joy in My heart is caused by the love you have for me, and the prayers and works you perform for your brothers and sisters in the world. Be at peace, My dearest ones. Know that your place in Heaven is assured when you remain faithful to My Son; and all I call you to be. We will be victorious, My dear ones, never forget that for an instant. The future is filled with chaos for all who have not chosen to answer My call. Just please, continue to act in trust, to live in the peace of Jesus, and to stay ever so close to Our Two Hearts. Great signs will be given soon to convince many of the truth of Our words. Our little ones who serve will be blessed with a special place in the Father's Kingdom. Do not wait to be convinced by signs and wonders. Convert now, pray more now, come closer to Us now as We prepare to lead you, with the Angels and Saints, against the powers of darkness. Remember, each event must occur in order to fulfill Scripture and the Father's plan for the salvation of His children. Persevere, My little ones. Is it not wonderful to be loved in such a way by your Heavenly Mother and, most of all, by the Triune God? Give praise and thanks at all times, children, to be called children of the Most High God and of Me, your loving Mother."

1/20/98, Jesus said:

"Daughter, please take My words. You are filled with love and devotion for Me, little one, and I your Jesus Who loves and adores My Father in union with Our Spirit, tell you I am so grateful for this degree of surrender on your part. All of the time wasted, the time lost in the Father's Plan is now erased, is now made up; and your place renewed in His desires for you. Continue to praise My Father, Carol, and rejoice in His goodness to you.

"The events are closer than ever, I promise you, little faithful one."

1/20/98, Jesus said:

The world is truly on another path, away from all Our chosen ones. The casual attitudes of many who once listened and responded is a sign of the growing strength of evil in the world. Yes, the Antichrist will make his appearance to the world during this year of 1998. Much will happen so quickly, and you will all be living closely together in prayer and deed. Do not worry about any aspect of the future, please My little faithful ones. You are all held deep within My Heart.

"A serious and sad tone is present in My voice today, My daughter, which you also feel in your own heart. Know that the events about to unfold will fill you with this greater degree of focus and awareness of suffering. You will be given strength to minister to the needs of all and will lack nothing in word and deed. The times, for which you have all waited, and prepared, are on the horizon. My Father's Will acts on behalf of the *innocents who are rejected by their own mothers*, their own kind! Be at prayer this night, as you are able, child. Be one with Me now to praise and plead with Our Heavenly Father to begin the cleansing of men's hearts and souls most quickly.

"'**Father, we kneel before Your Majesty and ask Your action in our lives and in the world. Enact Your plan now, Father, to bring all Your people back to You in love and remorse and repentance. Allow Your justice, guided by Your mercy, to pour forth upon the waiting world that knows not Your love and power. Bring us back to Your loving arms and scoop us up in Your mercy and forgiveness. You are Our God and Our Creator, Our Savior and Our Sanctifier. We beg You, Father, receive our prayers and answer us. Amen.**'

"Child, I wish you to distribute this among Our faithful ones. Wait in joy and peace now for the hand of My Father to allow the events to occur to the end of this age of evil. Watch and wait with your brothers and sisters in the world who share your faith and trust in Our words."

1/27/98 Jesus said:

"Yes, My dearest one; I desire to speak to you this night. Thank you for stopping to listen to My words of loving encouragement. You are wisely filling every moment, daughter, I assure you. Each chore is being put behind you in completion. I admire your ability and tenacity, gifts, of course, from My Father in these recent months. Expect good things, little faithful one. Expect miracles of love to abound.

"The discomfort you are feeling will never completely leave your body, as you can well imagine. This is a great aid to help you remain quiet and focused on Me and My dear Mother. The Angels and Saints are hovering near you now and send songs of cheer and love. All of Our faithful ones form one great body of believers in the company of their Angels and Saints, and number in the millions! Be filled with nothing but joy now as you wait in total trust that all Our promises will be fulfilled; be ready, daughter, be very ready. In the love of the Triune God, I am your Jesus."

PRAYER GROUP

1/27/98, Jesus said:

"Daughter, you are bravely following Our requests and can expect some response from many people who delight in judging and acting as overseer for other's discernment. Just continue to remain silent in the face of opposition. As I have promised you in the past, events will prove the truth of Our words to you...all of them. You are so much better prepared each day as you reread these words given with the greatest love for you and Our people. Those who listen in love will stand by you through every attack and be with you till the end of the Age. All of Our faithful ones form one great body of believers in the company of their Angels and Saints and number in the millions. Be filled with nothing but joy now as you wait in total trust that all Our promises will be fulfilled. In the love of the Triune God, I am your Jesus."

1/30/98 Jesus said:

"Events in the world and miracles and signs (Mother Angelica's healing!) begin to point the way to the imminence of the Warning. Our people will first be rocked by tremendous events that will occur shortly. The events will follow so quickly as to keep all who are not aware (of things prophesied) in great chaos and fear. Do not be alarmed, please daughter, at all you see. Just remain focused and prayerful.

"Thank you, Carol, for coming to praise and adore Me. The peace and love you feel are real and will only increase. I join your eagerness to begin this journey. You are blessed by all the Angels and Saints, by the Triune God, by your Holy Mother. Be of good cheer and sleep in peace, My dear one. Know that you are standing next to My Mother and Me and act accordingly! It is with great joy in My Heart that I bless and embrace you, My faithful one."

2/19/98, Jesus said:

"Listen closely now, daughter, for My words are most important this day. World events are poised for a *criminal level of aggression by your country*. It is no longer the greatest country in the world, and *will soon become the greatest aggressor*! There is no honor in the activity about to be perpetrated in the name of justice. There is no justice in the *monstrous plot by world leaders to decimate the world's numbers and push ahead the agenda of the one world order.*

"Remain in prayer for peace, My children. Remain serious and focused on the events developing at this moment throughout the world. Be aware of the treachery behind the actions of those who *work in secret to destroy, all the while presenting justification to the world for reprehensible decisions*. The time for frivolity and parties, distractions and self-glorification, gratification and laziness is over.

People of the world: I, your Lord and Savior, call out to you. In the Name of My Father and of Our Spirit and of Myself, I implore you to implore the Father of all to act swiftly now to bring His own justice to bear on all who seek to destroy His world. You will know stunning defeat at His hands, Pagan World. You will see the Son of Man in the sky, pouring out graces on all who will accept them. You will know the might of the One Who created you. You will weep one day in horror over the results of your pact with evil. Be on guard, My people. The prophecies uttered to so many, and by so many of Our dear faithful ones, have begun. No longer will you wait in comfort, but on your knees in pleading for peace. The beauty of the world will soon disappear and be replaced by the most difficult and painful oppression.

Stay close to Us now, Who love you and have promised to protect you. We have great need of your dear hearts to minister lovingly to all who will wander in confusion. Bring them to Me and explain My Father's Plan to bring back to His fold all who will allow themselves to be 'captured' and led. The Divine Shepherd will lead you into the Heart of the Father and Son and Holy Spirit, the Trinity of God Who is One. Repent! Repent, all who will listen, and return this very day in humble surrender to all you were created to become and to be. A last call, dear people of every nation, from your God. Listen and act My precious ones. I love you. I await your return. I beg you to hear and respond. In the Trinity, I am your Jesus of Mercy."

3/3/98, Jesus said:

"My child, please take My words. Be with Me now as much as possible each day now, dear ones. The hours are not important, but only our presence together in front of My Sacrament.

"The world is about to explode (speaking figuratively!). Be aware that people are being done away with in many countries without the knowledge of the world. This annihilation of the needy and destitute ones is part of Satan's plan to set up his one world religion that will truly only worship himself! My dear children, the only answer for survival during these times is to stay focused on My face. Wrap yourselves with My love and My Presence with you. Be removed now from the world and all its busyness. Know that prayers of reparation are impacting all those you pray for. Just continue, please, to persevere and believe in all you have heard. Be at peace, dear children. Know that you are cherished."

3/12/98 Jesus said:

"My dearest child, please take My words in joy and trust. Daughter, you are persevering well and praying mightily. I, your Jesus of Divine Mercy, come this night to bring you added strength along this path of waiting on My Father's Will. These are not easy days for anyone, especially those who pine over the removal of My Precious Presence and Tabernacle from its rightful place in My own house! Be filled with holy indignation, My friends. Defend Me as long as you can and be docile and holy and demure in your defense! The days are numbered that see any one of My churches with the appearance of a Catholic Church. The liberality of priests toward My Sacred Presence, their lack of respect, is astounding to all who behold. And yet, I have told them (all of us) in the recent past that everything will be removed of a sacred nature, and ultimately all of My churches will be closed. Yes, this is an unbelievable development in the history of My Church, but you must remember that these events must occur in order to fulfill Scripture before I return.

"The Body of Christ will undergo a scourging just like Mine. You are all asked to carry this cross and walk every step of the Way with Me to My Crucifixion. **This Passion and Death is relived now by My entire Church and, just as in days of old, persecutions of Christians will result. Those who follow Me, and Our beloved John Paul, will be asked to suffer greatly for the sins of the apostates who attempt to tear this Body asunder. The Gates of Hell are open to destroy all those who profess belief that I am your Redeemer and Messiah Who died once and for all to open again the Gates of Heaven to all who choose to follow, love and serve Me.**

"The Gates of Hell will never prevail over My Church, although you will now suffer its greatest persecution of modern times. People will quake with fear in the coming days. Areas already weakened by severe weather will suffer new attacks of the wildness of the weather. The coastal areas are increasingly vulnerable to the effects of the enormous storms that will only continue. Please, daughter, beg all to continue to pray that the people who live in these regions will turn to My Father in surrender and ask for His help and His mercy. The Father allows these events to continue in order to force people to listen and acknowledge their need for their God Who alone can help them. The devastation that continues to escalate is a sure sign of the living out of many of Our prophecies regarding these end times. See how unimportant and fragile are the possessions of those who see them ruined by the destructive forces of nature. Hear how many voice the importance of life in the face of overwhelming loss.

"These dear ones need to be the focus of your prayers, My little faithful remnant. Begin to share again your prayers and personal wealth and goods to all who have lost everything. See the difference in life-style required of those whose homes and property are washed away by wind and rain and fire. Many of these weather events are reaching through minds and hearts that have been hardened previously to the voice of their Father and Creator. Here is My Mother with words of love."

3/12/98, Blessed Mother said:

"The time, as you can see, is here for the illumination of your minds to the state of your souls, dear children of the world. You see unmistakable signs and words being given to all who wait for the Father to send His merciful justice into the world. This need not be awaited or anticipated in the future. It is happening now! Be assured, My dear, dear ones, that chaos and unrest exists everywhere as the forces of nature ravage so many areas. Your winter will last far into the months usually experienced as mild and warmer. Do not be surprised at the devastation that continues and the violent behavior, which accompanies it. The Father is announcing an extended time of hardship for those who refuse to listen to His commandments; for those who refuse and reject His precious gift of life. For all of My faithful ones, who listen to My voice and obey My requests: Please, pray that these events will soften many hearts and lead them back to their loving Father Who waits to heal and comfort them; back to My Son, Who desires to nourish and renew them; back to My Spouse, Who waits to heal them and fill them with grace. Be assured, My faithful soldiers, that this is a battle. Be assured that these storms are an answer to all the evil in the world. Be assured my soldiers, My special children, that you are fighting the evil one, My enemy, when you pray for peace; for an end to killing and plans for war; for the weather to return to its normal patterns, for God's mercy on all who suffer. These prayers are the weapons you use to fight the battle for Me and with Me at your side.

"The Angels and Saints have joined all who pray in order to cement closer relationships in the great Communion of Saints to which you belong as a militant Church of My Son. Please, dear children, allow nothing else to fill your thoughts and your time. What very, very brief time remains must be spent in the joy of loving and serving all. The days are changing rapidly at this time in the plan of Our Father. It is so necessary that you continue to wait with calm and patient hearts, offering this waiting to Me for My prayer intentions. You are so greatly loved My children of the earth. Remember to share with those you meet that I am the Mother of all people on the earth. I am watching over you and share in your tears of frustration, pain and suffering. You are always before My eyes and in My heart, and in My prayers and protection. The heartbeat that exists before the Father's plan is escalated and becomes even more obvious is still time enough to repent, to confess your sins, to reach out to others to help them live out these days, to explain to them the reason each event occurs. You, My dear soldiers, are prepared for any event, any disruption in your lives, any letting go and emptying deemed necessary for you by Our Father and Creator. Be at peace, My little faithful ones. Be assured of My Son's return and His victory over all of the evil in the world. Expect to see miracles occurring for millions of dear ones who will need a strong sign of the Father's great love in the midst of so much chaos and confusion. Remain faithful to My call, My beloved children. Expect continuing and total love from your God and His (and your) Heavenly Mother."

3/18/98, Jesus said:

"The days seem to hang in balance against all the expectations in the hearts of Our beloved faithful ones (everywhere). They are so blessed by My Father and filled with the gifts of Our Spirit. My Mother looks forward eagerly to the time ahead when all will fight for her honor and the Father's Plan of Salvation for His world. She prays in quiet anticipation of His renewed action in the world for the sake of bringing many more back to Him in repentance. This is an awesome time to be alive; to await the coming of the Son of Man; to anticipate the defeat of evil in the person of the Antichrist (and his many cohorts).

"At this time, there will be no more delays on the part of leaders of the world before a full engagement of powers, a few at first, then escalating into a full world war and enormous devastation.

"Little children of the world, do not be surprised at the number of people who will be removed from the earth through the action of destructive forces, hostile aggression, and simply evil intentions. The world is about to disappear, that is, the world as you know and see it now. By the time I return, you will hardly recognize the shape of the land and the numbers of countries. Masses of people will be decimated. The color of the earth will be scorched. The air will be filled continually with cries of mourning. The air will be so unhealthy that you will need to protect yourselves whenever you are outside your dwellings. All of these developments will be sudden, and people will be frightened by the many changes and awful conditions.

"I tell you these things again in order to allow you to be prepared for them. Even with this knowledge, it will require great strength to maintain peace and trust and joy in your hearts. Please tell all (you can reach) to live in the joy of the hope present in your hearts, as you await My return. I am coming to be with you and walk the earth with you. The astounding facts of My victory over evil will serve to give you the patience and perseverance that will be needed all throughout the coming events. You are poised on the brink of total change in your world and all who remain! Await these events, My beloved faithful, by hiding in My arms and taking refuge and strength from deep within Our Two Hearts. I bid you be of good cheer, filled with great expectations for a land flowing with peace and love, harmony and joy.

"Oh My dear, dear ones, you are loved beyond words, beyond feelings, beyond your understanding. Please, please hold out, hold on, hold on to My Mother's hand as together, We form the renewed Kingdom on earth. Do not panic, but quietly prepare for these events. Be in deep prayer from now on as much as possible. More is possible! I am your loving Jesus Who showers you with love. Reread all My words, My dearest ones.

"Carol, My dearest child, be filled with more strength and good health now. Sleep in My love for you."

4/4/98, Jesus said:

"My dearest one, you may take these words of comfort and solace: I am your CRUCIFIED Lord. I come with a Body full of wounds caused by the INDIFFERENCE of My faithful children!

You are by no means alone in your disobedience and selfishness." [which Jesus had been showing me all week! -C.A.] "The wounds in My Heart are increased daily by the carelessness of those who think they are serving Me and are without blemish, without pain of sin. Your suffering, daughter, must be offered for all those who are not aware of their weaknesses. It is so necessary that all be completely purified at this time.

"It is necessary for each of you to take so very seriously the words of My Father, of My Holy Mother, and of Myself and Our Spirit. NO ONE is praying ENOUGH! For this next week I desire all action but the MOST necessary chores, to STOP in the lives of My Remnant people. If you are to survive this time of the Tribulation and suffering imposed by the Anti-Christ and his followers, you will need to be emptied of ALL stain of sin and be filled with My strength, My goodness, My power, and My Presence. You must be living tabernacles for those who will need to find Me within the darkness of his reign.

"You must turn away totally and at all times from the world, and remain with Me in silence and peace, and be open to the grace and healing I desire to give to each of you. Make no mistake, My faithful ones, it is necessary now to completely DIE to your own will, your own desires, your own waste of time in frivolous pastimes. The Will of My Father MUST fill your plans for every moment of each day. The pleading of My Mother for increased prayer for the salvation of souls, and the repeated requests for a greater amount of time spent before Me in My Sacrament, MUST BE ANSWERED wholeheartedly by each of you IMMEDIATELY!

"Remember all the preparation you have made to be ready for these final events of this time before the illumination of your minds to the state of your souls as your God and Creator sees them. You have remained true to these requests and are nearly fully prepared to serve Me through your brothers and sisters.

"Until this Warning occurs so very, very immediately, it is very necessary that you answer this call for all of your time and attention to a focus on My Face, and My Father's plans and need of you. You will help the Triune God with your service and aid to His Lost Souls. They will need every sort of help and support from you.

"I can NOT too strongly state the importance of the mission each of you is being given now. I can NOT repeat too often how much I love ALL of Our children, and long to hold and comfort and heal each one in the world. There are so many gifts to receive, so much joy to experience, so much Peace to be known, if you will once again consecrate yourselves to My Mother's Immaculate Heart and to My Sacred and Merciful Heart.

"Bind the WHOLE WORLD to us with your prayers and your love. Be ready to serve beyond any normal capacity with Our help.

"We will NEVER abandon you, no matter how difficult and painful your journey may become. A complete trust on your part in My Power and Victory will sustain you throughout unbelievable terror and bloodshed.

"I do not wish to frighten you, My children, but I need to hold your ATTENTION, your HEARTS, in My Heart and in My hands.

"You are each blessed beyond words to describe. You are loved and CHERISHED by your Lord and your God. Whatever you see, whatever you must endure, is for the purification of your souls before My glorious return. A life of Peace in My Kingdom on earth, or in Heaven for all eternity, is worth ANY hardship, ANY time spent in difficult circumstances.

"DO NOT BE AFRAID, My beloved ones, be filled with JOY and EAGERNESS for My return. It will not be much longer, I PROMISE you now.

"Be filled with My Peace, children of the world. It is your Lord Who will save. You need do nothing but serve and pray and spend all of your time with Me, with My Mother, with the Angels and Saints! Come NOW and discover the bliss that is possible in Our Presence, receiving all the graces We wish to give you at this time.

Believe, My dearest ones. TRUST, and PERSEVERE!"

4/17/98, Jesus said:

"Good evening, dearest daughter. Please take My words of love and appreciation. This week, child, has been so healing for you, and you can be assured of being stronger than ever. Mary closes with these words: My daughter, thank you for taking this message for the world. You will be receiving many more important words in the future. Please continue to rest and take care of yourself. You are a joy to My heart, dear one, and a great general in My army!! Thank you for all the love in your heart for Me."

4/18/98, Jesus said:

"Daughter, listen now while I bring words of grave importance. I am your Jesus Who loves you as no other. I am the Son from on High Who died to save you and Who brings mercy this night on the eve of My great Feast of Divine Mercy. Dear Faustina is here with Me and filled with joy at the numbers who will gather tomorrow to pay tribute to My mercy, and who have prayed the Novena these past nine days for My requests. There will be great signs tomorrow that many will see as a result of My great mercy. Many will be renewed in My plan and advanced in their service to My Father. The dawn will bring new tragedies to several parts of the world as another sign that My justice is replacing My mercy in some instances. People must see the difference in these events and make the connection between nature and My power. Do they think that all is still just a coincidence?

"People of the world, awake from your slumber and look around you. Before there is added destruction that may find you still slumbering, wake up and read the signs everywhere in the world that point to the displeasure of My Father. Do you not believe that your God might be angry with the behavior in the world? Keep watching then, and be convinced by the crashing of the sea and the battering of mighty waves. These are times for desperate action on your part, My people. People in desperation are often moved to take huge risks and heroic measures to maintain safety for themselves. This is what I, your Lord, am suggesting to all of you! Be energetic in your prayer and your spiritual preparation for the storms that will continue. Fall on your knees and beg for My mercy upon the land.

"On this Feast of Mercy, I wish to pour My graces and forgiveness upon the whole world. Please come and ask Me, beg Me for this mercy for the earth and everyone on it. Expect a mighty response from Me when you come seeking shelter in My Merciful

Heart. Please, dear ones, believe that I am preparing you for My return to the earth and all that will occur prior to this great event.

"Your world is filled with the finest and most advanced systems of communication ever known in history. Yet, very few listen or believe what they hear! The sadness that fills My Heart is a result of all the terrible destruction I see you experiencing, not at the hand of My Father, but at the hands of each other! Greed for power is the terrible force that will annihilate so many members of the human family. When people are of no use to those in power, they will be destroyed as a means of controlling those who remain to be used to further plans to control the world! This sounds too fantastic, I know My beloved ones, but it is not news anymore. Some of you are watching and listening and praying, and to you I say, 'Thank you for having mercy on Me, your Lord and your God!'

Tomorrow, I ask you to DOUBLE YOUR EFFORTS TO IMPLORE MERCY FOR THE WORLD. Believe that it will be given in proportion to what you ask. My Mother is here with her Angels and many Saints, and wishes to send greetings. Please listen to her who loves you so much. Be filled with the fire of My love, dear people. I love you, My faithful ones."

Blessed Mother said:

"Beloved children, I send greetings to you on the eve of this great feast of My Son's Divine Mercy. All of Heaven has joined you this week as you pray your Novena of Chaplets. We will continue to accompany you as you redouble your pleas for mercy for the world.

"Children, please be serious about the ongoing need to listen and respond to Our requests to all of you. Very shortly you will need to act on the requests of Heaven in an even greater way. This will be a matter of life and death, salvation or loss forever in Hell. Stay closer than ever to Me, my dearest little ones. Be humble, obedient children of your heavenly Mother who needs you to be ever at her beck and call. These times are most serious and call for a serious attention to Our words. You have been so faithful, and I thank you for this. You will only know in Heaven how many treasures you have stored and waiting for you. But **you must be even**

braver and stronger now. You must fight evil with all your might in this short time before the gift of the Father's Warning is given to the world.

"My dear ones, you do not know, nor could you ever understand, the great hardships that await you. In trust, I ask you to simply wait in peace, and pray for the people of the world that they will respond to the graces offered at this time, that they will persevere in faithfulness to their choice to return to the Father of ALL people. It will be very, very difficult to accomplish, My little ones. In spite of strong intentions, the fear of the moment will lead many to abandon their promises in order to save their lives. You must not follow them, children of my heart! My heart bleeds for those who will be lost on account of choosing a momentary pleasure. What looks like the easier way will lead only to the hardship of slavery in the ranks of the Antichrist.

"Believe me, dearest children, when I say you will need every ounce of strength to hold out to the end of this Age. Be assured of my help with all my Angels and all the Saints. This will be enough protection! Continue to remember the victory that is assured, that is already won. Wait in peace and trust, children of the world. Be ready to greet My Son when He comes again to claim you for His own and walk with you in the Garden of Our Father, as the earth is returned to its former grandeur and beauty. Be filled with delight, My little ones, and realize each event brings you that much closer to the realization of all Our promises for an era of peace and purity. You will all see Me at that time, for I am always with My Son and He is always with Me! Be strengthened once again now with new, hope and joy; new expectations of peace and mercy.

"I am your Mother who comes this night to build up your trust, to bring happiness to your hearts."

5/4/98, Jesus said:

"Dear one, please take My words before any other prayer. Today was a peaceful one in your life, daughter, with much prayer and dwelling in My Heart. But this pattern is soon to be interrupted by the plans of those who would conquer the world.

"Right at this moment (yes, in your time!) there are people planning the takeover of neighboring countries throughout the world. This will be well orchestrated, child, and a reason to send troops in many directions to further dilute the defense in your own country. Please, dearest spouse of My Heart, spend the rest of this day with Me, praying for the salvation of many who will be entering Eternity as a result of these aggressions. The need for all to continue in increased prayer only escalates, as many prophecies begin to be fulfilled and many lives are lost. Know that every word you hear from My Mother and Myself will be fulfilled very shortly.

"We in Heaven realize that you, Our faithful ones, have all been subjected to many delays, and are weary and puzzled by these delays. It is only that, as We have reminded you in the past, the Father waits as long as He can to allow events to begin that will subject His beloved children of the world to great struggles and even eventually displacement from your homes. These are not games We play, My sweet one, but the mercy of God acting to protect all of you from as much chaos as possible.

"Please, people of the world, remain serious about spending all available time in prayer and quiet. Reread all the words We have given to faithful messengers who have dedicated their lives to taking Our words of warning for all of you. They act in love, knowing how many have already walked away from them; how many are the criticisms and accusations leveled by those who think they are able to discern so well, all the while bringing harm to My Body. Please pray for them, too, My people.

"Only peace and mercy must reign in the hearts of all who serve Me. Only kind words and prayer should come from lips that receive Me daily in My Eucharist. My Mother is greatly saddened by those of you who attack each other, causing even more confusion in the minds and hearts of those who wish to follow My Mother and Myself.

"Seek forgiveness and reconciliation, My followers who quarrel about each other. Seek to remain in prayer of remorse and silence, and ask Me to forgive you. The time has disappeared before the events that will turn your world upside down. There is no time left for personal attacks and arguments. Put your anger and harsh words to rest, and come to My Mother and allow her to soothe the turmoil within you. Trust that My Father, Our Spirit and I will deal directly with those who stand in the way of the reception of Our words for the preparation of all Our children who still listen.

"This is a rather harsh message, yes, but there have been many harsh words given among many of you. The time for living in peace and harmony has long been upon you. Do you not trust your Merciful Lord?

"I am your Jesus of Mercy Who died for you, your Savior Who is ALWAYS with you, Who will NEVER LEAVE YOU unless you turn away from Me through your rage, setting yourselves up as judges when God Alone is the judge of man. You will see justice given now at the hands of My Father. You will see the diabolic ones exposed and caught in their own traps.

"Oh My dear people, I call to you with love and plead with you to stop these endless contests, this war of words and accusations. The Adversary gains much when there is war among the children of God.

"Come back to Me, My loved ones, with all your heart. Allow Me to lead you to peace, to the land where enemies will lie down together in peace, (Is 11:6), and hearts beat in rhythm with My Own Heart, My Merciful Heart.

"Beloved children of the world, UNITE!! Present a strong united front against which the enemy of good can make no advances, cause no crumbling of your fortified walls. If you have honest concerns, bring them to Me before My Blessed Sacrament. Give Me the pain and anguish you feel, the things you see that cause you worry. Bring to Me your questions and concerns, and I promise to resolve every one. Am I not a God Who saves, a God Who has repeatedly brought My people out of slavery, out of the deception of the evil one?

"I will not fail you now, My children. Ask Me for Knowledge, for Wisdom, for Understanding and for the Peace only I can give you. Call upon Our Spirit to heal you of anger and distrust. Spend many hours in front of Me, all of you, but especially those who suffer serious doubts and anguish.

"I am coming to free you, once again. I am returning to walk among you in a purified world that has been emptied of anger and hurtful accusations. I know that you would protect My Mother with what seems to you like sincere word and deed. Remember that Christians love one another (Jn13:35) and are constantly practicing the virtues of My Mother: her gentleness, her patience, her trust in the power of the Holy Spirit, her very Spouse!

"I call all of you now, beloved of My Father, to put away all hostile words, all contemptuous attacks upon each other. I call upon you to live in peaceful resignation to My Father's Will, before the power and fury of Satan is loosed upon the world. These events are all part of My Father's plan to ultimately rid the world of all evil completely; to fulfill every word of Scripture before My return. But We, the Triune God, ask you to unite in peace under the banner of Our Beloved Mother, under the Mantle of her protection. She will see that deception is uncovered. She will crush Satan's head. But, please, do not crush her heart now with words designed to crush each other!! We count on all of you so very much to help Us in this battle against the malignant enemy.

"Be one with Us, My children whom I love, to whom so many gifts have already been given. We rely on your help during these ever increasingly difficult days and times. Be united in the love of the Immaculate Heart and trust your Lord and your God to protect you from deception. I have promised to save you from the evil one. I WILL!

"Thank you, little one, for taking this call to Our people. Please add the cause of unity amongst the soldiers in the Army of My dear, dear Mother who grieves at all the unrest and personal attacks she sees. Take all this energy you might use to denounce each other, My followers, and give it to prayer for conversion and peace of as many as possible who do not yet know of the Love and Beauty awaiting them in My Father's Kingdom. Thank you, child. You are greatly loved by your Lord, the Spouse of your heart. Be at peace now, dear ones.

5/11/98, Jesus said:

"My dearest child, I am your Eucharistic Jesus. Please take My words meant for your enlightenment. Daughter, the day has been filled with beautiful prayers from your heart to Mine. Thank you, child, for your obedience and surrender today. Such little time remains for hours spent in this way, and I am grateful you are filling them (with time spent) before Me in love and submission.

"Dear one, do not do anything other than this prayer of unity. Be focused on My Presence with My Mother, your special Angels and Saints. Daughter, the world is not ready for the events on your horizon. Please inform them that danger lurks behind the Chinese attempt to engage your country in trade. The willingness of your government to overlook human rights atrocities, and suppression of all but State approved religions is an affront to all this Nation has fought for in order to win freedom for all who would live in peace (in this country). Your government gives away that freedom carelessly and with no thoughts of protecting the American people. It is too late to effect a change in these policies now, but I warn you to expect many surprise moves by foreign governments in the very near future.

"Daughter, plead with Our people, wherever you go, to expect mighty events of a destructive nature. Encourage them to be at peace, trusting completely, and praying much for all who are unprepared. Events are so near. I speak in this way because I wish to remind all that the Father's Will is about cleansing the world of the evil that confuses the minds of so many, the duplicity that covers the actions of evil men who must be exposed and revealed by the Light of Truth.

"The love of My Father is the first thing all of My followers and soldiers will need to present over and over again to frightened ones who come to you. Look at all of the reasons you have discovered for loving and praising and thanking the Triune God at every moment.

"MAKE A LIST, MY PEOPLE!!! Come before Me in silence and write down what you will say to strangers who need to be fed with Scripture stories and teachings that portray a loving God. Write down what experiences you each have had in your lives that convince you of the love and forgiveness and mercy of My Father. Why do you love Me, My children? What has convinced you to trust in My promises? What words have you heard proclaimed that have moved you to prepare for My Return to the earth to fight the great Battle of Armageddon?

"Are there psalms and Scripture passages that you use constantly to bring a return of peace to your hearts, in order to still your fears. Are there some that you refer to immediately as a comfort in times of sadness or loss, times of doubt or confusion, times of the need for comfort and nourishment, times of near despair, humiliation, sorrow for sins; and times of personal need for consolation, for a deeper understanding of God's great love for you or a loved one?

"Make note of these places (in Scripture) in a little booklet. Make note of the words you might wish to use in dealing with many people who will be in such need themselves. Keep this small notebook with you at all times in order to add new ideas or thoughts that will come by means of inspiration from Our Holy Spirit.

"THIS IS A SERIOUS CALL TO YOU!!

"These are serious suggestions for all My people who wonder what they will say and do in a time of crisis when all are in chaos.

"Record words you might use from the great number of teachings you have all received from Me and from our dearest Mother. Do this now, My beloved ones who wait to serve Our people. Be prepared in a new way as you stock up on supplies...of loving, helpful words in order to feed Our lost souls who will be hungering for the truth and words of peace and direction. This will be a great help to each of you, too, My dear ones who love Me.

"Be ready to fire at the enemy with weapons of prayer and preparedness, words of instruction and reason, words of truth and logic that will serve to fight the plans of Satan to divide and conquer Our people who need to rediscover the Way back to My Father with the help of Our Spirit.

"Please, dear beloved ones who listen and pray, receive My suggestions and act upon them immediately. Be ready for the onslaught of huge numbers of people that will nearly overrun all of you in their panic. Be the calm center of truth and instruments of love and grace, channels of peace and mercy from now until you each join Us in Heaven at a time predetermined by the Father's plan for the salvation of all His children, you, His beloved.

"Arm yourselves with the breastplate of truth, the armor of love with which to repel Satan and his hideous throng who believe they will overcome all of you with tactics designed to lead you to despair, and surrender to empty promises of power and victory.

"It is a time, just before a battle, to gather all of your resources of prayers and the power of the Word of God and all His promises. You must stay quiet and totally removed from the world from now on, My little soldiers. You must stay closer than ever to My Mother and her Angels, to Me in My Blessed Sacrament, to the Sacraments with all their graces and strength, to your consecration to Our Two Hearts, to the whispered guidance of the Holy Spirit Who leads you in safety, to your Angels who will lead you at the right time away from the dangers of the Antichrist and his henchmen.

"You will be amazed at the organization that is already in place to accomplish the plans of Satan to destroy churches and all religions. In order to overcome the entire world, things will happen in an instant, and you must be ready to flee these evil men with their plans for your life and ultimately, your soul.

"The time is here for you to take every precaution against the plans of Satan to isolate you from the truth, and cause you to lose your way in the darkness descending rapidly.

"We have told you about the safety and protection possible, hidden away from the Antichrist, within the Mantle of My Mother, within My wounds, and within the peace and comfort of the Two Hearts that beat as one.

"You are prepared, My beloved ones, when you do all these things in a trusting and peace filled way. You have the might of My Arm and the gentleness of My Mother to bring you through incredible difficulties. DO NOT BE AFRAID, MY LAMBS!

"Do not give in to the pleadings of loved ones who may beg you to take the Mark of the Beast, the easier way, the ease of life offered by those who administer the chip that allows you to continue to buy and sell in a seemingly free way.

"You must continue to remind yourselves of the finality of the results of your choice for God or the world!

"You must remain convinced of all My promises and the love offered by My Mother and the Triune God. Go about these preparations in peace and trust, believing that the Kingdom of God is the prize. You will live in a renewed world or in the Kingdom of Eternal Life. Either way, you have won the crown! You will have accepted the victory I have already won for you. You will have accepted the peace and salvation waiting for you in union with Love.

"I send you these words to ponder and act upon quickly, My dear, dear people. You are loved without end.

"Thank you, My beloved, for listening closely. You have done well taking My words today. There are many more words and warnings in the days to come.

"Dwell in the peace and joy of Our love for you, people of the world. Peace to you, My little one."

5/28/98, Blessed Mother said:

"Beloved daughter, it is I, your Mother of Sorrows, come to ask your help this night. I come to you and the few faithful who continue to pray, requesting a day of fast and prayer tomorrow (today, Friday) for all the threats that now lay poised on your horizon.

"The world plays games with power and taunts, with abilities to destroy; but without the reasoning necessary to make sound decisions based on humane principles.

"The confusion present in minds of world leaders, who barter lives for the opportunity to be first in the eyes of each other, is about to result in terrible destruction. Even an understanding of the possibility of a Third World War cannot prepare anyone for the terror and destruction about to be unleashed upon innocent people who are pawns in the terrible game of power and one-upmanship.

"The goading of one country by another is a situation being spawned by Satan. It is a delightful dilemma to witness for all the power hungry leaders of the world who simply await their turn at flexing nuclear arms and muscle.

"The killing of people means nothing to men who gloat over the power amassed by anyone who conquers the nearest country, and on and on until near total destruction of the world results. What does it matter if so many innocents are killed? To be on top of the heap of dead bodies is to be victor in the eyes of madmen. Power drives men hatefully and fearlessly toward whatever will conquer the greatest numbers.

"Be serious, child, about this request, please. Know that I will be with you and all who pray, closer than you know, uniting all your prayers and offering My own, as well. These gifts you offer united to mine will be taken by the Angels to the throne of the Father in Heaven. They will be thrice blessed and returned to the world as graces and protection, mitigating the destruction allowed by the Father as much as your prayers and fasting will obtain. It is so necessary to be in prayer from now on, My dearest child, because time has run out. Events will no longer be delayed.

"When you remain close to Me, united in prayer, you are the safest you can be, you are the most blessed and protected you can possibly be, you are helping Me and doing the Father's Will as much as you are able. This alone is a great gift to each one who spends a day with Me in this fashion. It is another reason for you to be free to respond to any and all requests for your time and energy on behalf of the entire world. You will be spending many days like this from now on.

"Do not, please, think that all of you who respond can do only a little good because there are so few of you. The Angels and Saints will multiply your prayers and endeavors. My pleading for mercy will result in far more than you alone could imagine or acquire in the way of graces for the world. Do not think, no matter what occurs, that your prayers were not heard, or answered, or beneficial. It is only in Heaven that you will learn the results of all your efforts and obedience to My requests. Please assure everyone of the special place they all occupy in My Immaculate and Sorrowful Heart.

"Dear children of the world, pray as much as you can this day. All of Heaven is united with you in love and prayer. I am your Mother and friend who loves each of you beyond telling. You bring so much ease to the aching in My heart, and I thank you, dear ones who love Me and join Me in prayer now.

"Thank you, daughter, for taking these words. You are loved by your Mother in Heaven (and in your heart)."

6/15/98, Jesus said:

"Daughter, please take My words. Listen carefully, and with love, as these are serious words.

"The world is spinning towards disaster, as its leaders spin webs of deception towards mortal combat. The warlike actions of certain countries put the world in the greatest danger. Powers are lining up for a confrontation of epic proportions designed to defeat the weak of this world and decimate as many as possible.

"A nuclear attack will bring major powers into positions as defenders of freedom, protectors of the world. But, in reality, all of this is planned and agreed to by everyone who makes decisions to take over the world and dominate, as a one world government, all of its people. I tell you truly, people of faith and belief in God, you must prepare yourselves to face God at any moment from now on. (I got the feeling and understanding that this was about being ready to live or die at any moment, not that everyone was going to die. Just be ready for anything). Be focused on the preparation of your souls so that you are in a state of purity and grace, ready to be taken into Heaven at My Father's Will. (In an earlier message this year, Jesus said many of even the chosen will be taken to Heaven where they will pray for all of us left on earth)

"I ask you to pray for insight from the Holy Spirit Who will show you hidden faults and weaknesses, Who will lead you to the Father in My Name for a great healing of your hearts. All the world's people who believe in God must be able to freely serve Him at the call of the lost souls who come to them. The Holy Spirit will lead them to you when the second Pentecost will occur on earth as a result of many graces poured out by the Father. Pray, please, that all will accept these graces, and serve and nurture the many souls who desire to return to My Father, their Creator and Lord.

"Dearest ones, you are in the final days before major developments and destructive events are allowed by My Father to cleanse the earth before My return. The Father always allows a human agent to be the instrument of His Will for purifying his people. As you are begging for His mercy upon all who do not know Him, realize that you are building up the Body of Christ, and that I am the Head of this Body.

"As your Leader and Lord, I wish to urgently request that you do all things necessary to be reconciled with family and friends, to pray in order to be strengthened and convinced and accepting of this great mercy for which you are praying!! Let Me be your

All, your Everything that you need in order to be properly cleansed of sin. To trust in Me is the most important part of your preparation now.

"YOU MUST BE EMPTIED OF PRIDE AND ATTACH-MENTS in order to be a vessel of the peace of Jesus.

"The Father of all desires you to practice having mercy on Him, too, by receiving the Sacraments and praying the Mass every day. Do not forget the power of My Father to forgive, to renew the world, to protect you from harm through the Most Holy Trinity and the graces obtained for you by Our dear Mother and yours.

"Children of the world, you cannot continue to ignore Our call to you and expect to be saved from the Antichrist.

"Please do not become anxious and worried about developments of possibilities that may never occur. Your active imaginations can create an unnecessary fear that is not of Me. I am your Jesus of Peace and Mercy!! Empty yourself of all anxieties, as you sit before Me in adoration. Allow Me to fill you with this peace, and with it will come trust and a conviction of the truth and power of all Our words to you.

"WORRY NOT ABOUT WHAT MIGHT HAPPEN, BUT ONLY REJOICE IN WHAT IS HAPPENING NOW, as you seek My face, as you honor My Name, as you reconcile with others and with your God.

"My Mother offers her help and protection to all her children, that is, everyone in the world. She showers her love and graces on all who will accept. She stands by at every moment waiting for you to accept her, to call upon her, to come to her. This is an opportunity you must not refuse! Your life and salvation depend upon these, more than suggestions, invitations from the Triune God Who wishes to save forever in Heaven ALL His creatures. His love for you is an absolute fact, whether or not you believe it! His ability to overcome evil is an absolute fact! For this to occur in your lives, you must just believe in His mercy and forgiveness on souls who return to Him in humble contrition and sorrow for sins.

"Pour out the sinful habits and resolve, once and for all, not to repeat them. Believe that you can overcome with the help of God through Whom all things are possible. Do not continue to war against each other. Do not continue to speak with harsh words. Do not continue to be self-absorbed, but abandon that selfishness to Me, waiting for you in the Sacrament of Reconciliation. These suggestions are given by your Lord and Savior in very serious tones. Failure to repent of sins will result in drastic possibilities of each one succumbing to the might and evil of the Antichrist.

"Please believe Me, dear people of the world who listen to Our words, and take this opportunity, this very week, to relinquish control of your lives and souls to the Supreme Majesty Who waits for your return. His Heart is open wide to receive you, to wash you in the waters of grace, to change you: reformed and remolded into the vessel of the Presence of Jesus, Merciful, Eucharistic and Loving. This is not a lofty, specialized call to only those who desire Me, but especially to those who are in such great need of Me. Understand, I AM STANDNG BEFORE YOU, LOOKING DEEPLY INTO YOUR EYES AND HEARTS! Allow yourselves to be comforted by My love and all the tenderness that I Am! Stop your frantic running, dear ones, and rest in My arms.

"As My faithful are praying for an increased outpouring of the Father's great mercy, take advantage of this deluge (of mercy) that has the power to overcome your sorrows and your weary life. ALLOW MERCY TO LEAD YOU TO FORGIVENESS, TO HEALING, TO YOUR SALVATION! Believe that you can be forgiven. Without forgiveness in your hearts, the erasure of sin from your souls now, you will be easy prey for the Antichrist and his power to persuade and corrupt!!

"These words are sent with great pleading and My own loving concern for your spiritual welfare. I know what the Antichrist will do! It is from a knowledge of the events of the near future that I come to you about the absolute need on your part to be cleansed, to be free from the slavery of sin, to be comforted by the peace of knowing forgiveness and becoming a new creation.

"My people, you must listen and act, if you would avoid the evil and power of Satan loose in the world. LET GO OF THE WORLD AND ALL YOUR WORLDLY WAYS AND BE REBORN AS THE CHILDREN OF GOD YOU WERE CREATED TO BE, REFLECTING MY MERCY, MY OBEDIENCE AND LOVE FOR OUR FATHER IN HEAVEN. Believe these words, beloved ones, and reach out to others in patience and love. When you do this, you will have solidified your consecration to the Two Hearts and the perfect Will of the Father.

"I come to you with warning of a grave future for which you must be prepared in all ways, but especially with a clean heart and a faithful living out of the commandments of My Father. To love yourself is an important part of your renewal. BE HEALED NOW, MY DEAR PEOPLE. Take advantage of reconciliation quickly and sincerely. Our Holy Spirit will give you knowledge and strength to return. Come to the waters of grace, My people, please!

"I am your Jesus of Mercy Who waits continually for your visit. I am the Jesus Who hears your sins recited, and offers forgiveness, and takes away those sins. I am Jesus Who loves you and begs you to hear My voice."

6/19/98, Jesus said:

(I must share this personal portion and Jesus' wonderful humor before He gets serious again. This was said with a very 'smiling' voice!)

"Do you suppose, daughter, that you are alone at any time? You KNOW that you are not! Do you suppose that you are not protected every second of the day and night? Recall that you are not!! And do you think the Angels have stopped chanting your name and thanking My Father for all of His gifts for you? Please know that they have not.

"And do you really believe that the special Saints you have been given only pray for you when you invite them? I assure you, little one, that is not the case!!

"You see, daughter, you must talk and interact with Us more often, as that is the only way you will become truly aware of Our presence with you at all times. This will be so important in the future when snares will nearly surround you; when you are in hiding from the plans of Satan to harm you. This will be the time it is even more necessary to believe that We are with you, so that you will not succumb to fear or panic or even despair.

"It will be necessary on several occasions to call upon My Mother and her Angels, St. Michael and the Archangels to come to your defense in a very real and powerful way. When you do this with total trust, with expectations of protection, they will, of course, be at your beck and call immediately.

"You have no idea how much your life will continue to change, as you surrender to all you are called to do and to be. Just believe these words, please child, and trust that all events and occasions, no matter how dangerous or hopeless it looks, will be overcome by the power of My Father. You must believe this, daughter, and practice Our presence at all times of the day and night. Continue to persevere in the outline (routine from Jesus to improve my lack of discipline!!) you have been given and you will accomplish more of every chore and project you hurry to complete.

"My Mother is with Me, dear one, and wishes to give you words of explanation and new understanding. I love you, daughter"

Blessed Mother said:

"Yes, child of My Sorrowful Heart, I am truly standing in front of you with My arms stretched out to you, sending graces of peace and comfort to your mind and heart. Thank you, daughter, for filling My heart with joy at your continued progress. You must believe that you will overcome yourself(!) no matter how many times you forget and must (it seems to you) start over again. The ideal is always the goal while we travel the earth. The soul's response is a heartfelt answer to the interior call of her God. You know and feel it each time you are called by the Father through the words of My Son, their Spirit, or Myself.

"Daughter, the world is being completely fooled by the false quiet it perceives. Please tell everyone that this peaceful time will not, cannot last much longer because of the ardent feelings of patriotism every leader of smaller nations harbors in his heart. These are backed up by the ability now to attack a neighbor first, in order to display power. Numerous soldiers are not needed when nuclear devices can be deployed at the push of a button. Wars and differences are quickly decided when massive destruction can be delivered in a matter of minutes. The innocent ones who sleep unaware of imminent danger must be the focus of your prayers at this time, daughter.

"EVENTS THAT WILL LOOK LIKE THE END OF EVERYTHNG FOR SEVERAL COUNTRIES WILL ONLY SPREAD AROUND THE WORLD EVENTUALLY, RESULT-ING IN THE DEATH OF COUNTLESS NUMBERS (OF PEOPLE) AND THE DESTRUCTION OF MANY PARTS OF THE WORLD.

"Do you wonder at the constant tears and pleading from so many of the Angels and Saints, along with Jesus and Myself, from knowledge of the days about to unfold. Please tell Our dear, dear ones they are loved so much by the Father of us all. There is nothing to fear, even though you may (fear), and certainly hear about frightening and sorrowful events and occurrences.

"THE FATHER WILL PROTECT ALL OF HIS ELECT FROM DESTRUCTION OR ANNIHILATION BY THE EVIL ONE. SATAN WILL NEVER BE ALLOWED TO STEAL ONE OF YOU AWAY FROM THE PROTECTION OF MY MANTLE IF YOU LISTEN CLOSELY TO THE VOICE OF MY SPOUSE, IF YOU PRAY AND SERVE THE DEAR ONES WHO COME TO YOU, IF YOU REMAIN OBEDIENT TO THE NEEDS OF OTHERS AND THE CALL OF JESUS AND YOUR HEAV-ENLY MOTHER.

"Be at peace, little faithful ones. There will be events that may shock or alarm you. If you will recollect yourselves and call upon the peace of Jesus, it will be given immediately, and you will return to the strength and calm behavior so necessary to serve the needs of so many. There are no more messages that will tell you of new happenings at this time. There are no new requests from Heaven. There are only your prayers for mercy, for each other, for peace, for perseverance, and for My intentions that truly contain all of your intentions, that the Father's final realizations for cleansing the world will begin to play out in the world to their swift completion.

"OH MY DEAR ONES, I LOVE YOU WITH ALL OF MY HEART. I weep for the pain and struggle I see already in the world and all that is to follow. Do not be frightened by My words, children of My heart, but stay close and pray with Me; believe that I am there with you when you invite Me; believe that all your prayers are being answered, are being used for the good of all, for mitigation of certain events, for the purification of your own souls and the comfort of all who will be suffering even more, and the reparation of sin.

"I call out to you once more, dear people. Reach into your hearts and draw upon all your compassion, all of your obedience, all of your surrender to everything We are requesting of you, even though this may mean long hours in prayer and silence. Change places in your mind with all who will be suffering. Realize these truly are family members of yours in the Body of Christ. Accept even more responsibilities now to love and pray for people everywhere. They have great need of you, My dear, dear loved ones.

"Be one with Me, now, children of my longing. Accept the increased responsibility, the increased gift of yourselves to all who do not know God, or who have rationalized Him away with proud words and callous refusals to listen and believe. More and more, I see you relating to the terrible pain of rejection My Son and I experience at the hands of the hardened hearts of the world. More and more, you come to love My Jesus and Me! So I ask you again, draw on all your love for Us and join Us as often as possible to pray with all of Heaven for mercy and a quick resolution to all the events that must occur to fulfill Scripture before My Jesus returns. With all of your strength, out of all of your love, be united totally from now on to Me, your Heavenly Mother and the Triune God.

"Thank you, My beloved ones who listen. Thank you for giving up so much of the world now in order to help to serve the needs of the world. You are pressed to My heart, dear ones of My heart! Feel it beating with love for you. The love of the Two Hearts burns brightly for you, My children!"

6/21/98, Jesus said:

"Oh child of My Eucharistic Heart, if only more of My people would come to an understanding of surrender and giving all their burdens to Me. These crosses (that we are all bearing at this time) are nothing compared to what awaits each of you in the future. How important and necessary it is for each of you to allow Me to take these trials, share them with you, carry the weight that might otherwise crush you. I have promised not to overcome you with your sufferings. I desire all to share their troubles with Me and then give them to Me. This is what makes your cross a joy! It is in your trust, in Our being more closely united, that you receive the joy of being nearer to Me, united more closely to My life and to Me; being transformed into another Me through suffering in union with My Father's Will, in union with and hidden within My Heart.

"Praise and thank the Father today with every step and task and breath! Spend this day in prayer, as you can, and nothing else. The distractions you still experience will always plague you, as long as you are not totally committed to Me in focus and mind and heart. My Mother has words for you. Stay in My arms, daughter, and be immersed in the feelings of My love for you."

Blessed Mother said:

"Child, please take these words: Dear people, you are praying and responding to the pleadings of your Heavenly Mother for mercy for the world. I thank you and ask you to continue. Do not let up in your efforts to help your family throughout the world that depends mightily on your help, your energy, your loving prayers on their behalf. As long as you are united with Me in prayer for them, you must know that the enemy will be fighting more than ever to distract you, to overcome your efforts with fatigue, to divide your families and allow you to experience pain and rejection! It is difficult to believe that God would allow prayer, obedience to My call to you, trust in all of Our words, to cause husbands and wives, parents and children, families and friends to be torn apart.

"Just remember that each one has a free will to choose between the world and My Jesus' promises for a renewed earth for all who remain faithful. To continue to persevere will be more and more difficult! You will have your hearts broken again and again. That is why you must continually cling to Me, as My Jesus did after so many hours and days of preaching and performing miracles. How many times He would run to Me in exhaustion and grief over the hard hearts of so many.

"Do not be reduced to ashes and bitterness, dear little soldiers. Be filled now, as you read, with new courage, new strength, new ability to hold out until My Jesus' return. Offer each heartache as a great sacrifice and penance for the conversion of all who hurt you, of all who add to your doubts and feelings of loneliness and dejection.

"Jesus and I are with you, My darling children. You are held in the Two Hearts with the greatest tenderness and appreciation. Allow Our love to smooth the furrows of your brow, to ease the pain in your hearts, and to wash away the fatigue that causes the spirits of all to lag, to feel the weight of the needs of the world, but also the burdens of ridicule and rejection. Be lifted up, My dear ones. Be filled with hope and the joy of promised victory for you and all you pray for. Be assured of Our continued presence with you at every second of your lives.

"Allow Our love, Our words today, to heal you and remove the weight of these burdens.

"Give them to My Jesus now by nailing them to His Cross. Be refreshed by His strength, His ability to carry them with you. Please be at peace, faithful ones, and offer your waiting, your struggles to the Father in exchange for His great mercy on the world. You are accomplishing mighty deeds for the world. You are loved, My dearest children.

"Daughter, thank you for bringing the world to Us in your prayers and petitions. I will speak often in these weeks and months of floods and fires and events which add to Our people's needs for encouragement. I am your Mother of Sorrows who loves each one in the world, who prays for your needs and struggles."

6/26/98, Jesus said:

"Daughter, I think you already know that this will be a very serious message to Our people. (I could feel this for hours before receiving it.) You are praying well and listening very intently to Our words, and so you are chosen to take long and important instructions for those who listen.

"Tonight, child, a serious and secret meeting takes place between your President and foreign powers. THIS BEGINS A SERIES OF MEETINGS AND DECISIONS ABOUT WHERE TO ALLOW THE FIRST NUCLEAR STRIKE. The entire world is set up for this possibility. (In other words, I believe He means, this can occur anywhere).

"The prayers of so many HAVE and WILL make a difference, little one. You must all believe this! Loss of life and severity of damage is already mitigated to a degree; and so each must continue to plead for mercy on those who go into Eternity from now on.

"The area targeted by the super powers will destroy many people and cities. The escalation of these plans goes on behind closed doors, with one country goading another through devious people sewing discord and discontent in the minds and hearts of many leaders.

"Be at peace, daughter, as you record these words. (I had just then remembered that I had not cast out demons in His Name and asked for protection from my own imagination or agenda or desires, that I had not asked Him to identify Himself.) I tell you all of Heaven prays for you at these times. You are surrounded by many Angels tonight, who keep the demons away from any ability or plan to deceive you.

"These words are of great importance to all of Heaven: to My Father and Our Spirit, My Mother and, of course, Myself. We are grateful for all the time you give to this mission, the surrender of your heart and self to take Our words and minister to Our people. Be assured that you are protected and able to take My words unencumbered by any evil or distractions. You are deeply loved, My little soldier of the iron will(!) You are being molded into a perfect fighting weapon and have nothing to fear. Now we will continue.

"The world will not truly believe the imminence of nuclear war because of believing so much propaganda all these years. The possibility of destruction to your own country is more than likely, once an attack is made anywhere in the world.

"I tell you these things tonight for all of Our dear ones who believe in Our words and in the protection We have promised according to My Father's Will for each one.

"I COME TO ASK YOU TO BE PREPARED TO SEE AN ESCALATION IN YOUR NEED TO TAKE STEPS TO BE READY TO LEAVE YOUR HOMES AND TAKE REFUGE AGAINST NUCLEAR FALLOUT! This sounds like a scare tactic on the part of evil, if you are a person who is filled with doubts and anxieties. Please, daughter, assure everyone that it is I, their Lord and their God, Who comes to warn you of growing plans of evil men!

"Please know that the deep love of the Triune God calls out to save as many as possible from terrible pain and wounding. You will not have a great deal of time to pack up things to take with you, My people. This alarm is sounded in enough time for you to assemble things you would wish to take along.

"YOU WILL BE ABLE TO RETURN TO YOUR HOMES IF THERE HAS NOT BEEN TOO MUCH DAMAGE TO THE AR-EAS WHERE YOU LIVE! RADIOS WILL ALERT PEOPLE WHEN IT IS SAFE. THIS TIME OF DESTRUCTION WILL NOT LAST LONG, AND WILL SET THE STAGE FOR THE ANTI-CHRIST TO VERY CONVINCINGLY APPEAR WITH SOLU-TIONS AND HELP FOR THE WORLD.

"Your government, child, will be at a loss to solve its own dilemmas and will reach out to foreign powers. I have mentioned this several times to you, My dearest little one, and to many of Our messengers in the world. There will be great confusion during these times. You will all need to be brave, trusting that you will be sup-ported by the might of My Arm!

"PEOPLE OF THE WORLD, PREPARE TO EXPERIENCE MANY HARDSHIPS FROM NOW ON. THE FIRES AND FLOODS HAVE ONLY BEGUN.

The bizarre weather patterns are the result of nuclear testing and weather patterns that are more intense than usual. My Father allows these in order to alert people to the need to come back to Him; to experience the need of His power, the might of His plan of salvation and safety.

"IF ALL PEOPLE WILL BEGIN NOW TO PRAY, THERE IS STILL TIME TO CHANGE THESE PLANS OF THE FATHER. THERE IS STILL A POSSIBILITY THAT PEACE COULD BE-GIN TO DEVELOP BETWEEN ALL PEOPLE AND COUN-TRIES OF THE WORLD! IMAGINE! IF EVERYONE WOULD STOP SCHEMING AND PLOTTING, THERE WOULD BE NO NECESSITY FOR A TRIBULATION, AND THE EARTH COULD BE RENEWED IN AN INSTANT WITHOUT ALL THE SUFFERING AND CLEANSING FIRST!

"But Satan holds too many hearts in his evil and powerful grip. He has been made more powerful by the increasing numbers of people who worship him and themselves! As parents, so many in the world will understand the great sadness in Our Hearts about all that is to begin so soon. We do not wish to see God's children destroy each other.

"Oh child, there is such peace and true happiness available to the world, if it would only accept the proper and blessed lifestyles so possible. A life of grace and love and prayer is a healthy, happy, carefree life ... free from any worry, free from the slavery of Satan, freedom of mind and heart and body for the whole world! You shall have these freedoms and all of this promised beauty, My precious children, but not without a major battle: one you have begun to experience already against increased attacks on every area of vulnerability that threatens your resistance, your perseverance.

"My Mother weeps tears of blood to help you see the intensity of her grief. As a Mother to the World, she will never wish to see even one destroyed from the greed of plundering men who want the whole earth (and everyone on it) AS THEIR SLAVES. I will continue to call out, as long as the Father allows, even though few are listening anymore.

"Give constant praise to My Father, dear people who have given their hearts to My Mother and to Me. Thank Him for delays that have allowed you to live in peace and fresh air and sunshine until now. Some areas of your countries have already lost those gifts of your Creator! I will continue to warn you for as long as I am able in the great and perfect plan of My Father.

"Whatever you see, wherever you flee, however long you must stay, be assured, please My beloved faithful ones, of Our presence with you every moment. Be convinced and comforted by Our great, great love for each of you, as though you were the only person on the earth! Your God has enough love for all, and wishes to save all and bring you to Heaven forever.

"Please, please hear My serious words with open hearts and a serious resolve to comply with every request from Heaven. Reread Our words to you, dear loved children of My Sacred Heart. Know well what We are telling and promising you; what We are requesting of and needing from you for the good of the entire world's population, their souls and your own. There are only so many ways to plead with you, to say the same things over and over. The consequences of your disinterest (and turning away now) are beyond your imagination.

"Please, more seriously than you ever have, listen and react by praying and preparing (until you cannot anymore!) each day. Then sleep in peace and trust, believing that you will be doing the Father's Will for you at every moment.

"TURN OFF YOUR TELEVISION SETS AND RADIOS, DEAR ONES. TUNE IN TO MY VOICE!! LISTEN TO THE MUSICAL VOICES OF THE ANGELS AND SAINTS SINGING THE PRAISES OF ALL WHO PRAY WITHOUT CEASING, WHO PRAY WITH YOU AND FOR YOU. HEAR THE HEAVENLY MUSIC THAT ACCOMPANIES THEIR PRAYERS, AND BE SOOTHED BY THESE BEAUTIFUL MELODIES OF LOVE AND PRAISE. THE FATHER BLESSES YOU WITH STRENGTH AGAIN THIS NIGHT, LITTLE SOLDIERS OF THE WORLD.

"The more you pray, the more graces can be showered upon all of you and your families and loved ones. Be at peace, I tell you again, people. Pray, prepare, love your God and your precious Mother, and love yourselves and each other! My Mother sends tears of joy and love for each of you. She is so grateful for your love and obedience to Our call."

7/2/98, Jesus said:

"Daughter, hear now My important words of love and compassion for My people who listen and act.

"Thank you, so many of My beloved who are taking seriously the words of warning to Our daughter. She has been a diligent and faithful servant to you and to Us, and will continue to bring you important words of direction and solace. She has been prepared through many events and sorrows in her own life, and is ready to continue now (in a new direction) her particular mission and ministry.

"Please pray for all Our messengers who struggle to convert and become more purified themselves. You must cherish each other, all of My faithful remnant. You must be patient and loving with each other. You must continue to grow in the virtues of Mary, Our Mother, always remembering the gifts and graces that enable you to pray in the first place!

"My dear ones, you are so beloved of My Heart. Please ponder that fact. Ask to be filled with a greater understanding and appreciation of Our love for you. It is what sustains you!

"The love of My Father, revealed more by Myself in My life on earth and given through Our Spirit, is your Life Force. We sustain you in Our love, in Our constant creating and renewing of yourselves (your very cells), your spirits, your abilities, your energy, your response to life and Life!

"Know that the Presence of the Triune God is absolutely essential to your Creation, to your spiritual and physical maintenance, your abilities, all of who you are and what you do: the talents, the intelligence capacity. ALL OF YOUR GIFTS ARE FROM GOD. The Holy Spirit moves and inspires you to learn and to grow; to implement your abilities, culled from genetic contributions and environmental influences, yes, but given to you specifically according to the Father's plan for each life. You are given the means to sustain yourselves with work and enjoyment, relaxation and renewal of mind, body, soul and spirit. And these are meant to help you learn to appreciate the gifts and beauty of the world which is, of course, also God's creation.

"You were created to give praise and honor and gratitude to My Father; to realize that you are the beloved children of God and heirs to His Heavenly Kingdom. You were given the talents to know Him through My words, My life, My teachings, My example, My love for you which resulted in the ultimate sacrifice of My life, that you could be given the renewed opportunity to accept and be united with Us in that Kingdom. Every person alive is given that opportunity through Baptism.

"Each person must finally return to their Baptismal promises, and live them totally and joyfully. The world, by and large, does not do any of this! And for those of you who do, there are the promise and means, (for I am the Means, the Way, the Light and the Love) for you to someday achieve this unity offered in Heaven through the unity possible now with Me, with My Father, with Our Spirit and with the heart of My dearest Mother!

"Dear, dear people, take advantage of increased graces and blessings being offered in these days. You know yourselves a little better now and realize how dependent you are on Us for the strength and courage you will need in the coming days. The warnings you are being given through many of Our messengers now, must be heeded and acted upon immediately. Do not spend too much time sitting, questioning and wondering about what to do and where to go.

"Act quickly, My people, to prepare for any possibility in the very near future. You will know where you must go when the time comes. My children in certain areas have places readied, have knowledge you need. Listen to them and act upon their words and suggestions. Act and prepare for the good of your family and neighbor, for all who have nothing and do without. Be aware of treachery at every turn and be prudent, always focusing on My face, My love, Our words of direction to you. Begin to think more for yourselves now, My beloved little ones. Do not wait to see what another does, but concentrate on your own family needs, your own responsibilities. Long ago I told you to prepare to live a long time or a short time! That time is here. It has begun.

"Please, My loved ones, do not be afraid of Me, of My Father Who loves and sustains you, of Our Spirit Who enables you to respond, to cooperate now with all the graces that are being given with all of Our requests to love.

"Know that YOU ARE BEING LOVED THROUGH ALL THESE WORDS OF WARNING; THAT YOU ARE BEING REFORMED AND MOLDED INTO MY IMAGE! You are putting on Christ only as much as you shed the world and selfish pastimes. You are cleansed and purified by being emptied of sin and the corrupt ways of the world.

"You all desire to please My Father, I see that in your hearts and I am grateful. Take the last steps out of the world now, please, people. Please give yourselves to Me, to Us at the soonest moment. IT IS A MATTER OF HEART, OF ATTITUDE, OF MOTIVE AND DESIRE, OF BEHAVIOR, OF SURRENDER OF YOUR WILL! Stop struggling against Me, dearest of My Heart; stop resisting My grace, the gift of peace, the Way to Eternal Glory!

"Do these possibilities not appeal to you, My people? If they really do, hurry! There is not a moment to lose. Come back to Me completely, to the Triune God Who beckons, Who calls, Who waits, Who cannot wait much longer before this destruction is upon you.

"Be on your knees, children of God. Be filled with a deep sorrow for your sin. Bring them to Me in the Sacrament of love and reconciliation. Be freed of your earthly bondage. Be unburdened now and forever! Be one with Me in My love for My Father and all of Our people: your family on earth. You were created for this, dear ones. Accept your inheritance from My Father and be at peace forever.

"I am your Jesus Who speaks with great, great love for you; who desires that you would be one with Me in the Father and Our Spirit; that you would allow My Mother to lead you; to guide you; to teach you, and to bring you into this unity of My Sacred, and Merciful, and Eucharistic Heart. Come, My beloved, Come! Know that these words of Mine will touch many, many more of Our dear ones, and will bring new souls into the one fold of which I am the Shepherd."

7/7/98, Blessed Mother said:

"Dear one, please take my words. I am your Mother of Sorrows who brings words of direction and support for you. You have learned much in these years of service. Know that you will continue to speak, but it will be in a different sort of setting. The time of creative writing is over for you daughter. I wish for you to let go, once again, of all the things you have done for Us in the past. You can be pleased and grateful that each project has been successful, thanks to the help of the Holy Spirit: His inspiration and His thoughts and desires.

"Be at peace now, and rest and walk and read and pray in the coming days. (on retreat in Ca.). The quiet time will not last long, and you will long for a return to this peace and order in your life.

"The world is truly not even beginning to understand the very near events that will loose destruction on the earth. Already there are new atrocities against human rights and human life. Imagine, daughter, seeing your own children brutally attacked by gangs of savage men who have no respect for life or honor as individuals. (I had been praying for the women in another part of the world that I had read about on the Net, who had been repeatedly raped, some in front of their families, and then killed along with their children, and had been asking for mercy for all of them). My heart is so crushed by viewing this brutal behavior.

"Your own heart will be broken likewise, as you view loved ones succumbing to the torture of the Antichrist. Please continue to pray that more tragedies can be eliminated and holocausts mitigated. It is NEVER TOO LATE TO PREVENT SOME EVENT THAT BRINGS NEW SUFFERING TO OUR CHILDREN OF THIS WORLD, AS THEY BATTLE EACH OTHER FOR SUPREMACY.

"Daughter, the strength and discipline you are learning will never leave you, and you will be very glad you persevered! There is much to tell you in the days ahead, so keep your ears tuned to My voice and that of My Jesus."

7/9/98 Jesus said:

"Thank you for coming away to rest and listen. I need for you to surrender even more now. Will you agree to stay in almost seclusion from now on, so that you can allow Me to further work the Will of My Father within you? The days left to the quiet world, the waiting world, the perceived (to the sleeping world!) peaceful world, are so few. MORE PRAYER IS ALWAYS POSSIBLE! You have had so many good times and good friends. Now it is time to die to your own plans and desires. It is time to live as though you were not alive; to be as a sponge to soak up all of Who I Am, all of what I say and desire of you.

"Yes, you will accept any new invitations to speak, but you will be in peace and quiet prayer and seclusion in between from now on. I wish for you to stay away from the phone, the news, the weather (the last TV excitement in my life!) the world totally. These are important words for you now. No matter what anyone else thinks or says, you are to continue on this brief path of total renewal and transformation. (I only include these statements because they seem to reflect the urgency and nearness of all the serious events mentioned in recent messages as due in the world).

"I wish for you to praise My Father constantly. Be aware of My Presence with you at all times, always listening for My voice or that of My Mother. This is a serious final preparation of your souls and spirit before unbelievable agony and disaster are experienced throughout this country and the world. Humility is more than ever the virtue to practice, to pray and long for, to appreciate and understand. Please believe all I am telling you, little one, and rest in My arms and be at peace."

7/12/98, Blessed Mother said:

"Child, please listen to My words of joy and sorrow. You have succeeded in reaching many more in these past days, (after retreat, a talk in Vista) and so more words of importance will be given tomorrow. Please spend all of these next two days in prayer and quiet. This is the only way that you will survive this schedule of increased talks that awaits you. You will be stronger now, and more renewed in health, as you continue in obedience to our requests.

7/13/98, Our Lady said:

"Dearest daughter, please take My words, given by the favor of the Father of us all. The world, My daughter, must listen now to Our words of warning, or be lost in a whirlwind of events destined to enslave the people of the earth. All of the plans of the Antichrist and his people include the entrapment of the strong and the annihilation of the weak. I tell you this in order to warn all, yet again, for the need to beg mercy on the many who will be entering Eternity so very quickly now.

"People of My motherly heart, listen with all of your minds and hearts. Do not allow anyone, no matter who, to dilute or defeat your belief in Our words of warning and Our promises of protection. Dear ones, be firm in your conviction of the need to prepare to leave your houses at any moment.

"Once a strike occurs, the retaliation will be automatic and occur according to plans already agreed upon by leaders of major powers.

"You are being given information by Heaven at this time through the words of your Mother of all people. I am that Mother who calls to all to repent and come back to your God; to prepare for the eventuality of nuclear destruction in almost every country in the world. Terrorists are people without the means of caring for others; who are driven by a depth of hatred unknown to most other people in the world. The events will happen so rapidly that if you do not move immediately and quickly, you may be caught by the death dealing weapons that are involved in these attacks.

"My children, you wait for signs of your own design, of your own plans, that will finally convince you to believe. As with any occasion, the Will of God is what determines the gifts and signs that are given. Please do not ask for signs and miracles, ask for mercy on all who will die in these attacks and dreadful wartime decisions.

"Do you believe that you are loved, My children? Then recognize words of warning given in love. Realize that We come to you everywhere with special graces and whisperings of love and caution, begging you to heed the warnings that will precede the time when each person in the world will see their sins, their weaknesses, their selfishness and pride! I know Our faithful ones ARE praying more for My intentions. I thank you again this night for your fidelity and obedience. Continue to beg mercy for the hard hearts you see and feel all around you, everywhere in the world. Listen to Our messengers as they share Our words, and plan to be ready to leave in an instant.

"You have no idea of the degree of devastation and injury which occurs as a result of these weapons of such terrible destruction.

"My people, My dear, dear ones, I will continue to call out, to warn you, to beg you to listen and act. Be sure of this, when the devastation begins and the Warning occurs, many will come seeking your forgiveness for their doubt and their own hard hearts. Have courage, children, have patience and persevere!"

7/14/98, Our Lady said:

"Come, My dear one, and take My words for the world. Tonight it is more news I bring for all those who read and believe. Be at peace about all that must be endured in your mission for Us. Continue to give praise and thanks for every event, no matter how uncomfortable you are made to feel. You will have opportunity to pray much while you are away. Please bring as many as possible to the Altar and adore. The Will of the Father is unfolding for you at every turn, and you must continue to be brave and persevere. How much warning can be given? What good are My words and the words of My Jesus, when only ridicule and rejection are shown to them? And yet, the mercy of God deems it necessary to continue to call out to those who pray in hope that more will listen and respond.

"**Oh dear ones of the earth, do not decide how Heaven would speak!** Do not give proud and haughty judgement to the words from Ourselves to you through these brave messengers who accept your judgements in silence and humility, bearing with the snide remarks and sly smiles behind their backs. Truth and all that is hidden will be made known in the Light. Do not think you are not seen or heard by all of Us in Heaven who pray for all of you, no matter how you treat Our words or messengers.

"I come tonight to also ask you to add to your preparedness a visit to My Jesus in His Sacrament of Reconciliation. He is waiting there to receive your sorrow and repentance, your firm promise not to sin again, your belief in His forgiveness of every sin that is confessed; no matter how serious. He is waiting to shower you with His love and bathe you in grace; to give you a new beginning, as one born again into the light and innocence of your new found life as His child. There cannot be a sin He will not forgive. It is the Nature of God to be Mercy and Love. His greatest desire is to fill you with the knowledge and gifts He wishes to give you. Do not hesitate for a moment! Run to your priest and confess all with the help of My Spouse, the Holy Spirit. He will show you, if you ask Him, what it is you need to confess, what lies hidden to your conscious mind. He will assist your fainting heart with difficult sins and stories of failings you must bring to Jesus now while there is still time.

"With the great probability of so much destruction in the near future, won't you please take advantage of the opportunity and graces offered by the Triune God through this great Sacrament?

Bring peace back to your hearts and souls, My loved ones. Bring peace and joy back to your lives with the sure knowledge that you are forgiven; that your souls are as white as snow, and new strength and grace lives in your hearts. You can return your lives to order and the discipline it takes to refrain from the people and places and behavior that are part of a sinful lifestyle.

"You are loved, children of the earth. We are calling you to come now and receive a welcome from your God and Father, His Son and Their Spirit. Do not waste time again! Please be focused on the serious task of preparing to leave your homes; to gather what you will need to sustain you for a short period of time, and to be in the state of grace for the time of serving the people of God; or facing Our God Himself in Eternity.

"**If you knew, My dear ones, that you were positively going into Eternity very soon, would you not wish to be in a most pure and innocent state?** I am sure this will cause many of you to reflect upon the possibility, and realize these possibilities will be true for all people of the world.

"You must be serious about My words, children of My Immaculate and Sorrowful Heart. I am praying with all of Heaven that your response will be quick, and your faith and trust lasting. I will speak more in these days of summer, as you experience the discomfort of heat and increased storms and fires. Let these lesser calamities speak to your hearts, dear ones of the world. Ask the Holy Spirit, once again, for new eyes, new ears and a new heart. Each one will need all the grace and help and renewal being offered by your God and Myself, your Mother of Grace. As your Mother, I beg you with tears of love to listen and return quickly, lest you die of wretchedness and hunger! I love you all, My children."

7/17/98, Jesus said:

"Hello, My daughter, please take My words. I am your Jesus of Divine Mercy Who loves you. Be at peace within yourself tonight, little soldier.

"It is a great challenge to all Our people to be asked to accept a warning to prepare for almost certain destruction. The people who always listen do not like to make the mental jump into the action necessary now to actualize Our words with a personal response and follow through by all who believe. The mind balks at the acceptance of words that frighten, that threaten peace and stability...the status quo. Hearts recoil in fear at the thought of being uprooted, no matter what the threat.

"Our words are meant to reach beyond the natural apathy of people who believe most events or threats are just too much trouble to do much about, too much work to respond to immediately. Even heavenly suggestions are held off by Our dear ones who cannot conceive of the destruction of this beautiful land. Even with pollution and lack of tending in some areas, your country still reflects the beauty and results of careful planning and protecting by concerned people of the earth all these 200 years. How could a prosperous, powerful nation with such richness of culture and talent and freedom and diversity be in danger in a world that works together for peace and harmony, unity and equality? These are some of the immediate questions asked by qualified individuals who think they know the state of affairs in the world. I tell you, daughter, the arrogance of Satan would never hesitate to lie and deceive the people of the earth, causing any amount of destruction to further his plans to ultimately enslave these same people.

"My dearest children: Please hear Me. IF YOU DO NOT LISTEN TO THE WARNINGS OF HEAVEN, GIVEN THROUGH THE WORDS OF OUR LOVING MOTHER, YOU WILL CERTAINLY PERISH! This is an aim of the followers of Satan who have bought into his lies and promises of power. It requires a very corrupt mind and heart to welcome the seductions of Satan with his lures of world domination and promises of immortality and victory. It is not difficult to understand, once you understand how pride blinds one to the truth. Those who are bent on destroying the lesser nations in order to rid the world of an excessive number of people considered weak, marginal and non-productive, will not stop at anything that threatens to get in the way, or attempt to stop them.

"Another great value of prayer is the great defense it provides without being visible or calling attention to its effects in any way! The ways of God are often seen as mysterious. Your prayers and sacrifices are used to purchase souls, to snatch them back from the clutches of evil, to enable graces of conversion to be given to Our lost ones of the world. Be assured of the wonderful effects of your prayers and your trust, My faithful soldiers. Do not listen to voices of ridicule and humiliation. Be ready to increase your focus on Our requests and desires for all of your time. When you consider large destruction, you will do whatever is necessary to obtain the slightest mitigation of My Father's plans. It requires much time and prayer to balance atrocities; to make reparation for the terrible sins of apostasy and disobedience.

"This is another serious call from your Jesus Who calls to you to abandon the world, to believe in these words of warning and direction, and to rest on My Heart alone, wrapped in the Mantle of the Immaculate Virgin Mary. Walk with her; talk and then listen to her words of encouragement, and appreciation and love. I come tonight to fill you with new energy and commitment to the plans of My Father to purify the earth and its people.

"Dear ones, I AM YOUR GOD! I DO SEE AND KNOW EACH HEART. It is all right, it is understood that you will be waiting for a sign to convince you. DO NOT WAIT! The task is arduous. The energy required just to accept the truth of these words, and begin immediately, requires that you JUST BEGIN! Start after My Sabbath Day of Rest in the Lord. Be prompt in your heartfelt response. Galvanize into action your whole families. Make this a project to enjoy!

"Anticipate miracles and great assistance from your Lord. I am your Jesus, dear people. I WANT YOU TO SUCCEED! I DESIRE YOU TO PERSEVERE. I DIED TO AFFORD YOU THESE OPPORTUNITIES! Be grateful to Our Father for these opportunities to be saved for a new and renewed time after the Day of the Lord. Be at peace about all you must do. DO NOT WAIT TOO LONG, BUT ASK THE HOLY SPIRIT TO HELP YOU AND HASTEN TO COMPLY WITH ALL OUR REQUESTS. Most of you truly know that We love you without measure."

7/26/98, Jesus said:

"Daughter, welcome to My Presence! I have waited eagerly for your return (from Cincinnati) and our visit together. Dearest one, please remember not to worry about anything! You must totally relax (yourself), that all will be tended to by My Father. Listen for more words to Our people, little soldier. Give praise and thanks to the Father. Be at peace now.

"Daughter, an aggressive move will be made in the world this very week that will set up more animosity between neighbors, and set the stage for immediate combat. Please tell Our faithful ones not to hesitate another instant! It is not so difficult (to first write a list of needs) that you must wait on others to direct your intentions and decisions. I have told you of the necessity of being mature and beginning to act immediately for the gathering of clothing and food and utensils, bedding and all the rest required for a very simple lifestyle.

"You will be astounded and terrified when news of the first nuclear attack, is reported by your media. The world will then ask, "Why didn't you tell us about this??" I will reply that many a faithful messenger has called out on Our behalf with words of warning and direction. **As in Noah's day, no one is listening!** Child, do you know how much devastation this will cause? Keep your thoughts turned towards Me, My dear loved ones, and on each word I am giving to you. You must prepare for the possibility of very cold weather everywhere after a great atomic explosion. Many things will be destroyed forever.

"Many will be the one to accuse you of every possible fabrication, daughter, as far as the messages of warning. There will be almost no support for you from My priest sons, and your heart will continue to be saddened by the coldness and hardness of many hearts. These things must come to pass daughter, of My Father's Will. Do not dwell now on anything other than My Face and My words to you. All MUST be done according to My Word! We will finish for tonight, little one, so that we may continue after you are fresh and alert. Please sleep immediately and awake refreshed."

7/27/98, Jesus said:

Welcome, daughter, once again. We will continue these words for Our people, and to soothe your heart. I am your Jesus of Love and Mercy Who calls out to all who will listen.

Please, dear ones of the world, take seriously every word you hear or read from Me through this messenger for whom all of Heaven prays and pours out protection. Most especially when she is recording words from Heaven for your education; your understanding; your preparation to gather supplies, (spiritual as well as physical) in order to be ready to leave your homes to be protected against nuclear fallout. These words, My dearest people, are so hard to hear, so difficult to believe. Please pause now and ask the Holy Spirit to enlighten you; to open your hearts and minds once again in order to accept words of warning for each of you. Pray for all those who hear, that they will believe and hasten to ready their families' needs for a brief, but serious, stay away from the effects of nuclear radiation and fallout.

The time, My dear faithful ones, demands that you act quickly. Have boxes or large bags of food and clothing and water ready together in one room. From there, you will be able to move them quickly to a vehicle that will transport you to a place of safety. These words are meant to save your lives in order to serve all those in need after these destructive events and after the Warning of My Father. It is only through obedience to My call that you will be protected from the serious results of nuclear destruction.

"I know how these words are able to frighten you, if you are not firmly convinced that your God is trying to save you. Do you recall all of the stories collected in the Old Testament? Many deal with the call from Yahweh to His people, asking them to enter into battle with an army many times larger than their own. And they won the victory!! This is exactly what I say to you now. Against overwhelming odds, you are requested to take evasive action that you might be saved in order to fight another day with weapons of prayer and trust. It is I Who will be victorious, Who have already won the victory! However, you must be obedient, as soldiers of My Mother's Army, to each command, each directive; each call of your Supreme Commander.

"Children of God; know that you will not lose money or time or honor, if you prepare for the eventuality of a third world war. This, I have told you, will last a very short time because of the immense destructive capabilities of nuclear warfare. Why do you believe this will not happen? The Israelites, time after time, entered into battle greatly outnumbered. By their trust in the power of God, they were victorious at the end of the day. If you will follow these directives, you will be victorious also. You will remain on the earth without the terrible results of nuclear devastation causing any harm to you and your loved ones.

"If you are not able to take a position of defense, at least be ready to flee, even without supplies. Those who honestly find themselves in need, but who will obey these requests for your preparedness, will receive the sustenance you need. More important than physical needs, are the spiritual preparations through prayers for mercy, receiving the Sacraments of Reconciliation and daily Eucharist to remain in the state of grace and focused on My Face, My Mother's requests and My Father's Will. Everyone is able to visit Me in My Blessed Sacrament, who is not immobilized by a physical condition. When you prepare to serve My desires for you, My dearest ones of My Heart, you are free from the world already and ready to be with Me wherever the Father decides. His Will is perfect for each of you.

"DO NOT WAIT TO BEGIN SERIOUS PREPARATION, PLEASE, MY SPECIAL FAITHFUL ONES. YOU CANNOT MAKE A MISTAKE BY FOLLOWING THESE DIRECTIVES. ORGANIZE YOUR TIME AND SUPPLIES.

"Dear ones, why would you be suspicious of Heaven's attempts to save you from harm?

"Call upon Our Holy Spirit to receive His assistance in believing and preparing. The only time in a person's life that you make a mistake is when you choose not to hear God's Will for you! If you turn away from Me now, you are usurping My Will for you, My care and concern for your souls and bodies.

"Dear ones, do not be unbelieving, but believe! The only leader you can trust is the Triune God! Your politics, your possessions, your money, will not save you now. These are dilemmas and probable destruction that only your simple trust and obedience to my words will overcome. Work diligently, My dear people, at these preparations. Be ready to leave at a moment's notice. Trust that you will be led; that you will have more words of direction, as the time comes upon you. **You will know where to go, if only you believe and act upon My commands.** You are loved, dear ones of the world. You are cherished and chosen to lead Our lost ones back to Me amidst chaos and confusion. You will see a golden era of conversion among millions who will return in true repentance, and all of My words and promises lived out.

"Satan is a formidable power of evil, and your enemy. Do not attempt to cling to the world as he will strongly suggest to you! You are no match for his power. You will not survive as his follower. NO one will. Do not delay, My people. Do not resist My call or the help of your Heavenly Mother and her Angels. You will indeed be living as the Church Militant when you prepare yourselves with prayer. To flee from danger is only wise! To allow the power of the Triune God to protect you is purest surrender of your will and fears (and tendency to doubt Our words), to the saving and loving Will of your Heavenly Father, His perfect Will for you. This is a difficult task to undertake, I know, My loved ones. Again, take My Mother's hand and allow her to lead you through each prayer, each action that will result in your protection from weapons of terrible power to destroy."

7/30/98, Jesus said:

"My dear one, I, your loving Jesus, will speak. Daughter, the time of devastation is near and no one believes My words to you. Yes, We DO know the outcome of these requests (for prayer and to prepare to take shelter from nuclear fallout), but will always plead and try and call out until the last second before whatever event that is planned will or will not occur. It is so difficult for our people to understand why they cannot be told every detail beforehand! And I tell you, they are already being WARNED TO PREPARE ONLY BECAUSE THEY ARE PRAYING AND LISTENING, EVEN WITH MANY DOUBTS!

"Your heart is full of Sonshine, daughter! Everyone knows it who sees and hears you. The ones who criticize you have their own major issues and struggles with pride. Those who accuse you will be accused. It has already been written! Thank you for doing all in your power to soothe people's fears and answer their questions. Know that every ounce of strength you require will be supplied by your Triune God and holy Mother. Pray for each person's heart.

"Dear people of the world, please listen once more, as I call out to you in love. MOST OF YOU ARE STILL NOT TAKING SERIOUSLY THESE WORDS OF WARNING. I have spoken often in the past of a grave future, but you were not listening at all then. Now you listen with an attitude of disdain, of doubt and sheer disbelief. Or there are those who have reacted strongly out of fear. These are the very things I have asked you not to do.

The world is so used to gratifying every whim, it cannot believe that something might ever happen that would cause you real hardship, real struggle, the need to be serious and organize your possessions, the need to leave the comfort of our own homes for a place that is unfamiliar and awkward. I have been telling you, along with My Mother, all over the world to pray and prepare, to repent and return, not in fear, but in joy and sincere love. Please do not say you cannot believe the possibility of nuclear war, if you are honestly looking at the state of the world.

"**Your own President has no power or authority without the power of the One World people who allow him to get away with such immoral conduct and lack of responsibility to the people of this country.** The lesser powers of the world continue to bait each other and perpetrate acts of terrorism. The world, which was once so beautiful, so orderly and obedient to its Creator, is now sunk in the lowest level of degradation. Satan rules with ease the hearts of many thoughtless, mindless ones who are totally unaware of their degree of sin. Free license to sin is given by many of Our priest sons who have taken upon themselves the power of Satan and masquerade under the guise of a new enlightenment!

"Are you really surprised, people of the earth, that the Father will allow evil men to destroy each other? EVIL MUST BE DESTROYED. Right now, evil is having its day. It is written in Scripture that this will occur. Are you not familiar with My Prophets of old who wrote about these days? Do you not realize that God Our loving Father has always worked in this way; is once again sending prophets to warn and urge you to repent and return to your God?

"My Mother has spent herself totally to plead with you and for you. And now she must acquiesce to the Will and Justice of

Our Heavenly Father. He has been patient enough. He has been more than merciful, more than enough times. His Illumination of your souls is one more, and the greatest, act of mercy He could give you. Continue, My dear ones, to prepare for this also.

"Your prayers are always working to impact the lives of others for good; are always being heard by the Father and moving Him to give more mercy to the world, but you must ALL PRAY MIGHTILY TO STOP THESE THREATS OF NUCLEAR WAR!!! GREAT DESTRUCTION IS A HEARTBEAT AWAY.

"Please, dear, dear ones whom I love with all My Sacred and Merciful Heart, take the energy you are using on fear and doubt and arguments, and kneel in peace and humility, begging the Father to remove this nuclear threat while AT THE SAME TIME GATHERING SUPPLIES FOR THE GREAT POSSIBILITY OF LEAVING YOUR HOMES TO EXCAPE NUCLEAR FALLOUT. This then, My people, is a call to the whole world that lies in danger. Your leaders will not listen to your cries for mercy, but IF ENOUGH OF YOU CRY OUT CONTINUALLY TO YOUR GOD AND FATHER, HE MAY THEN BE MOVED TO INTERFERE WITH PLANS OF THE EVIL ONE TO ANNIHILATE DIFFERENT PARTS OF THE ENTIRE EARTH.

"Be driven by fear, if you must, but allow this to move you to pray in love for the saving power of God to act in order to save this planet from nuclear attacks and great destruction. Again, I tell you how much you are loved by your God and dearest Mother and all who are in Heaven. Reach out with all of your might and time now to storm Heaven. CHANGE YOUR LIVES. COME BACK TO YOUR GOD. REPENT AND RENEW YOUR BEHAVIOR. You can do this, My dear ones, if you truly wish to help the world to survive. It is up to you! We are waiting with open arms to forgive and receive your prayers and your souls into the true fold of one flock and one Shepherd.

"You are supported by all of Heaven, dear faithful ones. This now is the beginning of a major battle with Satan and all his followers and all of the demons of Hell. OVERCOME HATRED WITH LOVE, My dearest ones. IT IS THE ONLY WAY!! I am your Jesus Who waits for your response."

8/2/98, Jesus said:

"Child, please write. I am your Jesus of Mercy and Love, come to fill you with new and greater strength. You will be encountering increasingly angry people on these trips who will wish to discredit you. Please be extra patient and gentle with them. They are frightened, and you are the only person at whom to lash out with feelings of helplessness. Frustration is a constant companion these days with many who can only see things going from bad to worse. Please assure them of Our love and desire for them to return to Our Father in humble sorrow for all their sins, with contrition and a firm promise to amend their lives and behavior.

"The complacency of even the faithful remnant is difficult to encounter. IMAGINE HOW ALL OF HEAVEN IS FEELING, AS IT VIEWS APATHY AND RIDICULE ON THE PART OF THEIR RELATIVES ON EARTH! THEY ARE PRAYING CONSTANTLY FOR THE OPENING OF THE MINDS AND HEARTS OF LOVED ONES. THE NEED TO BELIEVE AND PERSEVERE AGAINST THE LURE OF EVIL HAS NEVER BEEN GREATER.

"Continue, daughter, to pray that lukewarm souls will wake up to the reality of a need for them to begin to prepare this very minute for all that is so very near to fruition. It will be rotten fruit that will be thrown across the lives of the people of the earth.

"Nuclear events of great destruction will be the fruit of evil intentions and industry. The weapons of the Antichrist are able to wipe out large numbers of people quickly. The only way to survive these plans to destroy much of the earth is to depart from your homes to areas that you will be shown. Trust in My words of protection, little one, and assure Our people that We will 'come through' With Our promises to save you from terrible suffering and death at this time. The Angels of the Lord are standing ready for each command of My Father. He waits only a second longer, children. Are you ready to act according to His Perfect Will to protect you from certain harm? BE READIED BEFORE THE WEEK IS OUT AND CONTINUE TO LISTEN TO WORDS GIVEN TO THIS MESSENGER ON YOUR BEHALF.

"Do not think it impossible that this is the vehicle chosen by My Father to deliver these serious words. This soul has not been found wanting after difficult trials and rejections from many acquaintances. This vessel has been emptied of superfluous thought and deed, and works only to serve the desires of My Father and needs of Our people.

"Watch and pray, people of God. Give thanks that your deliverance from evil is at hand. Give praise and thanks to God with every breath, little ones of My Heart. Be ready for events of immense magnitude. Evil will be removed from the earth and all people; but not before many are made to suffer and experience torment for their sins. This will occur on the earth, so that many can go directly to Heaven. Many will be renewed by My Mercy, and plunged into the abyss of My Perfect Love. Rejoice for them, people, and desire to come soon to Heaven forever! I will not abandon you, My dear, dear people."

8/6/98, Jesus said:

"All right child, please write these words of comfort for My people. Oh My dearest little soldier, I am your Jesus Who calls out with great heaviness of Heart tonight. I tell you, those who do pray are being given special graces and protection. Those who pray more will be give more of My gifts and power in order to heal those who come in search of aid. Great healing will be needed; and you, My faithful and obedient ones, will bring them to Me; first in prayer before My Blessed Sacrament; and then by the power of My Name. Many of you will have the ability to cast out demons and heal the sicknesses of body and soul. Count on this, My people!

"**Your God has chosen you to be instruments of peace and mercy and healing. Great signs will be given through you. I need you to persevere and be ready to serve in any capacity those who are refugees themselves after destruction decimates families.** Pray now for fidelity and courage and strength, My gifts of My power, not your own! Believe that you will see the good things of the Lord in the land of the living!

"Choose Life, My dearest people. Choose to serve God, Our Father, and all of His lost little ones who will wander in a daze.

Great will be the confusion until enough time goes by before order and some routine can return the great numbers to some semblance of peace. You will need to listen closely to Our Spirit speaking the words to you that will be right for each person. The many demands on your time and person will not deplete your store of energy, if you are meant to serve in this way. Do not give another thought to anything, dear ones. Do not let your hearts be grieved or alarmed, no matter what you see or hear. Remember that My Father's plan for your salvation and the renewal of the earth includes bringing very many people into Eternity from now on. This will not mean a long separation from them, as it has in the past! They will return to the earth with Me and My Second Coming. You will be reunited, although they will be in their glorified bodies. Do not be concerned with this please, My people.

"**Be concerned about the state of your own soul!** Be concerned about the degree of obedience you bring to all of your preparations to leave your homes to avoid nuclear fallout. You have much to do, My loved ones. I see that organization has begun to a very great degree in many homes. My children, as you pack and prepare supplies, remember to pray for the Heart of My Father to be moved to stay the plans of those who would bring nuclear destruction upon the world.

"Daughter, I wish for you to tell Our loved ones this very week that they must be more obedient to My call to them. You do not know the day or the hour that one single event will or will not begin; but you must follow My desires for you and the helpful suggestions your Lord and your God makes to you.

"**If you could see waters raging about you, or flames leaping all around you, you would leave the danger immediately. The danger is overwhelming before you can see it, dear children of Mine and My Mother's. Do not hesitate, I implore you.** Be open to Our words in every part of the world to so many, and gather foodstuffs and clothing to take along on the journey to escape this terrible fallout with its great potential to burn and disfigure. These words are harsh, but you must know I am warning you of actual possibilities. The world comes closer to full-scale combat everyday. You must be ready to move away from your homes for now, until the time when it is then safe to return. Do not grieve so, My dear beloved. Do not fear for those who answer My call to them. They will be protected according to My Father's Will for them. You can know that those faithful ones will come immediately to Heaven for all eternity!"

8/12/98, Jesus said:

"Dearest one, please take My words. I am your Jesus of Mercy Who comes to thank you for the great energy you have poured out upon the people of Our longing. They are so important to the plans of My Father. It doesn't matter, as you know, where you are or stay, because you are always with Me! (I had been thinking earlier about all the places I am visiting now.) The present moment, in Our Presence, is your home! Be encouraged that you are always doing My Father's Will when you are teaching and guiding and loving Our people. I know you enjoy visiting different places! You will be delighted for the rest of your life! (I knew He was smiling here!)

"I have more words to share for Our people who listen and act on them, daughter. Again, please stop and pray to Our Spirit for openness and the peace necessary to record these words. You are totally protected, child, and have nothing to fear.

"The world waits in anguish for the next words of Mine. And I say to you, My children, rejoice! Be grateful that you are blessed with ears open and attentive to My requests. Ask Our Holy Mother to join you as you continue to beg for mercy on the world. Praise and thank My Father for the gifts He gives to you that enable you to hear and believe, to respond and prepare for the possibility of leaving your homes.

"BECAUSE OF YOUR INCREASED PRAYER, DO NOT THINK THAT ALL IS WELL AGAIN! Mitigations and conversions are given, yes, but only the Father knows the final outcome of His plans. So please, DO NOT BE CASUAL FOR A MOMENT IN YOUR UNDERSTANDING OF THE WORLD SITUATION.

"Because you are unaware of the great evil existing in the world, you think that this time is like any other. I tell you, IT IS NOT! You think you will pray for a week, maybe two, in this increased way, and all will be removed of a destructive nature. I tell you, IT WILL NOT!!

"The well laid plans of evil men are ready to explode on the world. Great amounts of prayer and sacrifice are needed to bring into balance the weight of evil in the world. With the prayers of My Mother, her Angels and Saints, your own efforts are enormously multiplied.

"Be encouraged about enabling mitigation and change, but be completely realistic about the need to persevere for long hours in prayer of supplication, and for a long time, that is, until My Return!

"Even as you serve all who come to you for help and instruction, you must be offering your service constantly to My Father, and for the people you serve. They will need ongoing consecration and support; continuous attention from all of you, as they will be in terrible shock and grief, terribly saddened and nearly without hope.

"You can imagine, My dearest people, how sad you will be at seeing the condition of their hearts and souls. That feeling would need to be multiplied many times to approximate the condition of those who have lost everything and everyone.

"Dearest people of My Sacred Heart, you are so important to the plan of My Father. I call out again to prepare immediately, and BE READY TO LEAVE AT ANY TIME. YOU WILL BE AWAKENED IF NECESSARY, AND ADVISED THAT IT IS TIME TO PACK YOUR VEHICLES AND LEAVE IMMEDIATELY!

"IF YOU WILL ONLY DO WHAT YOU ARE ABLE, YOU CAN TRUST THAT ALL ELSE WILL BE CARED FOR! But you must practice obedience to My call for a preparation of food and clothing and bedding, with the necessary utensils for any need or possibility.

"DO NOT THINK TO OBTAIN DANGEROUS WEAPONS! MY MOTHER AND I HAVE PROMISED TO BE YOUR DEFENSE.

"Allow yourselves to be protected by the power of God and His warrior Angels! This can be part of your expectations, part of your preparations to depart.

"Thank you, all who have begun serious attempts to organize your gear. Thank you for taking My words to your heart and acting upon them. The more all of you respond in trust, the more graces and strength and protection will be given by My Father. Every corner of your hearts is known to the Triune God! Remember that, as you contemplate games of rejection or lack of interest.

"Be assured that your God will not tolerate attitudes of ridicule and rejection. Be assured your safety is determined by your trust and belief in these words.

"I need you, My people! I love you and desire to allow as many as possible to serve in the coming days all who will be sent by My Father for the conversion and healing of their hearts.

"You must act out your decisions, your choices! Mere words are empty and sterile in the face of overwhelming need. THE POSSIBILITY OF NUCLEAR DESTRUCTION IN MANY PARTS OF THE WORLD REMAINS VERY, VERY HIGH.

"Do not be discouraged, please My dear ones, by these words. These plans have been in place for a very long time. Be encouraged to continue spending as much of your time as possible in prayer of petition to Our Father Who waits another second and listens to your pleas!!

"Thank you, child, for your serious attention on My behalf and on behalf of the world whose sad plight grieves your heart so. You are held in My Heart and deeply loved and sheltered there. My peace is yours."

8/20/98, Jesus said:

"Dear one, please take My words of love. Thank you for your trust. You will never regret following My Father's Will in all things. The past is forgotten until the previous second, when you live in the present moment with Me! Free your heart again and again of each new burden, each new event that is sent by the enemy to bog you down, tie your heart in knots! You are a warrior that We count on for many journeys and events that will seem to be risks; but will be protected, in actuality, by My Father Himself and all the power of the Godhead. Do not be alarmed to accept any invitation, as We are with you and will determine your every move in the Divine Will of the Father.

"These days are full of intrigue throughout the world. Events of today have opened many eyes to a new reality, when these eyes and minds thought they already knew it all, had seen everything! (Clinton bombing without telling anyone else about it!) The American people ought to be alerted to the need for increased prayer simply because of escalating events. Terrorists are people without decency, without the normal rational means of making decisions. No one can equate any of the present events in the world with events of the past. It is a world of intrigue at every level of government in this country, but especially of your leaders. It is with sadness, I know, that people view each reckless action of your President. It will not only result in disasters, but has been calculated and planned to do so!

"The world cannot wait any longer, dearest child of Mine, to be 'convinced' of the truth of Our words of warning. Simple, practical assessment of what is being promised by irresponsible terrorists and others must alert people to imminent danger. Do not waste time with questions or details. Please allow all My words of warning that are followed by fulfillment of My words to move you to immediate action and preparation and prayer.

"If you do not continue to argue; if you do not continue to attack and imply falsehood on the part of My messengers, you will be given the opportunity to repent and renew your lives. If you continue to seek opportunities to discredit My faithful ones who serve My Mother and Myself, you will find yourselves in a situation that is the same as that of which you accuse others! My Word says, 'judge not, lest you be judged!' (Matt. 7:1) This is a last warning and mention from Heaven about all the outrages brought against these servants of Mine.

"Each one determines the future path they tread by making choices to obey or disobey. It is up to you; and I call you all to repent and begin again in humble docility. Be reconciled with your God and with each other NOW, dear ones. The time is gone from your scheduled opportunities. You have used up all your options, delays, or tickets to ride on My wings of mercy! There is no more time for games and attacks. Worry not about what others do; look at your own behavior and weep! Beg forgiveness now, My people, and follow My directions with complete obedience. I only wish to save you from harm and from hurting yourselves! These are words of love to all who listen.

"Do you need to see destruction right before your eyes to be convinced? It may well be that this will be done! It may well be that you are not fully prepared to continue to serve Me! Only I know your hearts and I tell you: repent! renew! remain in My arms, in My shadow. Be protected by all the grace and warnings you are being given. Receive My love. Receive all of Who I Am!

"Daughter, you have done well. Please pray this night and continue to offer each event, each prayer for conversion and mercy for the world. I am your Jesus Who worships My Father and Our Spirit from within the Triune Godhead. My Mother sends you her gratitude and reminder of her presence with many thousands of Angels and prayers at every second.

8/22/98, Jesus said:

"Please write, child. Please tell Our people tomorrow that they must act in great haste now, as evil people around the world set into motion the plans to begin a nuclear holocaust! This is information being given by the great mercy of My Father. As each one hears Our words, pray first that they will be filled with Our Spirit of trust and acceptance of the Truth. I repeat, those who do not take steps to follow Our call, and leave when they are instructed, will perish!

"Each one is free to make a choice. Unfortunately, many will choose to stubbornly refuse to comply with Our requests and will not survive this tremendous nuclear attack planned to annihilate so much of the world. Be at prayer whenever you are not speaking or doing other activities related to your various ministries and duties. All will soon see how authentic are these words of warning, My little one. All will know the power of Satan to attack the children of God. These plans are made to destroy My Church and as many people on the earth as possible.

"Do not argue, My people, or defend your own beliefs in these words. Hurry to gather belongings and foodstuffs and water necessary to sustain you for many weeks. Pray that as many as possible will accept this advice and hurry to prepare to depart. Signs will begin to be given now to help convince all of the truth and validity of this message and this messenger. Do not wait for these warnings to be accepted by others.

"I repeat, hasten to gather what you can, and prepare to leave at any moment!

"It is unbelievable how many will hear and believe, yet NOT act upon these messages of increased intensity. Pray, My people, that you will be strong enough to act upon your own convictions and come away when you are summoned to leave for safety from the effects of nuclear fallout. THIS IS A REAL THREAT, A GREATER POSSIBILITY THAN EVER.

"Do not delay, dearest ones, but begin this moment upon returning to your homes (from the talk in Huntsville, Texas, Shrine of the Two Hearts) to gather in earnest all you would need to survive away from your homes for this brief period of time. I remind you to gather whatever you can, and I will take care of the rest, but do not be lazy or unmoved by the serious need to act now to gather whatever you have, or can acquire, in response to My pleading.

"I am your Jesus of Mercy Who sends words of love to you in an attempt to save lives from the terrible effects of radiation. Be ready NOW, My beloved people, and then pray constantly that more will respond and prepare. These are duties of an obedient soldier.

"BE ALL YOU CAN BE IN MY MOTHER'S ARMY(!!!). (can you believe this??)

"Be one with Me now, children of My Heart, and prepare. You will all receive increased energy and power to serve and prepare."

8/25/98, Blessed Mother said:

"Dearest child, I, your Mother of Sorrows, come with words of wisdom for the world. Please be at peace, little one, and know that you are blessed and protected in My Mantle. Be grateful, please Carol, at all that is allowed to unfold in your life. Do not be alarmed at the harsh words said about you by others, but offer these to the Father along with your prayers for their healing. It takes a great deal of suffering to heal hearts! Remember what happened to My Jesus, and how few were healed and converted. Be at peace about all that is happening in your life. It is always according to Our Father's Will for you and for all.

"My daughter, you know how very serious are these times which still take the world closer to war. So many are completely oblivious to the danger looming on your horizon. The media is underplaying the seriousness of each event, and thus the world sleeps without a thought or comprehension of the reality of imminent danger. The fear and frustration felt by so many is the reason for My visit this night. Please pray to My Spouse for strength and clear understanding of all I will tell you now.

"My dear people, please be at peace! You are wasting so much time in an effort to discredit these messages and this (and other) messenger. Do you truly believe that a loving and merciful God would allow the evil one to lead you astray, to confuse you on such important issues as preparing to leave your homes?

"My dear ones, please reread all of these messages and concentrate on every word. My Son is telling you all He is allowed to say according to the Will of Our Heavenly Father! He will continue to call out and promise protection, give direction and words designed to lead you to your destinations at the proper time. Your God wishes to save you from harm. He is giving you enormous gifts of knowledge and understanding. If you do not wish to accept them, that is your choice, My dear little ones.

"Know that I, your Mother, am filled with great sorrow over all of you who ridicule and reject the words of My Jesus. He loves you! I love you! IF THE FATHER DECIDES TO GIVE YOU WORDS OF WARNING IN EXACTLY THIS WAY, WHO ARE YOU TO QUESTION HIM? DO YOU KNOW A BETTER WAY THAN HIS WILL FOR YOU?

"Please consider the great numbers of people in the world today. Great means are needed to communicate with so many. Great confusion is avoided by using only one messenger to be the vehicle for these very, very serious words of warning about the extreme possibility of very, very serious destruction and suffering from the weapons poised and pointed toward different parts of the world by very evil men. We have explained to you already why and how this unholy madness could occur. We have begged you repeatedly for as much prayer from each of you as you are able to give. You are told repeatedly what the Father desires from those who would live as His children, away from the world completely now and in union with all those who pray.

"If you think your God would not act in a certain way, what do you think of all those who have not acted in a certain way, according to My requests to the world and My Son's repeated warnings? Please try to see things from Heaven's point of view, with a mind to the justice of God responding to the behavior and cruelty of SO MANY in the world.

"You have become so centered upon your own needs and desires, My children of the world, that you too forget that GOD IS NOT HERE TO SERVE YOU, BUT YOU ARE HERE TO SERVE HIM AND HIS PEOPLE IN PEACE AND LOVE AND MERCY! You are still too focused on your own wants, on your own agenda, on your own lack of love for anyone outside of yourself!

"In times of danger, a mother must speak harsh words to continue to attempt to gain the attention of her children. These are words of truth I speak to you, My beloved ones. Even those who have remained faithful, and have been serving Me for many years, are not taking seriously enough the need to prepare this very minute all you can gather for a quick departure from your homes.

"Never stop praying for mercy and mitigation of terrible events, but act in unison with preparations to be ready at the call to depart. You are soldiers whom I have taught and loved all these years. Does a loving mother frighten her children? Does she send those she loves on wild chases after untruth? After folly? After a waste of the precious time left before My Son's return?

"You are angry because these words about possible nuclear attack in many nations come upon you quickly! And so you wage a war of disbelief because you were not told sooner. If you are at peace and trusting My Son and Myself, does that not mean you trust in all of Our words and not just those you like to hear, those you find acceptable according to your own agenda? Be alert to every word that has been given to you, children of My Immaculate Heart.

"THERE IS NO MORE TIME TO WORRY AND BE ANXIOUS ABOUT NOW THAN BEFORE WORDS OF A NUCLEAR NATURE WERE GIVEN TO YOU. PROTECTION FOR 'THEN' MEANS PROTECTION FOR NOW! TRUST 'THEN' MEANS TRUST NOW!! LOVE MEANS A COMMITMENT TO WHATEVER HAPPENS 'IN SICKNESS OR IN HEALTH, IN GOOD TIMES OR IN BAD!'"

"Be grateful to your Father and Creator, people of the world. Do whatever you can to be ready, and leave the rest to Heaven. You are loved beyond your understanding, so it is only with human eyes and ears and the human mind that you attempt to decipher words of your God. Do not add complications to your life, My little ones. Be simple in living and loving your God and His attempts to love you, to save you from probable destruction. If you are convinced that this development has occurred very suddenly, THINK HOW QUICKLY THESE MISSILES ARE TRANSPORTED FROM ONE COUNTRY TO ANOTHER!

"We hope to galvanize you into action so that you will move quickly to prepare to leave at any moment. RECEIVE THESE WORDS OF LOVE BY THE POWER OF THE HOLY SPIRIT, MY BELOVED SPOUSE. Please, pray again to Him for the gift of peace and an open mind and heart. I, your Mother, am praying for each one of you, and ask your prayers and cooperation for and with each other.

"Be filled with rest and peace now. Worry about NOTHING. Continue to prepare. You are held in My arms as we wait together in joy and hope."

8/26/98, Jesus said:

"Dear one, I desire for you to write My words for you. I am your Jesus from Whom come all of the gifts and grace given you by My Father. I love you, daughter, with an everlasting love. I wish to prepare you for events that will occur very shortly and for which you must be alerted and readied. The evil one, My child, will be further attacking you now, as your mission for Us escalates. My Father wishes for you to be only in prayer and allow someone else to handle all of your correspondence and phone duties. This is most necessary now, daughter, because of the gifts about to be given on your behalf. Do not, please, worry or even think about, be distracted by or wonder about anything from now on!! You are, yourself, not even aware how close these serious developments are, or how soon you will all be leaving for safety.

"You are doing your best to make everyone aware of Our words of warning. These words are being passed along quickly throughout the entire world. My Father will have mercy on many more, and Scripture will be fulfilled. Please, little one, be at peace. Truly you have no ties now to hold you back from a total immersion in My Father's Will. He desires you to be completely surrendered so that you might be at His beck and call, to go wherever He wishes to send you; but most of all, to be more silent, more secluded, more able to be united with His Will and the graces and new gifts He has for you. This is an absolutely necessary next step in your journey toward serving Our people and the Father's plan for your life. Our people will be served in a powerful way, and you must be able to perform the special duties these gifts will entail.

"You are a daughter of Our longing, one after My own Heart! I am so grateful to you for your continued and increased 'yes,' your hard work for all We ask of you. Please, child, praise Our Father with Me now and thank Him for His gifts and mercy to you. We are so very close to all being accomplished.

"World events move quickly now to set up the nuclear possibilities you are aware of. Nothing and no one else must fill your time or your thoughts. If you will just dispose yourself to this possibility, I will do the rest. You can do nothing by yourself; but with the help of My Mother, you will do all you are invited to do and become all you are invited to become!

"I see in your heart all the trust you need, daughter, and I thank you for complete abandonment of yourself to whatever happens. You are highly favored by My Father, dearest one. Continue to go forward and soon the right priest, chosen and prepared for you by My Father, will be given to you. You have been most brave and patient, child, about every development. You are loved and 'called out to' at this moment by all your special Angels and Saints and dear ones in Heaven! Be at peace and hurry to your home now. My Mother sends love and blessing to you with a reminder that you travel together every step of the way. You are deeply loved, My dearest one."

8/31/98, Jesus said:

"My child, please take My words of love. I am your Jesus. Please give My Father thanks and praise with Me and in Me and through Me from now on, more often, every day.

"Please ask Our beloved ones to request in prayer that their weaknesses will now be built up and that the needs of soul and body, known only to your God and your Heavenly Mother, will be met with all the graces of healing and increase. Do not think to wait until the moment of need is upon you, when you are surrounded by people clamoring for help and attention! Begin this moment to build up a store of treasures from which to draw upon throughout the coming preparation of all these lost ones. Great organization will be needed among all of you, and each one must offer himself and herself according to the gifts you know God has given you. Humility means to surrender your gifts to your God Who gave them to you in the first place! Do not wait to be called upon, but come forward immediately, offering your services for the needs of all.

"I tell you, you cannot imagine the chaos and noise of so many who have barely survived great destruction, and the realization of the reality of their own souls and results of past behavior. There is truly no word that would adequately cover the situation you will face for many, many weeks. (of service to the people who come to us).

"I call out again, My beloved ones. Do not sit and wait to be motivated and led by someone else. YOU ARE THE LEADER I COUNT ON. YOU ARE THE ONE WE HAVE GIFTED AND PREPARED THESE MANY YEARS. YOU ARE THE ANSWER TO ANOTHER'S DILEMMA. YOU ARE THE SOURCE OF HELP AND ANSWERS SO MANY WILL SEEK! Our Holy Spirit will bring them to you, that's why!!

"Because you discount or dismiss My words of warning to you does NOT mean these words are untrue or will not be fulfilled. It is I Who see what is ahead of you. It is not you who have all the answers! It is I Who know the future plans of My Father to use you in many ways; and the great necessity for you to escape the effects of nuclear attacks, so that you might be protected and serve your new family that will gather about you in such dreadful condition, in such pitiful weeping and confusion.

"My people, WAKE UP!! Please, GET UP. Go TO A CLOSET. LOOK INTENTLY at the contents. What is there that you might use in a situation away from the house and hiding from nuclear fallout? GO TO YOUR KITCHEN and LOOK AROUND. What do you see? What might you wish to take with you for a period of time away from your store of food and cooking utensils? WALK INTO YOUR BEDROOMS and see what is there that you use every day. SEE WHAT YOU ARE LOOKING AT, My people, My dear wooden heads!! Allow yourselves to be touched, awakened, alerted to danger by My words.

"HEAR what I am telling you, people. ACT upon the directions I give you now. BE FILLED with a spirit of adventure and excitement. TRAVEL with My Mother and Myself in the company of Our beloved Joseph who led Us away from the danger of Herod's men. Today the SPIRIT OF DESTRUCTION IS AGAIN ON THE MARCH! Even more powerful and destructive weapons are in the 'hands' of maniacal minds that do not think of all of you as something to be valued, but as objects of their great, great hatred.

"Please BELIEVE My words, beloved ones. MOVE QUICKLY to get ready for My call to you to depart. I and My Mother, the Angels and Saints continually pray before the Father's throne that you will be convinced of the need to respond to these requests before it is too late to escape the effects of terrible suffering. Do not imagine that you can imagine what this will be like, My dear ones! You must be obedient to My call, and prepare in order to be saved and fight by My side against the terrible forces of the Antichrist who is renewed daily by Satan himself! If you believe and are preparing, My dear, dear ones, pray for those who choose not to accept the truth of these warnings. Do not believe the evil whisperings of Satan's demons that attempt to distract you and dilute your focus, your strength.

"GREAT STRENGTH IS NEEDED IN ORDER TO REMAIN FAITHFUL, MY SWEET ONES. I AM HERE TO GIVE IT TO YOU. BUT YOU MUST COME AND ASK TO BE OPENED TO RECEIVE, TO BELIEVE, TO BE STRONG IN YOUR BELIEF IN ALL OF MY WORDS.

"My dearest children, be stubborn no longer. Do not continue to play your games and run after distractions. There is no way to simply run away from Me or from the danger that will surely come if you do not pray. I love you, My little dear ones, and I beg you once again, to allow Me to protect you. Read all of the suggestions you receive and promise that today is the last day you will ever waste!

"PROMISE ME AND PROMISE YOURSELF THAT YOU WILL DO WHATEVER IT TAKES TO ANSWER MY REQUESTS! THERE IS NOTHING ELSE THAT MUST OCCUPY YOUR TIME NOW.

"My mother is on her knees at all times in humble supplication to obtain special graces for you. Be grateful for these gifts of help and prayer offered to you and for you. Be at peace and constant prayer, all the while gathering and packing supplies. Listen to the cries of the world: voices of poor suffering ones who are condemned to suffer the evil of many who are motivated by the hatred of Hell itself. Be moved with pity, but BE MOVED TO STEP OUT AND MOVE!!

"GET UP, MY PEOPLE. GO OUT AND ORGANIZE YOUR BELONGINGS FOR THE CALL THAT IS TO COME AT ANY MOMENT. OFFER THIS AS A PRAYER TO MY FATHER IN REPARATION FOR YOUR OWN SINS OF FAILURE TO BELIEVE, FAILURE TO TRUST, FAILURE TO RESPOND, FAILURE TO ACT UPON ALL OUR PLEADING, ALL OUR REQUESTS TO YOU. And then, dear ones, cleansed and renewed, begin immediately to do, to be the prepared soldiers We are calling you , NEED YOU TO BE!

"We call out in love, children of the earth. Respond in love and action, please. You are blessed this moment with increased gifts. Use them wisely and choose life, My dear, dear loved ones. I am your Jesus Who praises and prays before My Father in Heaven for you. Be at peace. Renew yourselves in My love."

9/2/98, Jesus said:

"Dearest child, I am your Jesus, your own true and faithful lover of your heart and soul. Won't you please invite Me to come into your heart and visit for a while? Will you not ask how I am; how I feel; about the fact that I am longing for all souls in spite of their continued rejection which fills Me with the greatest sadness?

"Hard hearted people do not understand My love and patience and mercy for them, especially those who mock and ridicule Me, strike My face and spit at Me. They secretly think in their hearts that I am stupid, a fool, someone to be scorned and avoided. This would add to anyone's grief, and I come to tell you I am no different! My humanity is completely united to My Divinity. Here in the Kingdom of Heaven My human nature can still react with sorrow at the rejection of Our people. I died for all people! I continue to shower all with graces and the call to return to My Father. Daughter, please realize that your Lord can truly be sad, truly has feelings, honestly needs to have My human heart loved in return by all of Our children of the earth. Many of you are moved to such great sadness because of your own rejection in your lives. Offer this to Me in union with all that I have and continue to suffer for your sake, because of My deep love for you." (This message was continued two days later.)

9/4/98, Jesus said:

"Dearest child, please write My words. I, your Jesus, come this night with words for My people. They wait for another directive, another word from their Lord. Please once again, pray to Our Spirit to be filled with peace, and open to these words.

"Our people in the world will be waiting for a new word, and I tell you there is not a word that is new!! The words are: PREPARE, PRAY, ADORE, TRUST, PERSEVERE, BE AT PEACE! These are the foundations of your spiritual journey. These are the weapons with which to arm yourselves. These are the bulwark against which Satan shall not prevail. These are your armaments. These are your sword and shield.

"My Father is protecting all those who will be faithful to Our call. There are so many events to occur that will empty the world of evil, ultimately. There are so many of you who look for one false word from My chosen messengers, and I tell you this. My truth, My word is the light that the darkness will not overcome! (John 1:5) THE TRUTH WILL ALWAYS BE MADE KNOWN AND WILL SET YOU FREE! (Jo. 8:32) There are many who themselves are deceived because they hold a set of criteria against which they judge you and Me. When you (anyone) continue to serve Us to the best of your ability in trust, in love, in obedience, you will be greatly attacked by the evil one; and each progress (no matter how small) that you make, will be pushed back, pushed on, pushed out if at all possible by the demons of the father of lies. To work for Me is hard work, as My Mother has told you. The rules of the natural law, employing natural decency and a rational approach to living, are no longer accepted or utilized by much of mankind. So you are not now dealing with behavior and events as you knew them in the past.

"The present has no parallel in time, but it quickly approaches the chaos present in the great chasm between Heaven and the earth before My Father created order, and began to crowd out chaos with the beauty and order of creation. The times that existed then were no different in darkness than the darkness descending rapidly now. I was sent to cure your ills as a society, to lead you away from the empty existence proposed by Satan; but no one would listen. No one could hear above the roar of their own ego!

"The present day is filled with the worst kind of pride and evil. The greater number of souls on the earth gives Satan a greater opportunity to come into the lives of so many.

"The goings and coming at great speeds by the entire population of the earth has negated the opportunity to build the family. All of these events have a great impact on the stability of the life in a family." (I am interrupted.) "Daughter, we will again continue this instruction on things I wish for you to understand. Continue to pray to know truth and be guided by it. You are deeply loved."

9/5/98, Jesus said:

"Child, please write. I am your Jesus Who gives praise to My Father in unity with Our Spirit. Dear one, thank you for coming here. Be at peace and pray, once again, to the Holy Spirit for openness to My words. Do you trust Me, little one? All right! Then you will worry about nothing and no one! Each detail will be tended to by My Mother who watches all, while at the same time, praying for each. You are protected in her Mantle.

"Nowhere in history since the beginning, has such hatred existed, such a determined effort to wipe out those who are ethnically and economically a burden to the world in general. Please realize and tell Our people, that the hatred of the death camps was only a beginning, only a glance at the hatred of Hell! Truly, My beloved little ones, you must be praying before Me at every moment. Give up your games now. Give up your idle pastimes. Pray as a group; pray as a family; pray in adoration and the solitude of your own room...hidden from all but the Triune God. Retreat to that special place in your heart reserved for Me alone, and we will commune in love and in sorrow and concern for the fate of the world.

"If you were in a place of war, helpless and hungry, cold and undefended, would you not hope that many people in a more peaceful part of the world would be praying for you? All Our children are alike, and cling to the hope that someone is interceding for them in their awful plight. Change in skin color does NOT change the way people think and feel, their hopes and dreams. Changes in location do NOT produce people who love differently. The very fact that you all belong to the human family means you each have a responsibility to your brothers and sisters who suffer.

"Praise and thank the Father Who gifts you with so much; but please take seriously that the object of many gifts and talents is a total sharing of them and all of who you are!! If the world lived in this way, there would be no poverty or need anywhere, since the Father created enough to sustain everyone on this planet. You will all be brought to a place of understanding who reject the call to be your brother's keeper! This does not cause, was not ever meant to be, a terrible burden on some, when all do their part to tend the great family of the earth! You will see, My dearest ones of the world, and weep with sorrow over your selfishness and self-absorption. You will mourn your lost opportunities to serve and live as happy, cheerful children of your Father: Creator and God.

"Food equal to the amount of waste in the world every day would immediately cancel hunger everywhere! Think of the women and children dying of starvation in Africa. Their men are thinking themselves to be brave warriors who protect the land when, in reality, they play at games of war which allow their loved ones to die slowly and painfully. Think of a land flowing with milk and honey for every person on earth! This was ALWAYS THE PLAN OF MY FATHER FOR HIS CHILDREN. How far you have all traveled from this peaceful path.

"Your media, I tell you, does not report every event in the world, nor do they honestly report the number of tragedies occurring daily. There is so much deception among nations, and these are used to further the evil one's plan to dominate and rule. These are not idle words! I only spend this time in explanation in another attempt to move your hearts to pray and share, to prepare and plan the steps you must now take to be ready to avoid the devastation that is still so very probable in every country. And I will continue to call out to Our priest sons to be ready for great, great numbers who will wish to return to My Father after the great destruction of the land and the gift of illuminating their minds to the sad state of their souls.

"You must all be ready for anything at every moment, I beg you. Please, My faithful ones, BEGIN NOVENAS TO OUR SPIRIT TO OPEN THE MINDS AND HARDENED HEARTS OF MANY MORE, ESPECIALLY OUR DEAR PRIEST SONS WHO HAVE DELUDED THEMSELVES WITH MIND GAMES AND LOFTY CRITERIA!

"The lambs and the sheep are languishing while the false shepherds play and dance in the streets! WOE TO ALL WHO HAVE ALIGNED THEMSELVES AGAINST ME. WHAT FOLLY! WHAT ARROGANCE! WHAT TRAGEDY. WHAT A WASTE OF GRACES AND BLESSINGS WHICH YOU NOW THROW BACK IN THE FACE OF YOUR GOD. Do you really believe that you are smarter and wiser and better at life than My Father Who created it? All in Heaven weep for your ignorance, poor lost ones.

"Pray, My children of My Heart. Pray and continue to prepare, all the while trusting in God's providence and great and total love for you who remain faithful. It will not be easy, My loved ones, so please respond quickly with all of your hearts. It matters not where you go, or for how long. THERE IS A LONG ROAD AHEAD AND A STEEP CLIMB AGAINST WINDS OF WAR AND EVIL. BE CONFIDENT, CHILDREN OF GOD. I HAVE WON THE VICTORY. YOU CAN, TOO!! Be serious and gentle in these preparations that will surely bring you through every kind of hardship, according to the Father's Will for you. Notice the difference in your lives, little ones, between times of peace and times of frantic activity! It will be so much better to be leaving for safety in a peaceful mode instead of amidst frantic activity!

"IN ORDER TO BE PEACEFUL, CHILDREN OF MY SA-CRED HEART, YOU MUST GATHER AND ORGANIZE NOW ALONG WITH PRAYERS AND PLEADINGS TO OUR FATHER IN HEAVEN FOR HIS INCREASED MERCY UPON THE WORLD.

"You can do all of these things well, if you begin now to act upon all the words of Myself and My Mother. The days hurry to the end of the golden summer! These days have presented great suffering to people in so many areas of the world. This is not what We desire for you, people of the earth. We have always desired peace and joy, prosperity for all and an equality among every person. Know that this is possible, dear ones, but can no longer be obtained without first cleansing and emptying the world of evil. This is not so difficult to understand, if you will look about you with honesty, if you will evaluate people and behavior in light of My Gospel teachings and the commandments of My Father.

"DO NOT LIVE ANOTHER MOMENT IN DENIAL, MY CHILDREN. GROW TO ADULTHOOD THIS VERY DAY! ACCEPT THE TRUTH OF MY WORDS TO ALL OF YOU. Oh My dear, dear ones, you are loved so very much by all of Heaven, by My Father and Myself, by Our Spirit. We wait in longing for your response, your return, your renewal in grace. CHOOSE LIFE, MY DEAR PEOPLE. DO NOT LOOK FOR WEAKNESSES OF MY MESSENGERS. LOOK TO THE STRENGTH OF YOUR GOD!! Expect all weakness and brokenness to be healed within that strength! Expect great signs and miracles to the end of this Age. Expect to be protected, as you allow this to be accomplished, in My arms and the heart of My Mother. Be eager to see My return, people.

"I AM RETURNING TO THE EARTH TO DEFEAT SATAN AND HIS HORDES, WHETHER YOU BELIEVE IT OR NOT!! DO NOT MISS THIS EVENT, PEOPLE OF THE EARTH. DO NOT BE CAUGHT BY THE CLEANSING ARM OF THE FATHER AS HE SWEEPS AWAY EVERYTHING (THAT IS NOT OF GOD) FROM THE FACE OF THE EARTH. COME BACK TO US AND BE SAVED AND LOVED FOR ALL ETERNITY. DO NOT WAIT UNTIL YOU ENTER ETERNITY FOREVER TO DISCOVER THE PRESENCE AND REALITY OF GOD... AND OF ETERNITY!!

"Come now, loved ones, all. Come into a land of peace and beauty. Surrender to your Creator Who wishes to renew you as a revived and more perfect creation. DO NOT RESIST MY CALL, PLEASE MY CHILDREN."

9/13/98, Jesus said:

"Dearest child of My Sacred Heart, please write for My pleasure and your instruction. (There followed a lengthy personal message). I am your Jesus of Divine Mercy Who spends My existence united to the Will of My Father. He is your Creator and Lord, He showers you with gratitude for your heartfelt service to His children. You are gleaming in the golden light of Our love and power of Our Spirit. Be at peace. Do not worry or be anxious. You have My love and great admiration, daughter. My Mother will speak to you now with words of great importance for the world."

Blessed Mother said:

"Hello child! I am here by the gracious gift of the Father. Do not be alarmed by anything. Again this night, the Father revives your spirits, your heart and body. If one were to test your physical and mental powers, it would be found that you have increased in ability and youthful vigor(!) Please work to get into the best condition possible with your busy schedule. You must work at this diligently and cooperate with these new gifts, dearest one. Child, be very attentive now, please. Word of your increased speaking abilities is spreading rapidly, and you must be on guard more than ever for the interruptions of evil people interfering in your life and presentations. This is really true, daughter. Take care to be ready for more challenges and attempts to humiliate you. Pray throughout your talks for greater protection and openness to the words offered by the Holy Spirit.

"Tomorrow there will be more devastation in the world by terrorists who are escalating their plans to destroy Americans, especially military personnel. The buildings that are destroyed and lives lost are another challenge to your leaders to move them to retaliate quickly. This, of course, is planned, and will allow your leaders to send more troops out of the country. There will be no delays in these events, daughter. You may trust and believe My words. Your courage has increased your opportunity for more gifts and warnings to be given that will be followed up by the action these words describe. Continue to be brave and trusting, little one. Please tell people of the world to be ready for weather aberrations to increase and grow in ability to damage. In cleansing the world, the Father sets the stage to remove a great deal of evil in order to beautify the world.

"Daughter, We realize your fatigue, but wish you to have these words. The belief of many, many more lukewarm and hardened hearts will bring joy to the Father and to your own heart. It is time to retire and awake refreshed and renewed. You are learning much about the plans of Heaven by just being obedient and patient. You will overcome all opposition one day and be instrumental in convincing much of the world to prepare to escape nuclear fallout(!).

"The Holy Spirit is pouring out His power at all times. We are standing next to you at all times. Be filled with peace now. Be assured of my love and gratitude, child. You are truly blessed."

9/21/98, Blessed Mother said:

"Dearest child, I, your holy Mother, am here to bring you good news! The world waits for a word from Heaven. The words of Heaven have been given by My Son. Please tell all of Our people that We are with them, that We are actively sharing their burdens and struggles, that graces are pouring out from the hand of the Father into the hearts of all who listen and pray and prepare.

"YOU WHO ARE BEING OBEDIENT HAVE NOTHING TO FEAR. I ask you to pray for your brothers and sisters in Christ who will not choose to be obedient and leave their homes in order to avoid nuclear fallout or actual devastation.

"I weep at the obstinate hearts that do not allow themselves to be moved by words of love and promises of protection. You are all deeply loved by your God and heavenly Mother. If you choose to disobey these words of warning, you must then deal with the consequences.

"My beloved people of the world, be serious yet joyful from now on. All is in the hands of the Father, and we wait together for each act of significance to the world. The world will become more anxious and irritable as the days go by and events begin. Please ask Our dear ones also to ask for increased patience and peace, as the waiting seems to become a greater burden.

"My children of My Immaculate Heart are loved beyond their understanding. HOLD EACH OTHER IN THE EMBRACE OF YOUR HEARTS AND PRAYERS. LIFT EACH OTHER UP WITH WORDS OF ENCOURAGEMENT AND MUTUAL AP-PRECIATION. YOU ARE THE MIGHTY ARMY THAT IS HELP-ING AND WILL CONTINUE TO HELP ME CRUSH THE HEAD OF SATAN AND DESTROY EVIL FOREVER.

"There are special gifts and crowns waiting for you in Heaven. Please, please, My children, persevere in love and peace with each other. You have all come so far. Please remain at My side in this greatest battle against My enemies. Be the ones who assist the faithful remnant to endure until My Jesus returns.

"You are held lovingly in My Immaculate Heart. I am your Mother who loves you, who prays for you and with you, who will never leave you."

9/24/98, Jesus said.

"I thank you for coming to be with Me today. My dearest child, I too await with trembling the first nuclear events. Please be assured that the words already given to you are absolutely true. Your trust has been so strong, and so you will be tried even more to bring you to the ultimate place of strength and obedience. The Father alone knows how to test each one. The results are always in accordance with His Will and plans for you (and everyone), dearest daughter of My Heart.

"Days are disappearing behind a rush of days and events(!) The time has reverted to a series of events between light and dark, day and night! Wait until your time is no longer kept at all, as the magnetic poles are reversed and the earth turns upside down! There is so much to see, to experience, to record, daughter. Do not, I tell you again, worry about yourself or anything now. When things are seemingly delayed, the Father is choosing what is best to keep you humble and hidden and obedient.

"At any second, the battle between countries will begin. Believe this, child, and prepare more. Be patient, little dear one, and give all your impatience and longing to Me. Please continue to offer and give all to Me for the salvation of souls. The time for these events is so near, and We need very many to respond immediately. Please get some much needed rest now. Persevere and be at peace."

9/27/98, Jesus said:

"Daughter, please write My words. It is necessary that you take them now in spite of your fatigue. These are important words for Our people. You must pray again to the Spirit for the grace to take them in a clear and concise manner. Pray now, daughter, with all of your heart for openness to the Spirit and My words. Now let us begin.

"My people, I, your Lord Jesus, Son of the Father, in union with Him and with Our Spirit, call out to you once again. The increased and escalated plans of the powers that secretly plot to rule the entire world are again the subject of My words to you. Please join My messenger in a prayer to the Spirit of Love and Wisdom to open minds and hearts to these directives.

"In the coming days, there will be more attacks on innocent ones who go about their duties unaware that Satan is about to deal them a mortal blow. Please pray for these servants of Heaven that they will suffer little; that you may make reparation for their sins; that they may come immediately to Heaven. You will all be given these special requests for prayer from now on (before the fact) when people are brought into Eternity by a dreadful act of diabolical cunning!

"You have no idea, My beloved faithful, how much your love and prayers have the power to affect and change the lives for which you offer these prayers. This is a new gift to you from Our Father Who brings you more intimately into His plans for the salvation of so many. You are working side by side with all of Heaven who has joined you in these special times to respond to these requests from the Triune God. This is a great privilege for each of you, dearest ones, given because of your fidelity to the call of My Mother and all We ask of you!

"The Communion of Saints shines with the joy of union on every level of life. A bond of prayer and community exists that is stronger than all of you on earth realize. This should be a motive for you to pray with greater joy and the excitement of a new and deeper awareness of the Presence of the Angels and Saints, of My Mother and Myself. My Father showers you with greater strength and willingness to pray constantly until the end of this present age. When I return, you must make sure that I will indeed find all of you waiting in faith and trust, praying until the last second for the Father's mercy to pour out on everyone who will receive it!

"You are preparing for the probability of leaving your homes to take the protection of Heaven during the reciprocal nuclear attacks that are able to so decimate the world. You are praying for the Father's mercy to stay the full fury of Satan, and so it will! You are praying for the lessening of destruction and suffering, and so there will be!!

"Children of My Heart, I love you!! I call to you in desperate pleading for your continued and increased cooperation. Without your prayers and the love you hold out to the world, this planet would be totally doomed! Never underestimate the power of Satan and his followers. That is the reason you must remain at constant prayer until My return.

"The Father will never allow Satan to be totally victorious because He is God, He is Almighty, all powerful, all loving, and all knowing. Yet, He chooses to be guided by the requests sent to Him through your prayers, your concern, your sincere love for your brothers and sisters everywhere who are helpless in the face of war and starvation, abuse of every kind and oppression that will only become more total as the Antichrist is allowed to grow in power for the allotted time.

"The Father loves you by allowing you to serve Us by serving them (our brothers and sisters) and offering every prayer and assistance you can. This will be the same kind of lifestyle My Apostles enjoyed as we walked together the hills and valleys. Ask them to pray with you now, to intercede for you and the poor suffering ones whom you serve. Together with all the Communion of Saints, you will touch millions of poor lost souls.

"The harvest has begun, and the Harvestmaster calls to all His faithful workers to help Him gather the wheat into His barns. There will be much work to be accomplished as He renders each grain of wheat suitable! The threshing floor will be cleared by the Master and gathered into His places of safety. Do not for a moment question His activity, as the harvest will continue for yet awhile. Never doubt His ability, My little brave soldiers. Be on guard and ready to protect the dear ones whom the Spirit will send to you. Tomorrow we will continue, and I will tell you secrets that will allow you to serve in yet unknown and unheard-of ways! Be at peace, My people. Trust and endure!!"

9/28/98 Jesus said:

"Dear one, please continue now. I am your sweet Jesus Who loves you beyond telling. Be grateful to the Father for all the gifts He is giving now to your heart and soul. For My people, there are more words of warning.

"Dear ones of the world who listen and pray, please note these words from My Heart to yours. In spite of many words of condemnation from many of Our priest sons, please continue to believe and act upon these words that are meant to prepare you further.

"The coming days will see more attacks upon Our innocent ones. This will activate further plans of the one world people who are ready now to initiate aggressive action. If you will continue to pray as requested, you will continue to save many of these dear ones around the world. The actions designed to decimate the world population may indeed come to fruition, but your prayers for mercy will assure the graces to be released that will bring many more directly to Heaven.

"Again I point out to you, My beloved people, you must not be discouraged when great numbers are brought into Eternity. Through your prayers and sacrifices, many who would not have chosen My Father's Kingdom are now doing so! Be encouraged and filled with joy that great numbers who are presently non-Christian will accept Me as their Savior and their God. They will come to Heaven to pray for their brothers and sisters on earth that they, too, will accept the many graces offered to them upon entering into Eternity.

"Your own families will all be healed as you pray and remain faithful, My dearest ones. Remember and believe this, no matter what you see them do now! Trust the words of your God that this healing will render them able to choose for God at (perhaps even) the last moment of their lives. What is most important for each of Our children (and your own loved ones) is that they choose to spend all of forever and ever in the Kingdom of God; that you will all be together at last in peace and joy, completely healed for the eternal bliss of Heaven.

"My people, this promise from My Father is one for which you should 'put up with anything' to help effect with constant prayer and surrender to His Will. You will see great destruction; you will witness many taken into Eternity; you will need to wait in difficult circumstances for My return; but you will see Me return on the clouds, surrounded by Angels and all who have gone before you in this era of the end times. You will persevere until the trumpets blow, and you see Me with your own eyes return to defeat Satan and his evil cohorts. You will be lifted up in joy to meet Me and gather with Me to fight this greatest of all battles! You will each have performed many mighty deeds by then and be prepared to participate in this final battle to defeat Satan and all evil. You will be able, each step of the way from now on, to accomplish all that is requested and required of you. Be comforted by offers of protection and the sharing of Our power Who are with you at all times, giving you the strength and gifts you need. Count on this, My dearest children. We will not let you down. Remember, the Father allows the best possible events to occur for each one, according to your place in His plan.

"Again I beg you, prepare and pray; gather and organize; trust and love Me, your Mighty God and Savior Jesus Christ Who pours out My love for you in pleading at the throne of Our Father in Heaven. My Mother (and yours) brings Him your prayers through her heart and Mine. Together, We pray constantly that more will take steps to be saved from the plans of Satan carried out by the men of destruction, who expect to rule the world.

"Be of good cheer, My people. Great gifts and power of the

Triune God pour out upon all those who read and act upon these words. All of the special messengers have words which support each other now. This is meant to strengthen your faith and trust in them and in all Our promises to you.

"We are relying on you, people of the earth, to reach out with all of your might, as there will be great destruction soon that will actually be the work of man. Whatever you see, please remember to praise and thank the Father that His plans to cleanse the world and its people are going forward. When you truly believe that He allows mercy and good in the midst of justice and chastisement, you will be comforted and able to be quickly at peace.

"Please come to Me daily, My people, My dear faithful ones, in My Blessed Sacrament. Sit there in silent adoration, and I will heal you, I will strengthen you; and My Father and Spirit Who are one with Me will completely heal and strengthen and bless you also!

"Dear one, hurry now to pray and finish all your chores for your departure. It is truly I Who gives you these words, daughter, and Who will continue to bless you. Rest and hide in My Heart."

10/8/98, Jesus said:

"People of the world, I am Jesus, Son of God, Son of Mary Immaculate Queen. I call out to you again today in order to announce a time of favor to all who listen and respond. The Father allows Me to promise you every protection in your homes from all the evil attacks that will be threatening each place in the world. (My understanding is that this is after we return to our homes when the nuclear attacks are over.) You will still need to avoid fallout. It will be a special act of the Father that will render your dwellings livable again after the fallout. (When we return).The promise of the Heavenly Father of all is to protect you at other times after you return when looting and pillaging will occur everywhere. You will be frightened and think to leave, but I (Who loves you into this protection) say that you must remain and pray for peace and mercy to be given to all.

"If you are praying and being obedient to Our directives for preparation, you will have as much food and water as possible in your homes. You will trust in protection from My Father whether you are hiding from nuclear fallout or returned to your homes amidst this chaos and anarchy that will follow. It will be so difficult to remain calm, My sweet ones. You will need all your strength and resources. You must reread all of Our words yet again to become completely familiar with each directive for each time frame.

"There is very much to endure in the coming months. You can only follow Our suggestions at every step, trusting that each step is protected according to the Father's Will for each person. You are doing better, My little ones of My Heart. You are becoming more serious as the end of the year approaches, and I am most grateful. There are words of warning being given through too many of Our messengers now, and events in the world as well, should calm your fears, still your doubts. You are praying more, My faithful lambs, and all of Heaven rejoices. You are being blessed and strengthened in so many new ways.

"Feel the excitement of the call to be ready, to flee from danger, to live within Our Hearts and the Mantle of My Mother. Worry no more about those who do not listen, but continue to ask mercy for the world. All will be done according to My Father's Will for each of His children if you continue to pray often and mightily.

"You are Our beloved ones!! Please be comforted by these words. We could not accomplish this task of conversion and the salvation of so many without your prayerful assistance, your total and complete availability for all the needs and requests of those We send to you.

"Children of the Two Hearts, rejoice that evil will ultimately be erased from the world. Be confident and trusting in your God and your Holy Mother. All of Our promises are meant to save you and turn you into Our instruments of peace and mercy and grace. Be grateful, people of the world who are listening. Your God is coming to save the world from total annihilation and slavery.

"Be prompt in your every response. Do away with scoffing and smugness. Replace these with sanctity and obedience, sweetness and compassion. I, your Jesus, bring the love and blessings of the Triune God, Father, Myself and Holy Spirit. Be all that you are called to be, My precious Servants of the Holy Will of My Father."

10/12/98, Jesus said:

"My dearest one, take these special words, please. I, your Lord and God, worship before the throne of My Father. All praise, honor and glory be unto Him, little one. Be at peace. I speak in spite of your weariness, in order to comfort your heart. Please, daughter, pray for all who pray and listen. We are so close now to earth changing events. Daughter, please tell Our people to spend their days in ACTION OF PRAYER AND PREPARATION. They must not feel hopeless or helpless, since the Father is offering opportunities to overcome danger. You are all at a place of new understanding, ready to cooperate with any requests of the Triune God. If these words seem to be repetitious, know it is because of the ability of the repeated word to change, to renew and reform a person; like the repeated drop of water striking an object slowly whittles at the surface and eventually changes the shape of that object!

"The new object which results from repeated action, repeated reception by the object, is able to then be used for more and different tasks! While still retaining its basic composition, this new object has been changed, transformed into a new creation: more pliable, one that better fits the situation, the local environment.

"Repeated prayer, repeated words of repeated requests, also have the power to do this: to effect a change of shape, a greater pliability, the addition of new abilities from and by reason of its new shape. Our people are transformed into instruments of the Father's Will by RESPONDING AND ALLOWING these repeated actions by the Father, the Master Carver, the One Who knows best how and what to use to most quickly reshape His people! When they are faithful, and remain obedient and patient to His repeated acts and requests for repetitious responses (done with the least amount of resistance), His people can most quickly be affected by His power to change them and make of them a new creation.

"I ask all of you now, dear ones of the world, to repeat often your task of reading the words contained in this lesson, pondering their meaning in your life, and reflecting on the results of the repeated action of your response to the repeated requests of

Heaven for repeated prayer, preparation of belongings, silence and obedience! See how much you have changed shape, changed in your perception of truth, and praise My Father and thank Him repeatedly!!!

"I am your Jesus Who calls out to you again to repent and come back to My Father for His repeated gifts and graces for your continued conversion. Receive these words of wisdom, My precious people, and all of My Love. This has been the story of a tiny drop of water: the water of grace and salvation. Go now, daughter, in joy and renewed hope."

10/19/98, Jesus said:

"Dear child, please write these words now. I am your Jesus Who worships at the throne of My Father in Heaven. Be assured that it is I, your Lord and your God, Who speaks words of love to you. Your whole life is taking another direction again. Action will replace writing. Travel will increase. THE ANTICHRIST WAITS IN THE WINGS OF HISTORY! His evil plans are ready to be deployed by his followers. Evil will have its day, and the innocent along with the guilty will suffer the results of hatred and dreadful plans.

"War has been narrowly averted for the moment, daughter. The plans of My Father to interfere with the plans of Satan have stayed the moment of destruction for a small while, once again. Be grateful for this last second reprieve before Hell is loosed upon the earth; first through war and death at the hands of the sons of evil, then at the hands of Satan himself and all his demons.

"Be filled with peace and patience for the moment when the Father's hand falls and allows Satan to proceed with all of his well laid plans to conquer the world with his greatest ally, the Antichrist.

"Yes, little one, you will see the Holy Father leave the Vatican very, very soon for a place of safety, hidden from the forces of Hell. I, Myself, will guard him at a special place away from all those who work in secret to destroy him and Our church. Continue to pray for him who spends his days in pain and the anguish of one who knows his enemies and all their devious plans. This greatly beloved of all in Heaven will be protected by the Will of My Father and the ongoing prayers of all the faithful.

"Daughter, please advise all who pray and listen that there are many who are in need of aid throughout the world, as the winter sets in. The weather patterns bring more destruction to different areas, and more of Our children suffer greatly. Ask for prayers for them in Our Names, and the kind of help each one is able to give.

"It is time now for all of God's children to come to the rescue of people everywhere who suffer pain and displacement as a result of these weather aberrations. The world family must respond to the needs of their kin everywhere on the earth. The time for self-gratification is over, I tell you, and each must feel the want of comfort (that wealth affords) by sharing to a large degree their worldly goods and excess.

"The Father allows success to the work of hands that are honest, but expects all to share their portion of the world's goods with those less fortunate. Be focused now on the needs of others in so many places; as well as your prayers for mercy on those who leave the earth in increasing numbers.

"Reach out with all your hearts, with all your goods and special talents, My faithful ones. Do not wait another moment to help those in need and those who have nothing with which to prepare for a journey to the places of refuge where you will all be protected from nuclear fallout. As the days go by, it is more urgent than ever for each one to finish the task of gathering food and clothing and supplies!

"Daughter, you will sleep now, if you will pray to My Mother and her Angels. Be at peace, little one, please. All is well with you."

10/21/98, Jesus said:

"Dearest child of My Sacred Heart, please take words overflowing with love and delight. Your prayers go before the throne of My Father Who blesses and graces you with new resolve, new strength and discipline that will never leave you. Do not focus on another item or person outside of these messages, Our voices, My Face, the Will of My Father and the power of the Holy Spirit. I will send Our Spirit of truth and increased Wisdom to you now. My Mother sends blessings of love and smiles of gratitude.

"The upcoming days in California will bear much fruit and set up the time when you will first warn this country and then the world (secular) about the need to seek shelter from nuclear fallout. Russia has its missiles pointed towards this country. Each of the major powers is ready to attack instantly. You cannot imagine the destruction that will occur once the firing begins. This will truly serve to convince many of the reality of these messages and the Warning of My Father.

"My Father would have you be here (at adoration) in silence tomorrow, daughter. This preparation is more than necessary in these final days before destruction is unleashed. Be assured of the truth of all Our words to you, Carol, especially about the danger of nuclear attack. The Father's plans are so near to the time of fulfillment. Believe that many will come in sorrow and contrition for their hurtful behavior, (those who disbelieved these messages).

"Continue to pray for all, daughter, and to come here (Blessed Sacrament) and absorb the peace of My Presence. I am your sweet Jesus Who enfolds you in My arms and fills you with strength. You will awake refreshed, My child."

10/22/98, Blessed Mother said:

"Dearest child of My heart, I am so happy we are able to visit tonight. You have been so very busy, and I am grateful these chores (finishing the book) are ending for good! Please let another do all the rest of the work on this booklet, which has the blessing of My Spouse, the Holy Spirit. Do you recall when you were writing your first book? How you struggled to find just the right format? And now you have completed a third compilation of the results of a great deal of industry over these past years. How much you have learned! Please praise and thank the Father and be at peace.

"This waiting is upon us again(!), dear one, and can be felt keenly by all in Heaven and Purgatory, as well as all of you who wait. Please pray as much as possible tomorrow, daughter. The events cannot possibly wait any longer. The world is at so many crossroads. The people of the world do not even realize the many dangers ready to explode upon them.

"Starvation is decimating whole countries already, and new diseases have appeared that will take so many children into Eternity. The plans of evil men will account for most of these diseases, as new ways of reducing numbers of people escalate every day. I know you are praying for all of them, little dear friend.

Keep the cry for mercy raised every moment, My people. Listen to the cries of sick children, and allow this to soften your hearts and galvanize you into service for their families. So much work will need to be done for millions of people. Please begin to help now wherever you can. Look around you, my dearest children, and see the helpless and the unfortunate ones.

Begin to give until there is no more surplus in your lives; and then begin to give from your own want, your own helplessness and your own neediness. Please realize how much Heaven is counting on you, Our faithful remnant, to serve throughout this entire era until My Son returns.

Long for this time, children. Call to My Jesus and ask Him to come soon and release the world from its Crucifixion; and raise it to new beauty, new dignity, new levels of appreciation and gratitude, new degrees of holiness and purity!

Be happy children now, My loved ones, as you wait in peace and trust for all that you have been warned about to play out in your lives. You are finely tuned and ready to respond to whatever chord, whatever response is called for by the Father. He is your Goal. He is your Creator, and the One Who will renew the earth and all those who remain into the new era of peace and purity.

Wait in peace and a subdued focus on all that is to occur! Be docile and accepting of each event, and praise the Father Who gifts you with love and His perfect Will. You are all greatly loved, My dear ones!"

10/27/98, Jesus said:

"Dear child, please write these words from My Heart to yours. I am your Jesus Who worships the Father and Creator of all. Though We are One, it is My delight to do His Will above anything else.

Please believe, My dearest one, that it is your Jesus of Love and Mercy Who speaks. You have recovered well and are ready to continue your journeys into many directions. As My Mother told you already, the hearts of all who heard Our words were deeply touched and changed.

"Tonight new plans are being made to finalize the advent of war upon the entire world. Until the world is purified of evil, men will desire to make war upon those weaker than themselves. They think they meet in secret yet, I tell you, they are seen by all in Heaven. The plans of these evil ones are counteracted by the prayers of all of Us and those on earth who listen and respond.

"Games are played by leaders everywhere, and the people of each country are led astray by lies and deception. The sorrow of compassionate hearts everywhere increases as new stories about atrocities surface daily. Pay no attention to the weak promises of one power to withdraw troops or live according to a peace agreement with another. Each of the events of this kind is contrived, and will be short-lived according to plans agreed upon by leaders belonging to the one world order.

"This group will stop at nothing, My people, to push forward their plans for world domination! In spite of pleading for prayer support to direct evil men away from desires to conquer and destroy, the leaders of large and powerful countries are more confidant than ever because of the ease with which these plans are accomplished. The recent delays by My Father will be short lived in spite of the extended mercy He desires to give.

"Child, continue to do nothing but pray and rest between journeys to Our dear ones who invite you. Be at total peace, please daughter, about each concern you have. I am your Jesus, and I love you!"

10/30/98, Jesus said:

"Dearest child, I your Jesus, come tonight to issue words of warning. Please pray at this time to Our Spirit for special strength to receive them. I am Jesus, Son of God Who died on the Cross for you, Who calls to all to come to My Father and claim your inheritance that I died for. This inheritance is a part of the Kingdom on earth, further unity with Me and an understanding of all Our gifts and graces, Our words and promises, the fulfillment of every word of Scripture until My return.

"Now daughter, take these words for all: 'People of the world who pray and persevere, please listen. The time of preparation is nearly over. These beautiful fall days are a gift of the Father to His children, but they do not reflect the serenity or condition of your world at this time. There is no sincere rejoicing over the beauty of creation when you are making plans to annihilate as many people as possible. There is no joy in hearts filled with greed and hatred. There is no trust in God in people who do not believe in Me, and laugh scornfully at those who do (believe).

"Be ready, My dearest ones, for the time approaching that will signal departure from your homes to be in hiding against nuclear fallout and destruction. A degree of this devastation already exists in hearts bent on destroying most of the world and controlling the rest!

"DO NOT, I BEG YOU MY BELOVED ONES, FOR A MOMENT DISBELIEVE IN WORDS OF WARNING BEING GIVEN TO YOU. THE WORLD WILL BE FILLED WITH NUCLEAR EXPLOSIONS AT ANY MOMENT. All the words of explanation you have heard are about to be accomplished. Be ready, My people, to leave and go into a safe sheltered place of My choosing.

"Great fighting has erupted this very night in several parts of the world. Many of your military personnel will be departing in order to patrol, to maintain, and to ensure peace for the victims of greedy rulers. This will never occur because defeat is part of the plans of the One World Order who wish for many to die, to cease to be a problem that government is adverse to dealing with!

"Your country will become very aggressive very shortly. The reason for each new delay, in spite of the Father's plan to begin cleansing the earth and His people, is the mercy in His Heart and great desire to save and protect His precious children. You are His precious people, My dear ones. You are bringing flowers of prayer and song to lay at the foot of the throne of God!

"Have you finished with all of your plans to put food and supplies into one room, and be ready to leave for safety at any time? You will overcome this destructive period on the earth by obedience to My Mother and Myself. Notice all of the events, warlike or natural, that continue to pound many countries and cause their inhabitants to turn humbly to God, Their Creator, and ask for help, for peace and healing.

"You will wonder at the obvious gift of being saved from all the terrible destructive events. NUCLEAR WAR IS A TOOL OF SATAN, BUT IT IS NOT THE WORST! WHEN YOU TELL THE FATHER YOU WILL NOT LISTEN, YOU WILL NOT BELIEVE, YOU WILL NOT SERVE, YOU ARE ACTING IN UNION WITH SATAN AND EVIL!! BELIEVE WHAT IS WRITTEN: 'THOSE WHO ARE NOT WITH ME ARE AGAINST ME.' (Mt 12: 30) Put that constantly before the eyes of your heart, so that you may help many who come to you.

"You are My instruments of love, not destruction.

"You are My instruments of peace, not war.

"You are My servant children and soldiers, not ones of anger and aggression.

"Please tell Our people to FOCUS NOW ON MY FACE AND MY PRESENCE WITH YOU WHEREVER YOU ARE. Satan labors hard to distract you with many new plans and projects. Know that My Father's Will for you desires only that you pray and fast, do penance daily, attend Mass, reconcile with all, trust, be still before Me in the Blessed Sacrament and be at peace! The world is at the brink of war and allows plans of evil men to barter away freedom from this once great country. I, your Jesus, love you."

Happy the man who stands firm
When trials come. He has
Proved himself, and will
Win the crown of life.

James 1:12

ATTEMPTING TO UNDERSTAND SUFFERING

Suffering is completely a part of living! We cannot get away from it no matter how hard we try, and can see this fact reflected in daily events. Even the human body develops different sections at a time! Artists who construct large paintings usually complete small portions of the whole at first. Often you will see and can buy these smaller segments. They may be very powerful in their own right, but don't give us the whole picture the artist finally paints; the message isn't complete. It is without the strength and character of a finished product. Not until all the pieces are put together do we see the entire story or scene an artist desires to present. Also, this paint is applied in layers, lots of black, dark umber, purple, somber tones of which we aren't even aware. These underlying colors give the painting depth, more interest and greater contrast. That darkness, which can be used to signify suffering or struggle in our lives, is what gives us depth, strength of character.

Without suffering, pain and struggle, we would probably spin off the earth. Certainly we would be completely caught up in lust, greed, self-gratification, self-absorption, (naval gazing), Jesus tells us.

There are two components to suffering, the way I see it. It's mystical and practical. The mystical part brings us direct understanding and identification and knowledge of Jesus and His life. We couldn't possibly know the total Jesus without suffering. Our Lady has been saying all over the world, 'Study My Son's Passion. Dwell on My Son's Passion.' There must be a very special reason for that...and not just to appreciate that He suffered and died for us and won our salvation. This never meant that the tough times are over. It only means that His death opened the Gate to Heaven that had been closed by Original Sin. Our fidelity to the path, the way of Jesus, found in the Father's Will for our lives, is what puts us through that gate!

Pope John Paul II has said that suffering is so much a pattern and part of our lives that one of the reasons Jesus agreed to go through His Passion, Death, Resurrection and Ascension is to show us how it works in our own lives. Studying His life will give meaning to our lives and aid us in accepting, in calmly living out what is happening at difficult moments.

Another characteristic of suffering is that it is very tied up with sin. We usually suffer because of our own sin or someone else's. This affects us our entire lifetime. However, if sin is identified with suffering, so is forgiveness. We know we can't heal without forgiveness because sin requires forgiveness: from God, within ourselves and to or from others. Suffering is related to sin. So much has been written on the meaning of suffering, it becomes obvious that mankind has always agonized over the necessity of this dynamic in our lives. And then we remember when, as a result of Original sin, God mentions to Eve, "...in pain shall you bring forth children." And to Adam, "...by the sweat of your face shall you get bread to eat" (Gn 3:16,19).

God brought suffering to fruition in His Son Who was born into the world to win our release from the inability to enter into Paradise, brought about by Original Sin; to announce a day of favor from the Lord; to proclaim liberty to the captives; let the oppressed go free; to grant recovery of sight to the blind.

We have a huge edge on people who are not Christians because we believe that by uniting our suffering to Christ's, we can be co-redeemers. Suffering is redemptive. That is an enormous gift to us. We will suffer in some way just like every person in the world. It is part of our human condition, our heritage as adopted children of God, made in the image of God, our Creator, Redeemer and Love, and we must make the most of it!

We can choose not to accept suffering, or attempt to escape suffering, by walking away from whatever is painful in our lives at the moment. Divorce, drugs, alcohol, total irresponsibility, gambling, compulsive behavior of any sort are a few of the escape routes people choose. When we walk away from such events, we are not accepting the depth of experience that Life has ordained for us.

Suffering defines us as alive, interacting with life, with the people in our own God-given history. It helps make us who we are! We see that most especially when there is a tragedy, for example, the hurricanes in Florida., floods in the Midwest, the fires, earthquakes in California or other parts of the world, a plane crash, an automobile accident that involves many people, the death of a young person. All of these bring out the best in people...taps our hidden strength, our nobility, our heroic endeavors, undiscovered abilities.

If we didn't have pain or struggle, we'd never need to develop patience, perseverance, all of the things that come to the fore when we need them. We would never know the existence of our stronger qualities. We learn more about ourselves and gain a sense of healthy pride about our abilities, that we have what it takes to get ourselves and others through a crisis. That builds the self-confidence necessary to help us "keep on keeping on" for next time when the going gets even rougher. We have knowledge of our own abilities to draw from when we have a history, a foundation to build on. On the very practical side, we can rise to an occasion, then look back and say, "I did that! Not bad, self!"

Pain is definitive in that it outlines or points to a problem area, one which needs attention! We are immediately shown the right direction for necessary choices and decisions. In response to pain or painful experiences we are often propelled into a leadership situation we might never have volunteered for at first. This might be the only way to discover that ability!

In emergency, pain, tragedy, illness, God is showing us the strength, the dignity, the talents, the character we have. We come out of an ordeal having made many discoveries about God Who wants us to realize they were actually gifts from Him. It becomes even more exciting to see who I am, who I am becoming, more of my potential surfacing. There is a revelation of gift and ability that only happens through struggle.

Back to the mystical element and a more total identification with Jesus and all He suffered. We would love to be able to experience this identification only on the mountaintop, when everything was miraculous, above the ordinary existence, larger than life, away from the mundane and everybody else! "Lord, it's good to be here. Let's build a tent and stay!" (Mt 17:4). When God does allow us an extraordinary experience of Himself, we are filled with wonder and awe and peace and gift. We are ozoned with grace! It feels great and we say, "Oh boy, I really know Jesus now and what He's like." Unfortunately, that isn't enough. We can't truly know someone thoroughly until we know all the aspects of their lives, "view" all of their experiences from the inside.

When we suffer, we can suddenly say, "so that's what Jesus went through at the hands of the Scribes and Pharisees and all the people of His day" — especially when it's the emotional and mental pain of rejection or ridicule or humiliation, lonliness, disinterest. Jesus probably came home to His Mother and wept because of his human discouragement. He wasn't being taken seriously or even listened to! He had emptied Himself totally, Scripture tells us, He counted equality with God as nothing to be grasped at (Phil 2:6-7). and left His lofty place with the Father in Heaven to be born as a helpless tiny baby, subject to all the cold and misery that accompanies being human, in order to teach us, show us the Father, save us, and nobody cared! What a sacrifice! He allowed Himself to remain helpless and meek in order to draw people to His gentleness and love.

One remembers His frustration saying to the Apostle, "after all this time, Phillip, you still don't know the Father!! You still don't understand." (Jn14:9). We can identify with this kind of exasperation which makes us crazy! All of these things must bring us to a place of enlightenment. We say, "Wait a minute, Jesus, this is what it must have been like for you. Oh, my dear Jesus, how awful. I unite what I am going through now with what you went through then." All of a sudden, the painful situation takes on a whole new character, a whole new dimension, a whole new graced opportunity for us. What a new gift! In 1984, Pope John Paul wrote an encyclical on the Christian meaning of human suffering. Please consider reading another gem from this spiritual giant!

St. Paul is highlighted in Scripture, giving us such a clear understanding of suffering as he boasts of continuing the sufferings of Christ in his own body. Perhaps praying to him would be a good idea when we are trying to find meaning or the courage to unite ourselves to the experiences of Jesus.

Pope John Paul quotes Peter, "Rejoice insofar as you share Christ's suffering, that you may also rejoice and be glad when His glory is revealed." (1 Pt 1:6) The Lord does not chastise, continue to punish forever, we know, and suffering does come to an end. New growth begins, new directions are taken, new understandings, wisdom and knowledge prevail and we proceed, armed with new weapons, newly discovered ability.

There is sunshine after the rain, a rainbow when the clouds part and the sun appears. Things always get better. Life goes on and we have to go with it or die! The strength it takes to live, to reach out even though we don't feel like it, to admit we need help, to open up and allow other people into our suffering, is what stretches our minds and hearts, expands our consciousness and understanding of ourselves and our relationship to other people. The Holy Spirit works through our suffering and opens us up to new realities of personal need, of the dearness of many people. Our boundaries are expanded, as well as our depths plumbed, by the spirit of others around us willing to lift us up.

We are opened up to people in a different way because, often, it's people we consider the enemy! Someone or ones have hurt us in the past, and we made the decision not to let them in again so they can't repeat the hurt. We have done that subconsciously perhaps, but we all do it!

Suffering breaks us open, breaks our hearts that are cold and hard with decisions to defend ourselves against rejection and betrayal, part of Original Sin, part of buying into the world. Studies show that by the age of two, a child has learned how to manipulate its parents by withholding love! He has absorbed this from his environment and learned how to do it! You can see in your mind's eye right now the time your own or someone else's child did that!!

Gradually, over the years, our hearts become hard and colder through that very dynamic of withholding or refusing to love...especially when we refuse to love God Whom many people blame for everything!!

Along comes pain and breaks down our defenses. God breaks through these walls in order to get to our hearts. He allows whatever it takes to make us receive the love and gentleness, the tenderness and sweetness He wishes to give us, the love that is God. So then, suffering is also about love. In a practical way, it brings people together to help each other and in the process, learn to give love and receive love. All these interactions are occurring at the same time, and healing begins happening immediately for everyone involved, even without our awareness. No one could keep track of all these dynamics except God!

Suffering is a vehicle by which people become human. Hearts are broken by events and they cause us to stop and reflect in ways that we never would have otherwise. Again, that dynamic of realizing our potential and becoming what God wants us to be causes us to take a look at our lives and question our values, our goals. Pain breaks down defenses and postures. We can't have a haughty manner or disdainful look on our face when it is crumpled with pain. We can't pretend to be better than everyone else, aloof, or above the rest of a world we have seen as less than: ignorant, poor or disabled. We can't do that when pain slows us down to cause us to take a good look at reality. We are brought to the awareness that we are like all people: the same in weakness and dependency, related in a new way, brothers.

As our heart breaks, our knees buckle, our stomachs knot, our bodies bend, we also discover our own helplessness...how dependent we really are, and not the highflying untouchable who doesn't need anybody! This is the only way to make a discovery we'd rather not accept. Perhaps we carry the belief that nothing will happen to us out of the exuberance and strength of our youth. The Lord has allowed us to be invincible for a little while and, of course, we get carried away, go too far. Then He abandons us to our sin, our arrogance.

We know when we are left to our own devices by God because, very shortly, we fall flat on our faces! This signals a time of learning in our lives about what's important, some ultimate reality checks: what values are necessary, who's real and who isn't. All these things are necessary to stop us in our tracks, to make us think, make us understand there's more to life than we thought. How sad for people who have never lived or interacted with others at any depth. This, of course, could be the result of abuse or abandonment. But, still, the God Who loved us into life, desires to show us what it's like to be fully human, fully alive and loved by Himself, in community with Him.

We experience pain at the deepest recesses of our being where nothing else touches us so deeply except...joy! In a very mysterious way, Jesus explains to us, when pain breaks us open and touches us at that deep level, it prepares the ground and drops seeds of joy. That seed of joy is nurtured and grows when it is watered by tears of remorse and repentance! Only when we feel suffering, can we feel joy. Only when we have truly dealt with and processed pain, (walked through it and not around it), can we have an experience of authentic joy!! We wonder, why is that? What a curious mechanism, Lord, for us to need! How does that work? Jesus is telling us it is a matter of being opened at this deep level of our existence where pain and suffering touch us, preparing us for the joy which can follow. This is the joy that Jesus wishes to share with us, His joy...not giddiness, not superfluous, not surface happiness, but having to do with a gift being given to another, perhaps, a conversion experience that we have been praying many years about. One of our children finally begins to go back to Church and we say, "Oh God, I never thought that would happen. Thank you, oh yes, You are truly a great and loving and merciful God. I love you!" We appreciate God's working in someone else's life, or in our own, that we would not have been able to appreciate had the ground of our being not been first exposed by our suffering. Pain prepares us to receive the gift of joy, to experience it at this deep level and then to appreciate, give thanks for it.

These huge dynamics are a part of life that we want to live, to feel, to revel in. Then He says in this breaking of our hearts, this breaking apart of our self, (literally) we find in Scripture the image of ourselves as earthen vessels. God deals with us as the potter deals with the clay. You know that clay can collapse on the wheel, can get bent all out of shape in a matter of seconds. Also, we know that the potter can take the pot off the wheel completely and break it when the shape is not pleasing to him, or will not fulfill the duty for which it is being made! Each time it is put back together it is a little more nearly like what the potter had planned for that vessel. That's us! Over and over again we are broken and reformed to be the person, child of God we were always intended to be. With each new formation we become, we are less resistant to the potter's hands, to the new form we find ourselves in, more pliable. He mixes in a little oil of gladness, a little water of grace and we become softer, less resistant to change...beautiful images of what the Creator Potter is really doing in our lives. We can console ourselves, nurture ourselves with these images as a means of "getting through" the difficult times. It's very real and very beautiful how God deals with us...never more often or more roughly than we can handle. When we are broken, He heaps on more gladness and grace, and kneads us into the supple vessel that can receive and contain and reflect His Will.

We rub against each other in this life and can get cracks when someone bumps us too hard! Right now you can think of the last person who caused a crack in your exterior or taken a chip off your vessel!! Especially those closest to us...and we say, "Boy, I'm not going to bump into that person again!" We learn these things . However, in the rubbing, in the bumping, we are buffed! We are polished. Our surfaces become smoother and shinier. Pretty soon we are glowing and begin to reflect the light of Christ. All these images and understandings are important for us to recognize. They are truly happening all the time.

It won't make us any happier that something hurts or has gone wrong, but perhaps it will make us more patient and grateful. We know that praise and gratitude expand our graciousness and God the Father loves them! He's waiting for our love and praise and thanksgiving. In a very mysterious way, it heals us and makes us grow into the person we were meant to be...part of the process of becoming fully human, fully alive. It happens in little ways and in big ways, over and over again. All of these dynamics are actually little deaths. I don't like to say that we're practicing for the big one(!) but we are, not practicing so much as being prepared. Being prepared for all the little ways in which we are forced to die to ourselves, our own illusions and goals and values, we are reborn with new understanding, new truth, new values, new life. Dying to ourselves is the road we take when we are turned toward, begin to live life in the Will of the Father. That's our ultimate goal!

Unity with God is where we're going and Jesus is the Path, the Way, the Means. It's the Ultimate Road Show, the Final Destination. Unity means accepting and living His Will, being one with whatever He desires for our lives. Discovering what is holy means finding out that we are people to be cherished as gifts from our Creator to each other and to Himself, outward signs, blessed by God, capable of being occasions of grace, Sacramentals. Created in His love to learn to BE love. We know that our vessel must first be emptied of our own "stuff," our self-centeredness, selfish desires, self-gratification (whatever fills us and crowds out God and His desires for us), so that we might be filled with the needs and desires of others around us, might hear and see their pain, their loneliness, their neediness.

These little deaths are always experienced in five stages because we are dealing with loss. Until we arrive at acceptance (the final stage), we go through denial, depression, anger, compromise, and only then arrive at acceptance. We experiences these different stages over and over again, sometimes getting stuck at a stage and we are dealing with these dynamics over many different events in our lives. We wonder why we are tired sometimes!! This is part of our preparation, our emptying and we must realize how much a part of our living is taken up with this dying and rising. This realization helps us to deal with life, face up to the need for acceptance and say, "okay, I'll do what is necessary in order to get on with my living, my learning, my growing."

We are always, to some degree, grieving, mourning loss when we are actively engaged in struggle and suffering; loss of function, some ability or level of function we previously had. The Christian Catholic person will unite his or her suffering with those of Christ and know and believe that it can make a difference in the life and salvation of other people. To save souls is another reason we are here, why we were created. The choices to fast, to do penance allows us to trade them in for spiritual coins we use to purchase graces for the conversion of others; to let go of a way of life and choose another (often lesser); to have former friends who laugh at our new lifestyle, for instance, creates a sadness in us even though we want to remain in this new way of being and doing, forsaking the old ways.

We mourn the old self, even when we're glad to be rid of it! Whether we wish to be that way or not anymore, we sometimes miss it and wish we were still "going along!" We are meant to mourn. It makes us more compassionate, more understanding, more sympatico. In the mystical sense, we identify with Jesus. On the practical scene, we are identifying with each other: a very necessary component to be good neighbor, good citizen, good community. We become a closer knit, more compassionate Body of Christ.

Suffering makes us a better person or a bitter person. It's a matter of identification, understanding the meaning of certain events, realizing that Life is not out to get us, or get even with us for something we did wrong. People can despair when they see no meaning in life. They join gangs or take their own life without a sense of belonging. Abuse and rejection and abandonment can be the cause of acting out, lashing out, bitterness when attempts are not made to heal, to understand, to forgive. Without forgiveness, there is no healing and only emptiness; bitterness can remain. If a person refuses to accept love or forgiveness, refuses to allow or admit brokenness, he is dooming himself to a life of resentment and hardness of heart.

Allowing ourselves to become closer to another or others through suffering opens up the avenue of the healing that occurs from being loved and accepted for who we are. The Holy Spirit cannot get through, get in, until we stop rejecting the love and help being offered to us. God wills to have mercy on people who, perhaps, we wouldn't consider deserving of mercy because He knows the sadness in their hearts, the reasons those walls were built, and why the acting and lashing out occurs. We don't know the contents of each person's life and cannot ever judge.

A question about fasting, and why do miracles happen afterwards, leads us to the conclusion that fasting, certainly a death or emptying of obstacles, a denial of our senses, will render us more ready, more emptied, more prepared to receive those "miracles."

It is the preparation which our spirits need to receive more of what Jesus wishes to give to us. Identification with Jesus Who fasted in the desert forty days, prepares us to be able to receive. Fasting breaks open the ground of our resistance; food is a comfort thing which energizes and renews our strength. When we are uncomfortable from fasting, being hungry slows us down, gets us in touch with our insides, our feelings of hunger. This helps us identify with the dynamic of being empty through sin, "My soul thirsts for the living God."

Redemptive suffering is the only glory that is ours alone and is kept for us in Heaven. All the other things we do give God glory! In being lifted up, Jesus was glorified. Not until He was lifted up was He recognized. That same thing is happening to us when we suffer and offer it for the redemption of sinners and reparation of sin. We are lifted up and recognized as children of God (or not) by the way we suffer, peacefully (or bitterly).

Yes, Jesus obtained our redemption by dying and rising for us, but we must accept it, process that redemption in our lives, consciously choose the lifestyle that supports living as saved people, redeemed people, children of God. We re-remember Jesus' life with our own! We identify with Jesus and understand His great love for us in the intensity of His sufferings for our sake. We continue, St. Paul tells us, Christ's suffering in our own. "We suffer with Him so that we may also reign with Him" (2 Tm 2:12). And "if only we suffer with Him so that we may also be glorified with Him"(Rom 8:17) and also "For to this you have been called, because Christ also suffered for you, leaving you an example that you should follow in his footsteps." (1 Pt 2:21) The thing to do is learn from His example, how He handled especially the sort of suffering sustained by accepting meekly and humbly ill treatment and being misunderstood by others. 1 Peter goes on to say, "When he (Jesus) was insulted, he returned no insult; when he suffered, he did not threaten, instead, he handed himself over to the one who judges justly." (1 Pt 2:23) Because of the tremendous influence of evil in our lives, especially in our world today, everyone so angry, bitter, critical, unkind, seeking retribution, the power of Satan is greater than ever. Not to strike back, not to retaliate, not to defend ourselves is a huge endeavor and accompanied by great struggle and suffering.

Chapters 3 and 4 in 1Peter talk about suffering and our role in it now. Jesus' sufferings opened the Gates to Paradise and gave us the opportunity once again to enter Heaven. They did not guarantee our salvation. We must do our share to win our own heavenly reward that is available to us now that those gates have been opened!

> **It is a redemptive act begun by Christ but continues throughout history. Like any gift, we must experience His suffering, keep it alive, process it, feel it in our gut, choose it, be the example now for those around it. It gives me that unity, knowledge and understanding of Jesus that only suffering can give. Hope is the fruit of suffering! The will to go on, to overcome, is an expression of man's greatness!**

God is constantly revealing Himself to us, but He is also always revealing us to us. This is who you are, this is what you can take, can do for My sake. We express the degree of love we have for others and for Him by the way we handle pain and adversity.

"Greater love hath no man than to lay down his life for his friend!" God says to us, this is how great you are. Our spirits are strong and beautiful and something to nurture and protect, to be grateful for and proud of. One is healed only by being patterned after Jesus' life. This must happen for everyone before they can attain the salvation for which He died!

Take with you words and return
to the Lord; say to him, "Take away
all iniquity; accept that which is
good and we will render the fruit of
our lips. Assyria shall not save us,
 we will not ride upon horses;
and we will say no more, 'Our God,'
to the work of our hands.
In thee the orphan finds mercy."
I will heal their faithlessness; I will
love them freely, for my anger has
turned from them.

                                   HOSEA 14:2-4

ON LIVING IN THE FATHER'S WILL

We don't have to search too far to discover that the Father's
Will for His people has always been to keep His commandments, to
live the Beatitudes, to accept His mercy and love and forgiveness.
All the gifts He wishes to give us includes Himself! We are invited
through His words in the Old Testament to "Be still and know that
I am God" (Ps.46:10). We are reminded in Psalm 40 that sacrifice
and oblation He wished not, but ears open to obedience. In Leviticus
19:1-2, He says, "You shall be holy because I, the Lord, am holy."
God the Father, Genesis shows us, created the world and then made
us to live in it in dominion over all the animals. But when man
sinned against His command, He cursed woman to give birth in
pain, and man to earn his food by the sweat of his brow.

Over and over again, God called the people of the Old Testament back to Him from where they had wandered so that He could

heal them, forgive their wrong doings and form a new covenant with them, one in which He would be their God and they would be His people. That has never changed. So, He desires that we continually repent of our wrongdoing, seek His forgiveness, and reconcile with Him, living as His children until the end of our lives here on earth. He asks that we would come to Him alone for all our needs, ask all from only the Lord, that we may further comprehend His Will. This is totally foreign to us who live in the very aggressive, independent world of today!!

Everywhere we hear someone say, "Oh, I just wish I knew what God wants of me, what He wants me to do!" When we do this, we are sidestepping the obvious, ignoring the most fundamental facts about our life as Catholic Christians.

If there were only one phrase we could carry with us from Scripture it just might be, "Seek first the Kingdom, and everything else will then be given to us." And then we need to ponder that statement, and what it means for us personally. How can I put God and His Kingdom first, make it the most important dynamic in my everyday living? Besides looking at each thing Jesus said and did during His lifetime, how can I live that way?

Living in the Father's Will simply and definitely means accepting each event that occurs in our lives as the Will of God for us at that moment! Now, often that's hard to believe, much less accept. Most often, we are sure the Lord must have someone else in mind for the scenario He has given us, and we walk away, attempt to escape. We want our own way and not something that interferes with it!!

There is an important parable from Scripture that helps me understand the tension and often huge difference between my will and that of God. I can reread Isaiah 64, vs.7, and be comforted, filled with peace and understanding. "Yet, O Lord, you are our father; we are the clay and you the potter; we are all the work of your hands." And the great story Jeremiah tells us: "He went down to the potter's house and there he was, working at the wheel. Whenever the object of clay which he was making turned out badly in his hand, he tried again, making of the clay another object of whatever sort he pleased. Then the word of the Lord came to Jeremiah: 'Can I not do to you, house of Israel, as this potter has done?' says the Lord. Indeed, like clay in the hand of the potter, so are you in my hand, house of Israel."

This story tells me why the Lord breaks us, remolds us so often; each time adding a little more water of grace, a little more oil of gladness and making us more pliable in His hands. He shapes us into a vessel that more easily receives and holds His Will! Because of Original Sin, the whole great plan for life in the Garden of Eden was altered. We know the whole story; we have the guidelines laid out in the life of Jesus and the letters of the Apostles to the early Church. Yet we try to complicate the simple messages of Jesus by giving in to our own will, our selfishness, self-gratification. We overlook the awesome love for His Father and obedience to His Will that Jesus showed us.

Pope John Paul II in his encyclical *Rich in Mercy* relates that another reason Jesus agreed to suffer and die on the Cross was to show us the pattern of our lives, so that we would recognize and more easily accept what is going on, especially during the difficulties and struggles. The Father loves us more than we could ever imagine, more than we could ever hope to be loved. That's what we are being reformed, transformed, remolded to realize, to accept, to receive. Why must the Father's Will contain so much suffering? Because we are a rebellious, unfaithful, ungrateful people by nature. As a result of Original Sin, our tendency is to live as pride-filled, self-gratifying, self-centered people. We don't remember that His Kingdom is not of this world and we try to build our own Kingdom.

Back to Scripture...the whole story from beginning to end is the story of each human being. We are created, God makes a covenant with us through our baptism; we become slaves to sin; God frees us; we wander in the desert, unfaithful. God renews His covenant with us and promises that we are again His chosen people; Jesus is born into our lives many times through conversion experiences; He then sends His Holy Spirit into our souls, enlightens and gifts us even more. We learn how to live life like Jesus did it, to focus on Him, trust Him, await His return. At the end of each life, Jesus does return and takes us with Him, hopefully, to Heaven. Not the end of the story, but the beginning of a fuller, greater, perfected life in the glorified state of Heaven!

"Greater love has no man than to lay down his life for his friend." That's living in the Father's Will, and we must surrender our will to His, abandon ourselves to His plans for our salvation, come to Him alone for all our needs, give our hearts to Him, thanking and praising Him for all of His gifts, and for his marvelous plans for us for all of Eternity. We don't adapt to this kind of living easily. It doesn't taste or smell or feel or look the way we like things to be!! I personally believe that we will never know the true peace that only Jesus can give until we begin to surrender to the loving Will of Our Heavenly Father. We might look at one more place in Scripture and that's the entire letter to the Ephesians. I invite you to please read it all and then read it again and then again.

And now, Mary, our Mother, reminds us that the best road to follow is to come to her and allow her Immaculate Heart to help us come to know that Will. She reminds us to listen to the still, small voice of the Spirit Who is always whispering in love the direction we should take, the path to follow to the Father. Today in the beautiful air and sunshine, let us close our eyes and see, once again the scene described in Matthew 17, vs. 5. Jesus has just been transfigured. His whole person glows with the radiance of Heaven, and the voice of the Father is heard above Him, "This is My beloved Son with whom I am well pleased; listen to Him." That's all. That's enough!

The days of punishment have come,
The days of recompense have come;
Israel shall know it.
The prophet is a fool, the man of the
Spirit is mad, because of your great
Iniquity and great hatred.
The prophet is the watchman of Ephraim.

HOSEA 9:7-8

CRISIS COUNSELLING FOR
LARGE SCALE DISASTERS

A key element is the afflicted person's deprivation of the ordinary guidance and information which they need to carry on everyday activities. Life is out of joint and anything can happen in the strange void that settles on victims. Thus, guidance will be invaluable. Assume some authority! A disaster threatens self-image and is intertwined with threats to supporting social systems (e.g. life goals) and values or beliefs that govern lives.

Disasters demand responses that are distorted from those of ordinary life. All involved are unable to function effectively. (In this case, the loss will be enormous, everything and everyone.) Clinical shock will have resulted. The survivors will be nearly dead themselves from the severe loss, unable to think or respond clearly. The grief will be numbing; strong tactics will be needed to "reach" them. Repetition will be important. Perhaps a written set of directives.

Time of threat: when the danger of disaster is imminent and inevitable — no longer general or slightly vague — there will possibly be evidence of panic as time approaches and feelings of helplessness grow. This will be the overriding environment of people's psyche (like rape), completely vulnerable and impotent. People will be emotionally overwhelmed.

More signs of shock: lack of emotion, low stimulation level, low activity, docility and the absence of demanding. However, people are still very resilient and can be ready quickly to fully participate in repair and restoration. After victims recover from initial sense that the incident was designed expressly for them and their family, they are able to help others. (It may be possible that many deaths occur and leadership will be so necessary to overcome the inertia of shock and disbelief). People are always capable of heroic feats of strength and endurance. At first the ordinary frame and setting (that is, the environment) has shifted radically and activity will seem random, but it is not!

The morale of people who shared event is high and they are capable of responding to sensible leadership and direction for their activities. (This will be true also in a spiritual sense.) Natural leaders emerge who remain calm, have an instinct of what to do, are able managers of many problems.

Recognize those who have these leadership qualities (instincts [grace!]) and join with them in marshalling. At first, people may need to be led to lead! In the period following, there will be physical complaints. Some will withdraw from reality through fantasies and delusions. There will also be a period for anger, depression, effects of social disintegration. This may happen over and over with some getting "stuck" in a phase.

Because of possible build-up of morale between victims, they may resent outside help. Here we will have people coming to us for help and this may not be an overwhelming feeling. (In some of these paragraphs, comments will be added to deal with the fact of the WARNING accompanying the disasters. People should be in a confused state of mind and need someone to make sense of what just happened from those who are calm and seem to know what all this means.) Help everyone to understand this is a much expected reaction.

If there is a descent of media, it is not to help victims, but to meet a deadline. Anticipation of the problems of managing aggressive news reporters should be an aspect of every disaster plan. (In the case of the "illumination," the evil one will be working quickly to convince all those inclined to listen to him that this was a trick, perhaps the work of aliens and not to be believed as far as the state of the soul is concerned. This could be the message of much of the media... [only a suggestion!])

1. Work to avoid being overwhelmed by the magnitude of this disaster. As the children would say, "get a grip!"
2. Limit range of activity to what we can actually do to help.
3. Gathering information and getting it out is important. Families need to know status of other members. (In case of full national devastation, records will be all the more important for future and reuniting families.)
4. Families split up, and the need to keep them informed will be important to their psychological reactions.
5. Get family members together again as soon as possible. (This may not be possible! Immediate prayer by those in shock will probably not be possible either, since we cannot even pray very well when we are just feeling sick or in pain.)
6. Try to mobilize survivors to help each other.
7. **Alienation and feelings of not belonging anywhere, fragmentation** and abandonment are some outcomes of massive disasters. (These practical approaches will be important because many will not have the understanding of the recent events that we have and will have great fear of God, massive guilt and fear of further events. Many will believe it is the end of the world).
8. Try to rebuild family units as quickly as possible. (Still important to say many Rosaries. Have a prayer team strictly for that purpose, who would be unable to help in more physical ways).
9. Disaster Syndrome, temporary withdrawal and paralysis. Not serious or permanent.
10. Explain exactly what has happened to give them framework/ structure about nature of what they are experiencing.

11. People with psychiatric disturbance should be treated as such by professionals when possible.
12. **No Pollyanna approach filled with mindless reassurances!** Honesty and practical solutions are essential.
13. Assist people to make a realistic appraisal of exactly what has happened.
14. This becomes a basis for their future responses. Not everyone who survives will know about the whole scenario and that this is really good news!
15. Avoid giving false assurances when there is no solid foundation to support these.
16. Only when able to face the possibilities truly, can one draw on inner strength to make the adjustments to live in a world that will never be the same again.
17. Problem area for some is letting themselves be dependent on others, despite crippling disaster.
18. We may need to let some become dependent upon us for some period of time afterwards.
19. Never good sense to let someone become totally dependent, i.e. encourage independence, but allow the time it takes. All people are different. (Again, a good balance of treating shock, practical solutions and explanations and sharing our understanding of this particular disaster as God's Gift to the whole world will be so necessary).
20. There will be a need for someone to monitor the workers and helpers!
21. Do not intrude needlessly. (Or suggest or force prayer too often or too soon).
22. Common sense and confidentiality are the bywords of the day.
23. Do not attempt to get to the bottom of erratic behavior with confrontation (or try to make people feel guilty for not having enough faith, if they remain frightened longer than we think they should!)
24. Expect some transference. This is a functional defense and should not be tampered with.
25. Transference reactions are marked feelings of ambivalence, and a helper polarizes the person for positive or negative, even though the feelings are intended for others (or God!)

26. Emotional involvement is the price paid for not understanding transference reactions. People can become very involved in feelings which in reality have no direct reference to them. A neutral ground is essential. It is the only place we can confidently stand. This also creates an atmosphere of trust. This emotional involvement (or playing God!) can lead to becoming part of the problem and for cruel entanglements in which you might find yourself ensnared. (We will not have all the answers!)

We want to achieve a positive relationship marked with good feelings on the conscious level! Make no effort to disturb or mobilize the feelings that are below the surface. Do not try to ferret out hidden meanings, even though we may be picking up clear messages from the unconscious of the affected individual (or in this case, confessions of guilt or actual sins being brought to their awareness and shared aloud in fear).

We want a safe passage across this depth (of the individual) without trying to plumb it for all the information it contains! Defenses are what allow a person to go on living without dealing with the unconscious reality of their lives. (And now, the Lord has shown each person each reality of their lives, and they are unable to rationalize or deny truth. This alone will throw so many for a loop, as it will be the first time this may ever have been experienced in some lives!!)

The most important and calming effect we can have is our own behavior and the promise of direction to a priest ready to hear hours of confessions from the many, many people afflicted. Promises can be made of the Lord's eagerness to receive them into His arms with unconditional love and forgiveness as soon as each one has confessed and honestly seeks love and forgiveness.

Those who travel anywhere for refuge will already have experienced some passage of time and greater hardship. Our initial reactions will have to do with organizing our own lives and belongings in order to serve those who come without anything or anyone left in their families. Assurances that God, the Father did not wish to destroy, but only to cleanse, will need to be repeated. A constant reminder to seek the love and peace of Jesus and Mary, and believe that each one is forgiven, will be necessary. Our own faith and peace will give credence to all we say. One day at a time will be the survival mode, but also the reminder that we are not ever alone [if we choose to accept Them]. The presence of Jesus and His Mother are ALWAYS with us each moment and will not leave us ever, but we must receive them into our hearts and lives and wish to live only the Father's Will for the rest of time and Eternity.

The addition of preparation for the Second Coming of Jesus can be gradually shared, as we see the information being accepted and absorbed. Again, each person is different. The fact that all of the recent events are a result of God's love for us will take time for some to believe!

Perhaps a list of things to say to people would help "workers" who would not otherwise remember everything that will be helpful to say. Jesus is the most powerful Ally we will have; prayer the most powerful weapon; Mary the most powerful protection; They will be triumphant over evil in the world when the fullness of time is reached, despite immediate appearances in the near future. People will need ongoing support. We make progress and then tend to regress as a matter of process! Daily support and prayer among "workers" will be essential.

The evil one will be working still harder to discourage all, and our own trust will be sorely tried. We will work till we are exhausted and then need to keep going. We will pour out and give of ourselves like we cannot even imagine. We must fight against and encourage and strengthen each other against the tendency to give up, to walk away, to give in. Only prayer will support us during these times. Good humor will be the sign of sincere love!

Each person must understand that all action is prayer when offered up and united with the Hearts of Jesus and Mary, that is, we may not always have time to kneel and pray. All can be lived out for the honor and glory of the Father and the success of His plan of salvation for His children. Everyone knows this, but tends to forget in the "heat of the battle," the exhaustion, the overwhelming numbers. It has always been known by strategists that ya gotta have a plan! And then not to worry. The Holy Spirit is in charge! He truly is!!

NOTE: I came across these in an old green folder in a Retreat House in Illinois. If there is some copyright operating to protect these, it was not mentioned there. If I am remiss in obtaining permission from whoever presented the information in the first place, I am sorry for not doing so and will do whatever you desire.

Bands of Love

REFLECTION

If we are hearing clearly and believing, then we know that time is indeed running out for this age in which we live and the world is about to be cleansed and all the people in it, purified through trials and tribulations.

In order that we may be most properly prepared in peace and security, without fear or anxiety, Jesus has sent us the Perfect Mother who prays for and calls to her children that it is time to come in now: out of the darkness, out of the cold, and enjoy nourishment and safety at her side. This is nothing new. This is what a mother does for her child. This is what Our Blessed Mother seeks to do for us, and to lead us to Her Son, so that Both, in turn, can lead us to the Father, the Source of all goodness.

Quoting words of Jesus she has reminded us: "Seek the Kingdom of God, and all else will be given to you." These words were given with the request that her little ones ponder them anew. We are her little ones!

Speaking about the value of patterning ourselves on her littleness, her humility, she said:

"...Be little and humble, as I was little and hidden in the tiny village of Nazareth. It was there I taught My Jesus the things He needed to learn, as He became a Man and prepared to do the Father's Will. It was there that I spent hours in silent communion with the Holy Spirit, listening to the words I would share with Our Beloved Son. It was then that I learned what was meant for the future of My Son and what was in store for Him. I explained the value of suffering and true obedience to My Jesus.

"Obedience is what is needed for each step of the way if you are to allow Us to guide you. Never look back to the life behind you. Never allow anything or anyone to hamper you in your response to God's Will.

"Remain in constant communion with Me, wrapped in My Mantle and listening to My words. Come to Me often in prayer. Seek Me every moment of your day, but especially in the quiet times. Seek My will and the Will of the Father. Pray more and offer sacrifices to My Jesus.

"Please, warn My dear ones of the shortness of time, the little time that is left to repent and convert. The Sacrament of Reconciliation is the place to begin. There is so much healing offered to My dear children through this Sacrament. Pray that My dear ones return to this Sacrament soon and often!

"A new day will dawn for all to see who will turn and be faithful to My Son. Be assured that all are always forgiven when they seek forgiveness. Tell them how quickly they must return to their Father's house, lest they die of wretchedness and hunger."

"And finally, we will be called upon to defend Mary, the Mother of God, and all of Her words to us. We will be called to support our personal convictions with action, fidelity and perseverance. Her only action upon the earth is to get our attention, call us to Herself so that She might lead us to Her Son and they both, in turn, will lead us to the Father Who waits in joyful hope Himself for the day when He can welcome us into Paradise and shower us with all of the gifts stored for us in the Godhead since the beginning of time! A promise to be listened to, a reason to give thanks and rejoice.

He is the image of the invisible God,
the firstborn of all creation.
For in Him were created all things in
Heaven and on earth, the visible and
invisible, whether thrones or dominions
or principalities or powers; all things
were created through Him and for Him.
He is before all things, and in him all
things hold together.
He is the beginning, the firstborn from
the dead, that in all things he himself
might be preeminent.

Colossians 1:15-18

ON THE EUCHARIST

Let us give praise and thanks to God Our loving, merciful Father for the gift of His Son in the Sacrament of the Eucharist.

Let us reflect on the Son and give thanks and praise to Him Who stays hidden by reason of His deep humility in this Blessed Sacrament so that we may dare to approach Him and give him our love and adoration.

We begin to beg the Holy Spirit for the gift of openness to a greater appreciation of this divine gift, this sacrament which, unlike the other six that communicate the grace of Christ, is Christ Himself!

We listen together to the words of St. Peter Julian Eymard, the Saint of the Eucharist, whose reflections on Jesus in the Blessed

Sacrament of the Altar are without equal in Church History. We hear the importance of the Eucharistic Lord in the lives of many saints and learned persons. And finally, we offer a prayer of love and thanksgiving to Jesus, Our Savior, for choosing to remain with us to nourish and strengthen us throughout our life journey back to Him in Heaven.

Traditionally, the Church views the mystery of the Eucharist from three approaches: First, it is the perfect worship of the Father through the Spirit in Christ, the unbloody representation of Jesus' true Body and Blood which we receive as spiritual food under the sign of bread and wine, the Real Presence of Jesus and all of Who He is and ever was in Heaven and on earth. Third, it is the Lord's Real Presence maintained in the tabernacle for later distribution to the sick and for personal prayer or adoration.

The Eucharist is central to the life of the Church (and we are the Church!) Even several years ago it was not necessary to say this to people. We know that, but now there are many people, even priests saying the Mass is not about God, it's about people! The Mass is not for God, it's for people! And others are saying that Jesus is not truly present in the consecrated bread and wine: A horrific development for the God Who made us, Who lived and died and rose from the dead for us and Who has stayed with us that we will not be without His Presence always, till the end of time. A tragic commentary on our times and those who hope to usurp the power and centrality of God in our lives and in the world. A tragic development for those faithful believers in all that Jesus taught us, in all the words of Scripture, in all the promises of God.

The fundamental elements of the Eucharist are bread and wine plus the narrative words from Jesus' Last Supper with his disciples, now pronounced by the priest, "This is My Body, This is My Blood."

Receiving the Body of the Lord under the appearances of bread or wine is a sign of full membership in the Church and implies personal acceptance of all the Church's teachings. Notice, we did not say the action of the consecration by a priest at Mass was only a symbol of the Body and Blood of Jesus, but that the bread or wine is a symbol of the Body of Jesus truly present under the appearances of bread and wine. This act of receiving is called Communion. Ordinarily, therefore, only Roman Catholics in good standing (that is, in the state of grace) may receive Communion. Conversely, Catholics may not ordinarily receive Communion at services in other churches of different traditions.

Much of the above material was taken from the book, *What it Means to be a Catholic* by Father Joseph M. Champlin.

Eucharist is a gift of the merciful love of God, the gift of Divine Mercy which is Jesus Christ truly present in the Sacrament of the Altar, His Most Blessed Sacrament.

Let us remember when we receive the Sacred Host that Christ is Alive.

Christ is not alone. The Trinity is present there united with Him.

Christ is totally present in the Eucharist without ever leaving Heaven.

We know this because He told us that He and the Father are one.

There is only one Mass, and Christ is celebrating it, and it is going on all the time in the Eternal Now! Our celebrant invites us, joins us to the heavenly sacrifice that Jesus is celebrating all the time, out of time into Eternity.

This is not just one miracle. The Eucharist contains all supernatural realities; it is a variety of miracles. It contains all of Who Jesus ever was and all He ever did and still is and does. In other words, we receive the newborn Babe, the Toddler at the knee of Mary, the Boy in the temple listening and teaching with the wise elders; the carpenter's Son working at Joseph's side; the Teacher, Miracle Worker, Healer; Jesus' Passion and Death, Resurrection and Ascension into Heaven. We receive all of Jesus and everything He ever did!

We can breath in the essence of Jesus as our bodies and souls absorb His true Presence. We can love Him as totally as we are able in the most intimate unity received into our bodies and souls. We can thank Him and talk to Him most present in ourselves at this time and tell Him how eagerly we have awaited this moment.

We don't just receive Communion, we enter into communion, a deeper union with Christ. He is able to enter more fully into our lives when we are properly disposed toward receiving Him. There is no limit to the number of times we can receive Christ. The value of a spiritual communion is that it can be repeated many times throughout the day. This can be more efficacious than sacramental communion when our attitude, our longing, our entering in to Christ is greater than it might have been when we received sacramentally!

ENVISION AND INVITE JESUS ALL DAY LONG!

The guest, Jesus, becomes the Host of the Emmaus story, in our hearts, of our person. When we receive Him, we too are received. When I drink the chalice, It drinks me. When I consume Him, He consumes me. I am received into Eternal Life which begins now, into the life of the Trinity to whatever degree I have entered into the Eucharist, into a new way of living the way God lives.

With Eucharist, we become what we eat! The purpose of this transformation is called divinization. Eucharist is full unity with all people, especially the poor, and enhances the truth that in the Body of Christ, we are all one. We are in Eternity to the extent that we receive Christ...in other words, to the extent that I am prepared, open to His presence, truly recognize and appreciate the Presence of the living Jesus and my unity with Him, I am entering into Eternity with this act of communion.

We are united to the entire Body of Christ on earth and in Purgatory when we receive Jesus in the Eucharist. Our transformation into living Eucharist is always through Mary and we can better prepare for this unity by consecrating ourselves often to Mary. We are united to all in Heaven who are united to Christ and are closest to our loved ones in Heaven at the moment we receive Him because Christ is united to all who are in Heaven.

We are receiving Mercy Itself, Himself, because Mercy is the Heart of the Eucharist. All of the graces and nourishment we need are given at the moment of communion with the Eucharistic Lord. We do not understand or truly appreciate the enormity of the miracle and gifts that are given in this great sacrament and must meditate and ask Jesus to send His Spirit into us with a greater knowledge of all that He is and wishes to be for us.

What awesome mysteries take place during Mass! One day we will know what God is doing for us in each Mass, and what sort of gift He is preparing in it for us. Saints and holy people can be heard from in the new book, *My Daily Eucharist* by Joan Carter McHugh.

Cardinal Edouard Gagnon, spoke in 1993 and made an appeal for greater devotion to the Real Presence as a means of keeping the family together. He pointed out that Pope John Paul II is fostering belief in the Real Presence of Christ in the Eucharist to "save the family." The Cardinal said, "Christ is in the Eucharist, in the Mass, in our churches, and we have to put the Eucharistic Christ back into our lives. It is the first thing parents should tell their children. It is never too soon to teach your children about the Eucharist. I say it is a duty to tell your child. Their whole life and their eternal life depends on Christ.

"We have forgotten that the Catholic Church was recognized everywhere for the Presence of God in the Person of Christ in the Tabernacle. We should all work to reopen our churches. If the churches are open, the people will come."

On June 16, 1675, our Lord appeared to St. Margaret Mary Alaquoque and requested:

"I ask you that the first Friday after the octave of Corpus Christ be consecrated to a special feast in honor of My heart. Receive Communion on that day, and offer it in reparation to my divine heart; make amends to me for all the indignities which I suffered while I was exposed on the altar. I promise you that my heart will pour itself out in abundant graces of divine love on those who thus celebrate this feast, and who by their words and example will cause it to be celebrated by others."

There is a great story about St. Anthony of Padua who lived from 1195-1231. He was speaking before a large crowd on the truths of faith when he was challenge by a Jewish person who denied the truth of the Eucharist, asking him to prove the truth of his words. The Saint accepted and three days later was saying Mass when the Jew brought a donkey in that had been denied food and water during that time. At Communion, St. Anthony took the Sacred Host to the donkey and said, "In the name of Jesus Christ Whom I, though unworthy, hold in my hands, I command you to come forth and do reverence to your Creator, that you may confound these heretics."

The Jewish man now threw a handful of hay and oats to the hungry animal; but at a sign from Anthony it left them untouched, approached him, bent its knee before him, and bowed its head as a mark of veneration. The man, as well as others, was converted, and a chapel stands today on the spot in memory of the event.

It is good to nourish our appreciation of the great love and devotion of Saints and the phenomenal lengths to which Our Savior will go in order to prove His presence to us in the Sacred Host.

Jesus told St. Matilda, "At the moment of Consecration, I come down first in such deep humility that there is no one at Mass, no matter how despicable and vile he may be, towards whom I do not humbly incline and approach, if he desires Me to do so and prays for it; Secondly, I come down with such great patience that I suffer even My greatest enemies to be present and grant them the full pardon of all their sins, if they wish to be reconciled with Me; Thirdly, I come with such immense love that no one of those present can be so hardened that I do not soften his heart and enkindle it with My love, if he wishes Me to do so; Fourthly, I come with such inconceivable liberality that none of those present can be so poor that I would not enrich him abundantly; Fifthly, I come with such sweet food that no one ever so hungry should not be refreshed and fully satiated by Me; Sixthly, I come with such great light and splendor that no heart, however blinded it may be, will not be enlightened and purified by My presence; Seventhly, I come with such great sanctity and treasures of grace that no one, however inert and indevout he may be, should not be roused from this state."

Finally, we look at St. Peter Julian Emyard who lived 1811 - 1868. He devoted his whole life to Eucharistic prayer, concern for the poor and preaching on the Eucharist. There are nine books which comprise the Eymard Library which are recognized as classics of Eucharistic piety.

As Blessed Faustina is the magnifier of the Merciful Heart of Jesus, Peter Julian Eymard is the magnifier of His Eucharistic Heart.

The Saint advises: "Speak to Jesus of His Blessed Mother whom He loved so much, and you will make Him experience anew the happiness of a good son! Speak to Him of His saints in order to glorify His grace in them. The real secret of love is, therefore, to forget oneself like St. John Baptist in order to exalt and glorify the Lord Jesus. True love looks not at what it gives, but at what its Beloved deserves. Then, you will listen to Him in silence; or rather in love's most gentle and powerful action, you will become one with Him!

"We must keep in mind that Jesus, present in the Eucharist, glorifies and continues therein all the mysteries and virtues of His mortal life. We must keep in mind that the Holy Eucharist is Jesus Christ past, present and future; that the Eucharist is the last development of the Incarnation and mortal life of our Savior; that in the Eucharist, Jesus Christ gives us every grace; that all truths tend to and end in the Eucharist; and that there is nothing more to be added when we have said, 'The Eucharist,' since it is Jesus Christ!"

"Happy is the Soul that knows how to find Jesus in the Eucharist, and in the Eucharist all things."

There is not time to continue with all the gems of spiritual truths found in Peter Julian Eymard's writings. Please consider obtaining the Eymard Library from Blessed Sacrament Fathers & Brothers, 5384 Wilson Mills Rd., Cleveland, Ohio 44143. Another book contains ten Holy Hours based on Eucharistic devotions, words of Pope John Paul II, Mother Teresa, many bishops, Scripture, fifteen decades of the Rosary with Eucharistic meditations and all the rich reflections of St. Peter J. Eymard. It is called *Come to Me* and I hope many of you are very familiar with it. Perhaps you would be inspired to read all of the Gospel of John, as well as the letters 1 & 2 John; 2 Cor. 9 and remember a quote from 2 Cor. 4:18

I will be as the dew to Israel; he shall
Blossom as the lily, he shall strike root
As the poplar, his shoots shall spread out;
His beauty shall be like the olive,
And his fragrance like Lebanon.
They shall return and dwell beneath
My shadow, they shall flourish as a garden;
They shall blossom as the vine,
Their fragrance shall be like the wine of Lebanon

Hosea 14: 5-8

ELEMENTS FOR LIVING IN COMMUNITIES IN MERCY, TRUST, LOVE AND FORGIVENESS: THE HOW-TO OF LIVING IN TRUST AND CONFIDENCE IN THE MERCY OF JESUS AND MARY BY DYING TO SELF.

There is to be a new awakening, a new dawning, a new realization of what and how people are to be living their lives, now and through the events unfolding shortly: proper preparation for all to be able to cope, to overcome, to understand and to accept events about to occur.

Living in community will mean to live in Divine Mercy and the Divine Will of God, Our Father: to be mercy and surrender to all the Father decrees for the earth. There will soon be a time when we are called to respond to requests to extend our physical and spiritual selves beyond what we now know our limitations to be.

Before souls realize how they appear in the eyes of God, it would be well to know ourselves better, to know Jesus and Mary much better, and to realize that fear is a devastating tool which the evil one uses in all hearts.

People must overcome the fear that most hearts now have, which comes from not enough prayer; not believing that Mary, our Mother, is always in each heart, that She and Jesus will NEVER ABANDON those who willingly surrender themselves, those who abandon themselves totally to Jesus through Mary in a personal offering of consecration and service.

We realize that all who are children of Jesus and Mary are to be consecrated to Jesus through Mary, to the Sacred and Merciful Hearts; to unite totally in trust and confidence in the mercy of Jesus and Mary.

Those who can put the needs of others first will also be open: To realize that Jesus and Mary are here to protect and help their people, to show us how to become true children of the Father, to become holy and one with them, so all can become Saints.

To realize that the anger of the evil one will never cease and that he rages to take as many souls as possible down into his eternal abyss of doom; that the times must be lived in love for everyone: living out the hope, the mercy we have been shown.

To realize that there is no time to do anything other than what Jesus and Mary request; to show and promote God's mercy united to Their Hearts and with Blessed Faustina's help.

To realize that those who are Mary's soldiers and live in new communities will be filled with Jesus' presence, as He and Mary will walk among those chosen to help prepare others in what is to come.

To call on the Angels for assistance when the need arises because it will!

To realize the importance of praying with Mary, uniting with Mary through a sincere and willing giving of ourselves to Mary through St. Louis De Montfort's Consecration.

To realize how Jesus' Divine Mercy will work in our lives and how, from now on, all are to live mercy, which is love and trust in God, Our Savior and His Mother. To come to an immediate understanding of His Divine Will, the ultimate goal for every soul, as there is no time left to ride the fence and postpone holy decisions.

To realize that the Blessed Mother and her Spouse, the Holy Spirit, will guide our endeavors to gather many more souls into

His fold, into the folds of their Hearts and under the protection of her Mantle.

When we consider living in trust and confidence in the mercy and protection of Jesus and Mary (and the surrender that this will require), we reflect upon particular teachings given to us by Them. We must plan and expect to:

Spend much more time with Jesus in His Blessed Sacrament, giving to Him the first fruits of our energy, our time, our talents: to be still and know that He is God!

To listen as He molds us into instruments of mercy, of peace, of forgiveness and of love.

To pour out all the hurts gathered within our hearts and abandon ourselves to our Divine Physician more completely, so that He can work His Will in us.

To spend all the time possible with our Beloved Doctor Who longs to bind our wounds with His Love.

To come to Him daily, consecrating ourselves to His Eucharistic Heart, and waiting for His healing peace.

To know the love Mary and Jesus share. To realize that Their Hearts are One! To welcome each other in Jesus' Name and show each one His love in our hearts. There will be many people numb with shock and grief who will need someone to tenderly, gently, patiently minister to them. We begin now by practicing this behavior on each other!

To seek to lead others (through prayer, example: word, deed and attitude and suggestion) to Jesus and explain the Father's great love for all His children.

To understand and share with others that the Father is waiting to bring all of our loved ones into Paradise. Each must pray and change in order that all may one day be together in His Kingdom for Eternity.

To realize that some people will be martyrs; that each must suffer according to his/her deeds and be purified, so that all may have a chance to enter through the Gates of Heaven. On earth, we will be praying for our loved ones, encouraging all to turn back to Jesus, preparing for His Coming.

To continue to seek Jesus and His love as a healing balm for the soul and strength for the time to come. To know that this love is a precious gift meant for all who seek it (the only gift we will ever need), that Mary will help us find this love if only we ask her. To live as strong, courageous people who are willing to help all who come to us and encourage them to move quickly, as there will not be a great deal of time left in which to repent.

To pray for people constantly that they will have the opportunities they need to confess their many sins and return to Jesus. To lead them to the priests for Reconciliation, the place to begin all conversion.

To believe in the love of Jesus and Mary for us; convince others that this love is real, that They are longing for all to come to Them in prayer, that the Blessed Sacrament is where Jesus will heal all our hurts and broken hearts.

To live with the understanding that all time is short with little time left to repent and convert; that there is so much healing offered through the Sacrament of Reconciliation.

To encourage all to allow our faith to be nurtured and our fears to be calmed; to return to the rightful path towards our inheritance. To believe that a new day will dawn for all to see, who will turn and be faithful to Jesus.

To assure all that we are always forgiven when we seek forgiveness, and must return to our Father's house, lest we die of wretchedness and hunger. There will be no time to waste on frivolity!

To realize that the people who come to us for help and direction will be like sheep without a master and must return quickly to the one fold and one Shepherd. We will lead them, support and pray for them.

To pray for the souls of the many who will be going into Eternity and be purified in the fires of Purgatory. To realize that the times are most serious and call for unity among all Mary's children on earth in order to offer one prayer of petition to the Father.

To continue to comfort the Heart of Jesus, devastated at the conditions in the world. To understand that it is now necessary for the Father to rid the world of all that does not reflect the goodness and presence of God.

To continually praise God for all our accomplishments and realize how short is the time left to repent and turn to our God and Creator, as there may be destruction on the earth that is indescribable.

To WAIT WITH PATIENCE for each event to unfold that will fulfill all of the prophets and that which Sacred Scripture has foretold.

To always trust in Jesus' Word and Presence in our hearts.

To be prepared to give ourselves totally and give our total selves: a giving which encompasses our whole being, which absorbs us completely and takes over our lives (like that of the Father when He gave us life, and again when He sent His only Son to save us), a total pouring out of self and of everything we hold dear in order to save the lives of those in need.

Never to cease praying and offering His people to Jesus; to persevere to the end and never give up on them; to plead their cause until the last possible moment with the last ounce of breath. To pour ourselves out for others as Jesus has poured Himself out for us!

To allow ourselves to be filled with the peace and power of Jesus after we are emptied of our sinful ways and harmful resentments; to allow Him to soothe and heal us forever. To understand that this will be a process and take time to occur and, of course, time is running out!

To understand that time spent in quiet will develop our inner quiet and a silence of spirit; that the Presence of Jesus will change us, strengthen us and keep us close to Mary and Jesus with the help of the Holy Spirit.

To avoid all that would disturb our spirit for our own sakes. To be emptied of all that holds us bound, and dwell with Jesus in His Sacred Heart ... because Satan attacks relentlessly. He wishes to defeat Mary and destroy the souls of all those who love her.

To pray fiercely to combat attacks of hatred.

To complete our arduous journey (in surrender) by allowing Jesus and Mary to lead and guide us, totally!

To continue to pray for Mary's intentions and call upon the Angels and Saints at any time. To believe that they are praying for us constantly and will help in our time of need.

To remember that the most important duty is that of prayer and living in the Presence of our God. With this awareness, a new peace will descend upon us and we will go from task to task with ease, making of each one a prayer to offer to the Father.

To be assured of the protection of the Triune God and our dearest Mother and allow this to calm our fears (which can only cause further anxious thoughts to develop).

To understand that one is happy whose trust is in the Lord and whose journey is tied to the pattern of His life.

To persevere in the love of Jesus because there will be great temptations and power to attract the chosen ones away from Him. We will see how strong we really are and how His love will protect and sustain us.

To always be of good cheer!

To stop and give thanks to the Father for each task (and all that He allows us to do for Him), after we have finished it and before going on to the next one.

To realize that gratitude is a necessary ingredient on our way to holiness.

To appreciate God's gifts will help us realize more and more what a PRIVILEGE it is to be allowed to serve God and His people.

To become aware of the different gifts the Father has given to us and how He is now allowing us to use them. To realize that all of the things we do are a result of God's gifts to us: all that we have has been given us by God and without His presence at every moment, we would have nothing and be nothing!

To live and act with constant praise (with every breath) to the Father for these gifts; to seek to please Him in all we do; to remain hidden with Mary and to learn quickly that to love is all!

To rally people around Jesus and Mary with words of gentle authority and loving force; to assure them of Their love and continued Presence with them; to bring them to Jesus and assure them of safety and protection and the promise of salvation in His Name.

To seek rest in the Sacred Heart when we are weary.

To seek comfort in His arms when we are lonely.

To take courage (when we feel empty) and be filled by the Presence of Jesus in the Blessed Sacrament.

To come to Mary and Jesus when all looks bleak and overwhelming and allow them to refresh us. To refuse to allow the evil one to distract us.

To appreciate that times of silence and quiet are precious moments meant to cherish and strengthen us for the days to come. To be vigilant and pray continuously for the salvation of all souls that will perish, that more will turn to Mary and be saved as she leads us to her Son and His Sacred Heart.

To realize the difficulty of the times and the struggles of each person for their own purification and to live with patience and understanding, unconditional love and forgiveness for all. To allow their mindset to be ours, as we listen and pray with them.

To dwell on the time when God will save His people from the power of the evil one who will then no longer torment us. No longer will we weep and mourn, for peace and prosperity will fill the land and we will belong to the Father forever!

In prayer, to bring to Mary the millions who will remain on earth to suffer in their grief and, together, take them to Jesus to be healed and cleansed, that they might seek God and the great care and tenderness that awaits all who seek Him.

To realize that the sickness of our day is a result of a lack of God in lives given over to earthly pleasures, without the love of God to sustain the health of mind and soul.

To believe that everything that happens has a purpose that is most often to build our faith, trust and obedience.

To understand that, although waiting is difficult, it is good for the soul and purifies the heart!

To remember that we must be white as snow and pure as a lily in order to enter Heaven. Each of the trials we meet with resignation and trust will prepare us that much more for the glory which awaits us in Eternity.

To persevere and have faith and know that we are not alone, that Jesus hears every single word we say and think. He knows everything and will stand by our side until evil is conquered in the world. (It will be most helpful) to remember that there will be a time when the world and all of Heaven will explode with the joy of victory and the Triumph of the Sacred and Immaculate Hearts!!

To live in complete unity with each other with the understanding that we cannot completely serve them or truly love Jesus and Mary if we are still at odds with a brother or sister.

To fight evil with the weapons of prayer and penance and fasting.

To believe that much can be accomplished by obeying the directives of Mary and Her Son; much can be accomplished by listening with our hearts.

To redouble our prayers for the salvation of our loved ones and the world, and know that Mary is with us, praying constantly for these intentions.

*To understand that we are invited to eagerly await the Second Coming of Jesus, that this event will be great, that the salvation of those who trust in Him shall be fulfilled, that we are blessed as we do this.

To FOCUS ON JESUS and be comforted by the love He has for us!

To be consoled by the fact that Jesus doesn't care what we have done. He just wants us to come back to Him and repent and renew our lives.

To dwell in peace and trust, knowing there is nothing to fear for those who fear the Lord, their Mighty God.

To praise the God and Father of us all and continuously give Him thanks for His great gift of mercy which has been extended so many times now.

To say as many prayers as possible before leaving in the morning for Mass, or whatever begins our day, in order to prepare ourselves to be open and listening for the voices of Mary and Jesus.

To feed ourselves and all God's people with Jesus, the Source of all Life. To shelter them in His arms and hide them in His Mother's Mantle. To lead them to the Father through the hearts of Jesus and Mary.

To remember that in the future not a building will be left standing. After a period of darkness, the earth will quake and all that is not of Jesus will perish except for a few who will be allowed to remain by the Will of the Father. Jesus will return and defeat the Antichrist and all the cohorts of Satan. They will be chained in the bowels of Hell and Jesus will live and reign among us in the beauty of the world as the Father intended it to be.

All who live will see the saving power of God. All who dwell on this earth will see His coming in glory on that great day. Happy will they be who remain faithful to Him during this time of purification.

To allow our hearts to fill and expand which will, in turn, increase our capacity to love more and hold more people in our hearts. In this way, our hearts will soon encompass the world. In this way, we will become more and more like Jesus and the love He has for us.

To begin each day asking Jesus for a greater capacity to love, to heal, to reach out and touch the hearts of all.

To live with rejoicing, for the kingdom is at hand!

To beg God to cleanse the soil, renew the air, return the waters of grace to their proper channels and build up the Body of Christ, the Lifeline to the Father.

To be serious about requests for prayer and fasting, and know that what counts is a matter of living in the moment with our God and being united to Him in prayer: one in mind and body, one in heart and soul, one in the holiness of God, one in the neediness of man.

To pray for trust, since that is most needed by all people who will remain faithful. Trust is the heart of (and 'triggers) God's mercy.

To realize that only constant prayer in union with Mary and Jesus will prepare us to continue to respond in obedience.

To understand that suffering is the vehicle by which the people of God become human (hard hearts are broken which, in turn, causes us to stop and reflect in ways we never would otherwise); that pain breaks down defenses and postures, affected strengths and rationalizations.

To realize that the Father, the Heavenly Potter, takes us, the earthly clay, and breaks and re-forms us many times until we finally are emptied of our sin and resistance to Him, until we most nearly resemble the vessel we were created to be, which will hold His Will and sweetness, mercy and love to be poured out upon all we will meet.

To believe that the more we trust in the promises of Christ, the more He will be able to implement them in our lives.

To be concerned only with serving Mary and Jesus and the many people who come needing our help and seeking assistance.

To pray to the Holy Spirit Who will be opening the hearts of many people and allowing them to come back to Jesus, and offer each one to Him and pray for them.

To allow time to "recover" (process of conversion) through the days and nights we attempt to live a new life of prayer, penance, fasting and service. We continue to be aware of Their Presence, as Mary and Jesus pray and work with us.

To believe that strength and energy will be available to us when the times demand it. To trust that we will be renewed when we call out for help.

To offer all our graces to Mary so that she may dispense them most efficiently to those in need.

To realize that nothing we do goes to waste, that all of our prayers are heard, accompanied and given great power by the prayers of Jesus and Mary.

To realize that we need never feel alone or lonely, as Jesus is waiting for us to run to Him (Who always awaits our company and our love). He is always with us and we have only to pause and notice His Presence! This is truly living in the Divine Mercy of God.

To give ourselves entirely to Jesus now in words and deeds; to reserve ourselves for His needs and directives; to obey Him and sit quietly in anticipation for His desires.

To resist the attempt to figure anything out, as this will only waste valuable time. To be in a mode of readiness now for instant response to Jesus' call and that of His Mother.

To listen intently, to be directed by our Savior and follow His commands.

To be attentive to the needs of our loved ones and companions.

To be compassionate and willing to do the Will of God.

To be eager to serve people.

To be patient and obedient, willing to lay down our lives for our duties.

To execute our Commander's (Jesus') orders without question.

To be faithful, honest and true.

To follow our Leader into battle, never running ahead or acting without His permission, displaying courage and valor in combat. To resist attacks on our person in silence.

To do nothing to interfere with the battle plan, living with discipline and never challenging our Superior.

To do what is best for others without considering personal gain or loss.

To love and care for the people assigned to our care, never betraying their trust in us.

To live with loyalty to our Superior, even if this means dying for His cause.

To give ourselves entirely over to the needs and destiny of our Leader. To remain true to the cause of our Leader, in spite of coercion or even torture.

To persevere, not doubting for a moment that the strength will be in us, the path will be clear, the way will be opened to us by Jesus and Mary.

To realize that whatever happens is the work of the evil one who has driven the world to the brink of destruction and that this will result in the justice of the Father cleansing and purifying it of all that is not of Jesus.

To realize that Jesus is about to return and reclaim His rightful inheritance as King and Heir of the Father, that we will then see things as they were meant to always be in the Father's great plan for His people.

To pray that the world will come to know its Savior, to recognize its God. To pray that many more will hear the call of their Lord and His Mother before it is too late.

To build our battlements on a solid foundation and believe that all will be well, that there is nothing to fear for those who trust in Jesus.

To abandon all of who we are and receive all of Who Jesus Is.

To take His gifts and use them for His people and each other.

To be a light of mercy and instruction and peace and love to the darkness descending even now upon the minds and hearts of mankind.

To call to all the lost souls in the Name of Jesus and acquaint them with His love and His promises of salvation, mercy and forgiveness.

To call people back to reason and a sense of truth and security.

To defend Mary and the Presence of Jesus in the Eucharist with words of love and logic, with thoughts of His promises, recalling all He has done for us, how He is a God Who keeps His promises to lead His children out of the desert and into the Promised Land.

To lend our faith and strength and courage to all who call for it.

To surrender to Jesus and His needs for us.

To say "yes" each day and be open to His demands on us.

To listen to His Heart and the words which issue from it.

To realize that all are being given a chance to enter through the Gates of Heaven. Those left on earth, after certain events, can pray for their loved ones. They can turn back to Jesus and prepare for His Coming.

To prepare as though the end is near and understand it is not the end of the world, but the end of things in the world as we have come to know and experience them. It is the end of an era and beginning of a new way of living and experiencing Jesus (here with us in Person).

To allow our faith to be nurtured and our fears calmed, and pray that all will return to the rightful path towards their inheritance.

To have mercy on ourselves and go to Jesus to be emptied of all that troubles and wars against us (our sins and weaknesses), in order to be filled with His sweetness, His strength and courage, His Wisdom.

To know nothing is as important as:

1. the salvation of the whole world,
2. our preparation for the Second Coming of Jesus
3. the battle in preparation for that great day,
4. living in mercy as a means of attaining these goals.
5. being obedient to every request of Jesus and Mary.

To prepare to fight evil and defend truth, justice and the rights of God's people even to our death, knowing we would come quickly to Heaven to be with Jesus forever.

To study and hold in our hearts the words of Jesus, the Word in Scripture, in the traditional teachings of the Catholic Church and all the words of Mary and Jesus given in our times. To allow ourselves to share our faith and trust and hope in an attempt to return others to their rightful place as heirs of Heaven.

To live and pray and work with the belief that Truth will work miracles in the lives and hearts of the poor, weak, lost lonely children whom our God is calling back to Himself through so many events in the world.

That we all may live as one, we reflect upon practical elements of a new community of believers.

This will be a time of redemptive prayer and suffering for all of us, for all of our brothers and sisters in Our Lord and His holy

Mother. We will be looking forward to the day Jesus returns. The remnant will be gathered up to meet Him and we will live triumphantly together forever.

WE PRACTICE TENDERNESS AND THOUGHTFULNESS, allowing the words we speak to all to reflect the love and concern, tenderness and peace of Jesus and Mary. Soft spoken in our journey back to the Father, we will attempt constantly to live in His Will for us, becoming more introspective and quiet.

Continuing to have mercy on ourselves, we offer all of our fears and doubts about ourselves to Jesus in the Blessed Sacrament. As we are emptied of these feelings, we know we can be filled in a greater capacity with trust in Him and His care for us at every step.

Many have not remained completely faithful to the purity of their first response, but we must strive to be faithful to all that is being requested of us at this time by Jesus and our holy Mother. "A clean heart create for me, oh God; renew in me a steadfast spirit." (Psalm 51)

We practice silence and humility (the only way for us to be completely prepared for what lies ahead), all the while praying for sincerity and joy, knowing that the ability to change is only a matter of openness to the gifts Jesus and His Mother wish to give to all.

We will not need to defend ourselves to others, as we know that all we do is an attempt to honestly respond to the commandments of our God: living the Beatitudes, accepting and being His mercy.

We prepare to be emptied more each day and filled with grace and peace and strength. We attempt to shine with love and fire for the cause of justice and truth. THE SALVATION OF THE ENTIRE WORLD IS IN THE HANDS OF THOSE WHO PRAY.

We pray to be united to Jesus and Mary at every moment, listening and obeying their commands and directions, constantly giving praise and thanks to the Father as a community, a team, a fighting unit being prepared and honed into instruments of truth.

Aware of the terrible events in the world, we pray constantly for mercy on those who are suffering now, that they may be urged to respond to God's call to them. It will not be easy to look beyond the feelings and attitudes of others, but we must learn this important lesson and practice unconditional love and gentleness, knowing that it is only love which can melt the hardness of people's hearts and touch people's hearts with Their love.

We live with the understanding that Jesus will be victorious over the forces of evil at the last possible moment. Satan will be crushed and hurled into the burning pit. We can always call upon the Angels to assist us and upon Jesus and Mary to accompany us at each moment.

We realize that each trial is a treasure being stored in Heaven for our return and we persist in love and truth, that more graces will be available to those who heed the call to return immediately to the House of God and raise their hands and hearts in supplication for sins.

We will trust in the Spirit and remember that Jesus, Mary and all of Heaven are always with us, praying for us and facilitating each word, each action lived in obedience and surrender on behalf of our brothers and sisters and the honor and glory of the Father.

We will live humbly, sharing with all the gratitude we will always feel at being accepted immediately into the fold and how Jesus went out of His way to bring us back. We attempt to allow graces to flow through us to each one we see. It will be a time to shine with love and conviction!

The prayers we offer on behalf of all people will help them to listen and begin to live more fully what is being asked of each of all of us, believing also that our cooperation brings comfort and solace to the heart of Mary, our Mother, filling her with hope and joy for the times to come.

We will strive to live a better balance between rest and renewal, preparedness and alertness, seeking more of Mary's help in order to maintain a proper pace. The more we pray for each other, the more we will be healed ourselves!

In the quiet of doing nothing, strength is built up. In the quiet of listening, obedience is developed. In the quiet of just being, love will flood our hearts because we have the chance to love each other (you and Jesus) and be further united.

It will be so important that we know Jesus will always be with us, even after all vestiges of His Presence are removed by the enemies of His Church; that He has not left us alone, even though we do not see the Blessed Sacrament nor have the Sacrifice of the Mass celebrated for a certain period of time. We will spend this time building and practicing faith in all Jesus' words to us and the promises that will be fulfilled upon His return.

We will dwell upon the goodness of God and how He longs to hold all His people in a warm embrace of welcome.

We will continue to come to Jesus and make His Presence our home.

We believe that we must continue to strengthen our inner selves (building up a reserve of energy and core of strength to call upon), through on-going reflection and recollection.

If we hold Mary's hand and remain close to her Heart, we can be opened more and absorb more of her virtues, her gentleness and peace, and be ready to greet all with patience, meekness and love: continuing to come to her at every moment.

SIMPLICITY is the key to reaching the people of God, learning to listen for the "still, small" voice of the Holy Spirit guiding our words and actions.

Praising and thanking the Father at each moment will remove all focus from ourselves and our own concerns, allowing a return of peace and progress in our work; will heal the world of its anxiety and self absorption.

In the descending darkness, the only light that will shine for all will be those who will rally the remnant people around the Mother of Jesus and protect her from attacks of those who choose not to know her, hear her, listen to her words and invitations.

We will live with the understanding (and on-going reflection) that the reign of God is about to become a reality upon this earth: every promise, every word of Scripture be fulfilled up to Jesus' Coming back into the world to claim His inheritance.

We will prepare for a new time to begin, a renewed Church which will grow and rise out of the ashes of all that has been destroyed that was not of God.

We anticipate a new creation, a new world resulting from renewed beauty in hearts and in the world, in order for new life to begin: the law of the grain of wheat, the law of change and growth.

We live in patience and trust for the time when evil and ugliness are no longer accepted and tolerated, when a merciful God comes to the aid of His poor suffering children: No longer can God allow His people to be objects of the whims of creatures bent on pleasure and greed. No more can He allow His innocent ones to suffer the sins of those who should be caring for them, cherishing their bodies and souls and thanking the Father for the gift of their lives.

We await prayerfully and joyfully the purified time when abortion, pornography, incest, fornication, lying, stealing and cheating stop! And we continue to pray for the precious babies being aborted by mothers who do not understand the precious gift of life.

A great reason to pray will be the many who still do not heed the signs of the Father's displeasure, as many devastation's will wreak havoc among cities, sending panic across the country.

Each time we feel panic, we must stop, refocus on Jesus and our holy Mother, ask to be reunited to their Hearts and be allowed to concentrate on truth and the reality of all that is. It is very necessary now that we live in a way that is serious and practical!

We are being called by God, Our Father, to greater holiness, more prayer, to a greater love for Mary, the Holy Trinity and each other.

Women can be signs of the mercy and other attributes of Our Holy Mother Mary, in a uniquely feminine way, having a deep understanding and compassion about what it means to be a woman.

Men can be the signs of the mercy and virtues of St. Joseph and the Father, Himself, all immersed in trust in the Merciful Jesus by the power of the Holy Spirit. They, too, can support and affirm each other with a unique understanding and compassion for all that involves being a man in today's world.

Trust is our word. Trust in spite of, in the face of, the evidence (which may look completely negative; totally, overwhelmingly against us).

When we have mercy, we trust and then do not count the consequences. If our trust is betrayed or denied, then we believe that God has a good reason in mind for allowing this. We move on, trusting that He will justify us, our position, beyond our greatest expectations.

There is no time left for bitterness, resentment, anger, unforgiveness, lack of respect, criticism, judgementalism, living with conditions on our love. This kind of behavior is death to the soul, to the spirit. We are considering another type of death here, one which leads to new life and is imaged in the grain of wheat which denies itself, falls to the ground and dies in order to become something new which gives life to others.

To live with mercy, in trust, is to die to ourselves and put the needs of others first. This requires surrender to the Divine Will of the Father on our part, the other necessary component for living in community wherever we find ourselves in these end times, preparing to greet our Savior when He comes again!

Mary, the Mother and Gift of Mercy: the most holy Virgin is given to us as the Masterpiece of the Father's mercy!

In order for God's love to be communicated to us, there must be a bridge and that bridge is Mary. We know that a gift is always meant to be shared with others. It is for others, not to be kept for ourselves. Am I sharing Mary?

The human nature of Jesus was assumed by Him, not created. This looks at the difference between Mary who was created and Jesus Who was not creature, that is not created in the sense that we were, but had an assumed human nature that was united to His Divine Nature! He is beyond the concept of mercy because He is the only Son, not one of mercy, (applied gift), but one of love (the unity of a love relationship). Love demands unity with the beloved. Jesus is the essence of mercy, the manifestation of the mercy of the Father. Creation is the first act of mercy.

This is mentioned so that we understand that Mary is creature and receives the mercy of God in her creation and throughout her life. When God's love is given to a creature, it is given as merciful love. God's gift of love is received and experienced within ourselves. That is agape love. His gift of mercy is applied, or experienced from without ourselves (applied love). His merciful love is personified in Mary and if we are in her and united with her, we participate in her graces, her virtues, her mercy. This mercy demands that one give without counting the cost!

Mary is, like Jesus though not to the same degree of perfection, the personified mercy of the Father: the fullness of mercy. One cannot live by the Father's mercy in a total and complete manner if one does not live in Mary. She is very close to the Trinity. All the Father (therefore the Trinity) gives, Mary is by grace. That is a phrase to contemplate often and long! The Cause always contains more than the effect!!

Mary is never identified with God, that is, she was not a person of the Holy Trinity, but mercy in her was full and total, without limits. Mercy was communicated to Mary without limit. Mercy constitutes Mary's life! All that the Father gives, Mary lives.

One should look at all the events of Mary's life as a result of the Father's mercy. Mysteries of Mary are like an entrance door to the Father's mercy for our nourishment and encouragement and sustenance, our vitality, our resting place. This requires an excessive love, which we must ask, beg for, as though possessing the source of love. This is the "bridge" to the Heart of Jesus Who is the Fountain of Divine Mercy for the world.

Mercy is the way of access to the Father's love. There is power in the service of Love. The sin of the world is love in the service of power! Sin is the divided heart!!! Sin is allowed.

Satan hates God's gratuitous love and he tries to negate Mary completely, get people to forget about her! However, sin allows, (facilitates as it were), God's gracious mercy! Not a reason to sin, but a reason to remember the action of saving grace in the face of our brokenness and weak, sinful nature. Permitting Original Sin would allow God's omnipotence to be realized!

Mary, on the other hand, is the purity of the Father's mercy; there is no mercy more absolute nor complete in a human creature. When we consider the Immaculate Conception, we realize the Father's antecedent mercy. It was there before she needed it. His mercy is that way for us, also! The Father is always antecedent (Remember... He loved us first) ...with His love, His mercy, His forgiveness, His care. We only need to ask for it to be continued, to allow its action in our lives.

Mary is the one who received mercy in a particular, personal, exceptional, unique way, as no other person did. She merits the particular mercy throughout her life. An act of consecration allows us to draw nearer to the fountain of mercy that Mary is. She, like her Son, is all merciful. Mary is a dimension of merciful love.

The Immaculate Conception of Mary is a demand to us to live in a like, though different and less perfect, manner. It is a gift demanding of holiness with which Mary corresponded completely. In Baptism we are called to live the Immaculate Conception! (Please reflect how this can be lived out). This is gift and mission for us.

We are on pilgrimage with Mary preparing for the Third Millennium. St. Maximilian Kolbe determined that the Holy Spirit does not act except through Mary! In this age of abuse, how can we explain to children that God is a loving and merciful Father? We look at Mary for the answer, and see His love and mercy personified. We realize the obvious need to participate in her lifestyle, her intimate relationship with the Trinity.

On the Feast of the Assumption, the priest at Mass reflected that Jesus loved His Mother so much He could not bear to allow her body to be corrupted, so He brought her body and soul to Heaven directly. All of the gifts Mary has, God wishes to give to us! We begin to prepare ourselves by consecration, by prayer (St. Louis de Montfort reminds us) in, with, because of and through Mary in an actual slavery to her, which will lead to the unity that allows us to participate in her graces and virtues, her merciful love. Our greatest struggles, de Montfort says, will be overcome when we unite ourselves to Our Holy Mother Mary as her slave in the healthiest sense of the word...not expecting payment, or special favors, but knowing success to be ours as a result of her loving concern and help, her ability as a channel of grace from the Father through her Son to change our lives.

It is interesting that August 5th is the Feast of Our Lady of Mercy and also, she has revealed in these days, the actual birthday of Mary.

When we look at Mary's life, we must consider that she is Mother of Mercy by reason of her role first as Mother, but also as Intercessor, Mediatrix, Advocate, Helper, Co-Redemptrix. Because of her unique unity with Christ as his Mother who gave Him His flesh and blood, Jesus' Messianic Mission is also Mary's: proclaim a time of favor from the Lord, give sight to the blind, free the captive, champion the disenfranchised and victim by preaching the good news of the Kingdom to the poor. It must also be our mission!

All the works of the Father's hands are crowned with mercy. Every act of the Father grows out of His mercy, is rooted in mercy.

If we accept this mission, we need unity with everything that we have come to understand about Divine Mercy. If we are to act in a way that is rooted in mercy, what a change must occur in our behavior!

If we accept Mary as the bridge to Jesus' mercy, as the perfection of that mercy in a human creature, we must embrace her more totally every day and run with love to her waiting, merciful, loving arms.

The greatest truth about Mary is that she is the Mother of God, "Theotokos," the God bearer. All her graces and privileges are for or are from her Motherhood, i.e. the fullness of grace, Immaculate Conception, mediation, Assumption, Queenship.

John Paul II's *Mother of the Redeemer* was written to prepare for the new advent of 2001. He shows that Mary's characteristics are to be those of the Church. Faith: "Blessed are you who believed" (Lk 1:45).

Several scriptural events point to Mary's role as Mediatrix in the order of intercession. It was Mary's intercession at the wedding of Cana (Jn 2) that led to the first miracle of Our Lord and the beginning of His public ministry. At the Visitation of Mary to Elizabeth, Mary's physical intercession in bringing the unborn Christ to His unborn cousin, John the Baptist, led to John's sanctification in the womb of Elizabeth (Lk 1:41).

This role of Mary as "Mediatrix," or secondary and subordinate mediator with Jesus, has a strong foundation in the apostolic tradition as manifested in this fourth century profession by St. Ephraem (d.373):

"After the Mediator, you, Mary, are the Mediatrix of the whole world." More recently, Vatican II ends its beautiful treatment of Mary as "Mother in the order of grace: by confirming Mary's role and title as "Mediatrix":

Therefore the Blessed Virgin is invoked in the Church under the titles of Advocate, Helper, Benefactress and Mediatrix. This, however, is so understood that it neither takes away anything from nor adds anything to the dignity and efficacy of Christ the one Mediator (Lumen Gentium, No. 62).

Mary's role as Mediatrix with Jesus, the one Mediator, has two fundamental expressions in the order of grace. First, Mary uniquely participated with Jesus Christ in reconciling God and man through the Redemption. For this role she has been called "Co-Redemptrix" (meaning a secondary and subordinate participator in Jesus' Redemption of the world).

Secondly, Mary gave birth to Jesus, source of all grace, and she distributes the graces merited by Jesus on Calvary to the human family. This is the role of Mary as the person responsible for the distribution of graces or oftentimes by the more general title, "Mediatrix of all graces."

Mary participated in Redemption by accepting the invitation of the angel to become the Mother of God and by giving flesh to the Savior. Early Church Fathers saw the Incarnation and Redemption as one, unified, saving act (since the Angel Gabriel outlined Jesus' redemptive act in his heavenly message). Mary brought the world its Redeemer at the Incarnation.

Mary gave His body to Jesus as the instrument for the Redemption of humanity. The body of Jesus Christ was the instrument for the Redemption of the human family. Since the very instrument for the Redemption was given to Him by Mary, the Mother of Jesus clearly played an intimate part in the redeeming of the human race with her Son, far beyond that of any other creature.

Mary offered the maternal rights of her Son on the cross to the Father in perfect obedience to God's will, and in atonement for the sins of the world. Mary's offering of her own Son on Calvary, along with her own motherly compassion, rights and suffering, offered in union with her Son for the salvation of the human family, merited more graces than any other created person.

Mary , in an act of obedience to the will of God, offered Jesus, (and with Jesus), His own suffering by sharing in the experience of the passion and death of Our Lord in atonement for our sins. It is in this sense that we say Mary offered her maternal rights on Calvary and rightly refer to Mary as the Co-Redemptrix with the Redeemer (completely and in every way secondary and dependent to the sacrifice of Jesus the Savior).

It is important to see that Our Lady dispenses the graces of Jesus because of her special participation in meriting the graces of Redemption. The Mother of Jesus, above all creatures, fittingly participates in the distribution of these graces to the Mystical Body.

Mary's God-given ability to distribute the graces of Redemption by her intercession is an essential element and full flowering of her role as Spiritual Mother. For true motherhood goes beyond the birthing of children to include their nourishing, growth and proper formation.

Mary mediates all graces of Jesus to the human family by giving birth to Jesus and bringing the source and author of all graces to the world and by distributing the graces merited on Calvary by her willed intercession. She has, in a very real way, given birth to the body of Christ and the Body of Christ mystically united with the Head in grace.

She merited graces (that redeems the world) on Calvary. From Heaven, Mary distributes the graces of Redemption to grant each open heart the saving supernatural life of Our Lord. Vatican II ascribes to her, "Mary is truly our Mother in the order of grace."

When the Church says that the Mother of Jesus is Mediatrix of all graces, she means that all favors and graces granted by God to humanity reach us through the intercession of Mary.

From Pope John Paul's encyclical *Mother of the Redeemer*, he quotes Vatican II, the "motherhood of Mary in the order of grace will last without interruption until the eternal fulfillment of all the elect."

Shortly after, in the same encyclical, he granted the Blessed Virgin a new title as "Mediatrix of Mercy" at the Second Coming of her Son. She also has that specifically maternal role of Mediatrix of Mercy at His final coming, when all those who belong to Christ "shall be made alive," when "the last enemy to be destroyed is death" (1Cor.15:26).

Finally, to quote St. Bernard of Clairvaux who has been called the "Doctor of Mary's Mediation":

This is the will of Him who wanted us to have everything through Mary...God has placed in Mary the plenitude of every good, in order to have us understand that if there is any trace of hope in us, any trace of grace, any trace of salvation, it flows from her..God could have dispensed His graces according to His good pleasure without making use of this channel, Mary, but it was His wish to provide this means whereby grace would reach you.

The above material is from *Introduction to Mary* by Mark Miravalle. Jesus is the personification of the Father Who is rich in mercy. Grace (and all the acts of the Father) is a result of the mercy of God. Therefore, all that Mary is (by the mercy of the Father), is a reflection of that mercy; and, Mother of God, she is Mother of all mercy.

From the Encyclical *Rich in Mercy* by John Paul II, we hear: Mary is a vessel of mercy. She has been able to perceive, by reflecting on Israel, by experiencing first hand, and then by seeing on-going humanity, that mercy which from generation to generation enables people to become sharers of mercy according to the eternal design of the Holy Trinity.

Mary merits exceptional mercy, particularly at the foot of the Cross of her Son, as one who continues to bring people close to that love He had come to reveal. In Mary and through her, love continues to be revealed in the history of the Church and of humanity. This revelation is especially fruitful because in the Mother of God, it is based upon the unique tact of her maternal heart, on her particular sensitivity, on her particular fitness to reach all those who most easily accept the merciful love of a mother. By her maternal charity, she continues to care for the brethren of her Son until we all come to our blessed home. Mary continues to obtain for us the graces of eternal salvation. She enabled the incarnation of mercy in the world with her "fiat." As she gave birth to mercy in the world, so she gives birth to Jesus within us and as we allow, through our own "fiat," that mercy to be more and more present and active in and through our lives.

I solemnly tell you, those who have left
Everything and followed me will be
Repaid a hundred fold, and will gain
Eternal life.

Matthew 19:29

WAR IS ALWAYS THE SAME

As I recall, the story in old World War II movies went something like this: a soldier was often drafted and sent to basic training, and to spend time with people who were total strangers. Many new skills were learned and many preparations made to ready them for battle. As the time to depart approached, these men and women were not allowed to leave the grounds. Tensions rose as battle plans were discussed and an air of secrecy prevailed. There were many new rules by which each one had to abide. The families and loved ones of these military people had to say good-by to them, often without even knowing where they were headed. In fact, often they didn't know their final destination. This was so there would be no chance for the enemy to find out and ruin existing tactical plans. There were many last minute dinners and parties and tearful partings.

Sometimes, departures lasted only a short time and they were returned to base, able to see loved ones again, but with greater difficulty, knowing they would be leaving again soon, not wanting to go, and wishing things were like they had been during peace time.

The more responsibility a person accepted, the more rules seemed to apply. These brave people shared with their loved ones how frightening it was to be going into battle and the difficulty found in following all these orders. No matter how everyone felt about fighting in actual combat , each one knew the necessity of obeying directions or facing a loss of their place in the march to final victory. The thought of letting everyone else down (who would be counting on them) was enough to convince these dedicated ones of the importance of not deserting their posts (no matter how much they wished for this), in order to go back to where they used to be and those they loved. Of course, the commanders were counting on this kind of attitude and continued to talk about the importance of duty and fidelity to the safety and needs of others. Some of them even had fleeting thoughts of quitting, but knew this was impossible because they were too deeply involved in the war plans and couldn't risk the possibility of being removed from the group forever! In fact, their future as a citizen of their country was at stake and no one would want to take a serious step that would affect the rest of their lives and even beyond!

The soldiers, however, also realized that since the really heavy training had begun to prepare them for actual battles, (the real thing) nothing was the same anymore, anyway. Things had changed too much. Too much was at stake for the outcome of the fight for freedom, and people had all become very involved in their own way. The focus and behavior of everyone was different, as each realized the seriousness of doing their part to hasten a victory over the enemy.

Sometimes, these soldiers didn't see their loved ones for years. After their return, it was extremely difficult to adjust and try to pick up their lives the way they used to be. One of the reasons many didn't want to leave in the first place was, an understanding that; even though they missed everyone, so much during their absence, things would never be the same; and they wouldn't be; not after returning from terrible battles; seeing many of their comrades die or be terribly wounded; perhaps even bearing wounds themselves! In the movies, the commanders seemed to know how everything would turn out and were always insistent on complete discipline and obedience as the means of winning the war and securing total victory. They needed to be personally very disciplined and totally convinced of the necessity for trusting the rules, so they could teach by example.

When each soldier went away, it was with the understanding that they might not come back again; at least, maybe not in one piece! The people who loved them knew this too, and were saddened and worried about the well-being of the soldiers and prayed for them all the time. No one ever wanted to be separated, especially in order to go off to battle and fight an enemy they usually couldn't even see!

Wartime splits up families and loved ones and changes their way of living and being. No one wants to do what is necessary for a victory, but the possibility of living without freedom is a worse situation and a strong impetus to persevere no matter how difficult the conditions. War is Hell. Jesus invites us to journey through hellish times and eventually arrive in Heaven!